ROOTS, RELIGION, AND DEPRESSION
Into the Infinite Loop

E.C.L. Lang

Cadmus Publishing
www.cadmuspublishing.com

Copyright © 2020 E.C.L. Lang
Cover image: La Barque a Giverny by Claude Monet.

Published by Cadmus Publishing
www.cadmuspublishing.com

ISBN: 978-1-63751-002-5

All rights reserved. Copyright under Berne Copyright Convention, Universal Copyright Convention, and Pan-American Copyright Convention. No part of this book may be reproduced, stored in a retrieval system, or transmitted in any form, or by any means, electronic, mechanical, photocopying, recording or otherwise, without prior permission of the author

To Elsie Culpepper
If Jesus of Nazareth ever had reincarnations,
she was one of them.

Joyce has attempted ... to show how the screen of consciousness with its ever-shifting kaleidoscopic impressions carries ... not only what is in the focus of each man's observation of the actual things about him, but also in a penumbral zone residua of past impressions, some recent and some drawn up by association from the domain of the subconscious ...

-Hon. John M. Woolsey, Judge, United States District Court; an excerpt from Opinion A. 110-59, December 6, 1933.

Table of Contents

Evolution of a View, in Progress	1
The Great Mystery	9
Good Intentions	13
High Verbal IQ and Psychotherapy	23
The Latest Approach to Depression in Women:	61
Dawkins and the Genes that Rule the World	77
In the Beginning	95
Those Little Things I Don't Want to Remember	113
Milepost Four on the Long and Winding Road	119
Go Ye Unto All the Earth	129
First Families of Virginia and Scarlet O'Haras	137
Loss and the Waste Land	151
The Pain We Can't Face	177
Forget Freud and Give Us Cesar Millan	185
Opposition	201
The Stand-Up Routines	215
A Mind-Body-Spirit Perfect Storm	229
The Longing for Listeners Who Want to Listen	237
Revulsion and Redemption	251
Lionesses of the Pride	265
Mitochondria Multiplied	281
Stop Attacking - I'm Dead Already	291
Help! I Need Somebody's Help!	323
Lead-Up to a Meltdown	345
From Basket Weaving to Shots in the Dark	365
Psychoanalitically Oriented Psychotherapy or Psychoanalysis?	383
Event at a Cistern, Re-Visited	403
The New Alpha	415
Revelations	429
Elsie	447
Acknowledgement	457

Evolution of a View, in Progress

If you are a woman suffering chronic intractable depression and you were hoping to find some opening door for you within these pages - a cure, an ameliorative, an escape, a psychic anesthetic - you are probably in for disappointment. I can't think of one book on depression I've ever read that says early-onset depression is incurable, but I believe that is the reality of the condition.

If you are a mental health professional looking for endorsement of some method of therapy which you or colleagues are currently using to treat depression, I can almost guarantee that you won't find it touted in the pages of this book. Not only do I think that mental health professionals have, to date, almost unanimously rejected approaches that could help at least a little, but I also strongly believe that most current treatments are highly debilitating rather than helpful despite what your professions' studies purport to show about the efficacy of therapy in conjunction with appropriate medication.

Having suffered almost all my life from depression (about fifty-eight of my sixty-two years) and having participated in just about every form of treatment afforded free propaganda by the medical profession and the press, I would think that somewhere in all that time I would have run across one of those from-childhood depressed women who has been lifted out of it by therapy and medication. I haven't. I have heard of a couple of women who said they responded very positively to Prozac, but those two women did not suffer early-onset depression. Where are all these women who have had the treatments that are reported in print and on radio and TV to turn lives around?

If as high percentage of the population suffers from depression as is reported in the media, and if depression is as easy to cure as media items say it is, how is it that in over five decades of life I have run into many, many currently depressed women and hardly any formerly depressed women?

I suspect that they are like the alcoholics in the psychological experiments and studies who were reported in the media to have been cured of their alcoholic-type drinking and turned into successful social drinkers through the use of aversive strategies - being given painful electric shocks by their therapists as I recall. Follow-ups by the studies' organizers reported that after the completion of their behavior modification immersions these subjects could practice controlled drinking thenceforth. However, follow-up follow-ups showed that these subjects and their families had evaded the truth about the subjects' rapid return to alcoholism, and, in some cases, about the subjects' deaths due to drinking or to suicide, when they responded to the organizers' follow-up surveys.

Why would these subjects and their families report treatment to be a success when it was, in fact, an abysmal failure? Why would depressed women claim that they had been helped by therapies and medications that not only did not help them but that often left them worse off than before treatment? Because, there is an unacknowledged collusion between clients and their mental health professionals to avoid admitting that worthless and damaging therapies are worthless and damaging. In general, clients need for their therapists to think well of them, and clients know that their therapists are more likely to think well of them if they make a show of thinking well of their therapists and keep their misgivings to themselves.

Clients who go downhill in psychotherapy incur not only the disappointment of their therapists but usually their disgust and ill will as well. Such a reaction from a person a client is counting on to keep believing in him is the last thing a client wants to see happen. But clients find out, when their time in therapy drags on and they don't get any happier under their therapists' ministrations, that their therapists will make them pay for their failure to become feathers in their therapists' professional caps.

Therapists can hardly afford to see themselves as lacking ability to do whatever they were taught in their training they were supposed to be able to do, and whatever the esteemed of their profession seem to be doing with clients. They've spent a lot of money and many years in training, all the while being led to believe by their professors and supervisors that they were mastering approaches that would be effective in changing those whom they were coming to see as "mentally ill" and defective in their current state. There are a huge number of people in this world earning very nice incomes because the public has been led to believe that there are broken people every way we turn and mental health professionals fix them.

If you are a person who has been through many years of therapy and a variety of medications yet have even less sense of well-being than you had before you began therapy, don't let a therapist or any other medical person lay the blame for that on your doorstep. The most therapeutically beneficial thing you can do for yourself (I think) is to trust yourself with a trust much greater than that you would place in any other human being - especially in a mental health professional.

If you can muster the guts to do so, and if it's true for you, tell your psychiatrist, psychologist, or therapist of whatever ilk that the resources you are expending upon your treatment are not only a bewildering eking away of your time and money with nothing to show for it, but that your relationships, your productivity, and your self-esteem are all going downhill steadily with each passing week or month of therapy. Your professional will probably quickly voice a reason for that which absolves him (or her) from any responsibility for your declining quality of life; probably something to the effect that your "mental illness" is so severe that no therapist could "reach" you.

I believe that many mental health professionals purposely undertake to arouse shame and terror in the hearts and minds of clients who don't behave as subserviently toward them as their (the professionals') egos demand. One effective strategy professionals use to do that is to imply to clients who - they judge - aren't bowing as low as they should, that they are delusional, have grandiose views of themselves, are out of touch with reality, are psychotic. Often a professional humiliates a client and clubs her behind the knees by telling her he has diagnosed her as having some condition that she knows is associated with violence or sexual depravity. Once, these strategies that mental health professionals use to make clients go limp in the spirit made me go limp in the spirit.

Therapy, for most of us suffering from childhood-onset depression, has turned out to seem like a hoax and a fraud for which none of the perpetrators have had to pay or be called to account. Nonetheless, we have kept going back for more. Why do we do that? I suspect that fear and self-doubt arising from the fact that we observe ourselves failing to "get well" under the guidance and regimes of our mental health professionals — a group of people which our society has identified as good authority figures who are successful at leading emotionally ill people to wellness — make us compulsively keep trying to erase what we perceive as our own personal failure in this project. The coercive nature of this almost unanimous public sanction is too intimidating for us who are suffering to stand up and say, "You are exacting a huge amount of money and emotional commitment from us and leaving us with less than nothing."

This book is, in addition to being my homemade conveyor belt for carrying off personal garbage, an attempt at whistle-blowing. We depressed women who have been used by mental health professionals as a source of revenue and personal status since before Freud are the ones who must agitate to bring about change in our present healthcare system's attitude toward us.

ROOTS, RELIGION AND DEPRESSION

EVOLUTION OF A VIEW, IN PROGRESS

THE GREAT MYSTERY

How many times have we read lately in printed articles, or heard on radio and TV documentaries that many more women than men suffer from depression, but "we don't know exactly why"? Who are the half-witted researchers and mental health professionals who "don't know why" women might suffer from depression in epidemic proportions as compared with men?

How many of you male researchers have had the everywhere, all-the-time, with everybody experience of being universally ignored when you tried to share some special knowledge - hard-won through your own independent study, experience, and work - with others?

When I took part in a writing class here in eastern North Carolina a few years ago, an assignment we had one night was to write a short essay on why we write. In our class was a little old lady, probably in her sixties, with gray hair and unremarkable dress, no striking makeup or jewelry, who spoke in a voice quite average to little old ladies - that is to say without excessive loudness, animation, or raised pitch. Her essay on why she wrote was short and sweet: "I write because that's the only way I can get anyone to pay any attention to anything I have to say." She was fortunate to write well enough that she had been able to, fairly consistently, get her writings commercially accepted - at least by local publications. Most of us don't have that much talent, so we are indeed short of potential co-communicators.

In the groups of AA in Williamsburg, Virginia, in the 70s, where I first began to experience being involved in the verbal give and take of true self-help groups (as opposed to self-help groups as conducted by Nurse Ratchet), I had other issues to deal with than analyzing why everybody in a meeting would say "Yeah, that's right, you hit the nail on the head, you have truly got the important idea out of it ...", etc. when a big, tall, man spoke, and then have a look on their face of ennui and patient forbearance when a woman's turn to speak came.

And that was in Williamsburg, the home of the intellectuals of the faculty of William & Mary, the place of the lofty exchanges of the Brookings Institute, and a watering hole of timeless culture. As I went farther afield and attended meetings in more rural settings, I could see a consistent pattern: when one of the "good old boys" spoke, everyone in the group gave him their undivided attention. If, after him, it became the turn of a woman to speak, half the people in the room began to shove their chairs noisily back, head off to the john, and refill and doctor up their coffees. By the time she stopped speaking, everybody was back in their place and ready to listen to the next speaker - if he was a man.

So, listen up you learned mental health professionals who want to enlighten us female depressives with all your findings about our illness and who say "We think more women than men suffer from depression because women have a greater need for close relationships than do men". Why don't you give a little thought to how it might feel when the valuable (to you) insights that you want so much to share with others and to have validated by others are listened to with all the gravity one attaches to chickens cackling?

THE GREAT MYSTERY

Good Intentions

Through most of my life, I've trudged forward under the belief that I continued to suffer from crippling depression because of my own obstinacy and failure to avail myself of the good and efficacious treatments of skilled and thoroughly competent mental health professionals. I didn't come up with this point of view entirely on my own. This is the point of view with which most mental health professionals leave their clients when their clients not only experience no improvement in their condition but even see devastating worsening of their life situations as treatment goes on.

When I go on the World Wide Web to research current developments in depression, when I watch programs on TV relating to depression, when I peruse newspaper and magazine articles on depression, when I read books on the subject, and when I talk to therapists, I get the same communication from all sources: depression is a snap to cure. The sources tell me that no one need suffer depression; that all one needs to do to be relieved of this agony is to get oneself to a properly credentialed mental health professional for therapy and medication. Some of these sources of information (mainly institutional sites on the Internet) do pay enough homage to reality to make mention of the intractable cases who are never helped by either therapy, medication, or the combination. But, they downplay this eventuality to such an extent that it appears as an almost insignificant aside to the overall theme of the presentations; the overall theme being that depression is easily cured, and that the only sufferers who aren't cured are the ones who don't avail themselves of medical help.

In contrast to this assurance from mental health professionals and the media that depression can be quickly resolved with medical help are the images in my mind of all the people I have known, including myself, who have undergone years of therapy and medication and have profited little or none, or who have deteriorated steadily and dramatically during and after treatment. What I perceive to be the ongoing state of affairs with regard to the medical community's relationship with its depressed clients is a state wherein each group of the dyad is locked in perpetual self-deception. Mental health professionals hardly ever bring about significant changes for the better in their clients whose depression commenced in childhood or teen years. In fact, based upon what I have seen in depressed individuals I have known personally, have read about, have seen interviewed in TV documentaries, and have lived with in my own skin, I can only reach one conclusion: that relationships with mental health professionals exacerbate their clients' woes.

The public has found books like Sylvia Plath's *Bell Jar* and J. D. Salinger's *Catcher in the Rye* to be works of great inspiration and hope for young people whose emotional downhill slides have brought them to the pit of despair; so much so that *Catcher in the Rye* is required reading for students in many high schools. In both books, the authors follow their protagonists' lives as they become increasingly alienated from their fellow human beings and increasingly overwhelmed by confusion and feelings of hopelessness. Then, at the ends of these tales, the protagonists come under the influence of a psychologist or psychiatrist, and we, the readers, turn the last page with the vision in our minds of people born anew - young people starting life all over again and headed toward sure happiness and social closeness with their fellow human beings. We, the readers of literature that portrays mental health professionals as being caring saviors of the lost, love this stuff. We give these books to young people to read so that when they feel despair, they will know that there is salvation - that salvation being in a relationship with a psychologist or psychiatrist. To me, giving adolescents the idea that these authors are presenting stories typical of the outcomes of meetings with psychotherapists is setting them up for what might turn out to be great disappointment. My own meetings with a psychotherapist when I was in my late teens constituted a really bad surprise, and there was definitely no feeling of being born anew.

This is the *real* outcome of the lives of Sylvia Plath and J.D. Salinger and, by inference, the outcome of their experiences in psychotherapy:

Plath's book is an autobiographical account of her own

emotional collapse and nearly successful suicide attempts as a teen, her resulting commitment to an institution, and her initial sessions there with a psychiatrist. The book ends showing the central character (Plath herself) reflecting, as a result of her meetings with her psychiatrist, that her life prior to this new association had been analogous to being under a huge upended bell jar, having only the stagnant foul air trapped under the jar to breathe. Now (the protagonist continues, in her metaphor) she feels free of the dark confines of her bell jar; it has been overturned, the stagnant air allowed to escape, and she is breathing fresh sweet air.

Plath finally was entirely successful at committing suicide in 1963, the same year that The Bell Jar was published. The fact that Plath wrote this book, which ends on such a beautifully uplifting note, shortly before killing herself, says to me that during the time she was writing the book, she had the sort of hope that depressed people often have during the days preceding their suicides, when they have made their plans for ending their own lives and foresee that they will not have to endure the agony of depression much longer - that they are packed and ready for their trip out. Plath's book is a fairy tale, one she and we the readers want to believe despite the fact that Plath's death proves that her own psychotherapy and psychotherapists were unequivocal failures at helping her escape her inner torment.

The closing of J. D. Salinger's *Catcher in the Rye* reveals the protagonist (Salinger's alter ego, Holden Caulfield) envisioning himself as being,, like the psychologist with whom he has just established the beginnings of a bond, a savior who stands guard at the edge of a cliff which borders a field of rye. The metaphor of the field of rye arises from the words to an old song, *Comin' Through the Rye*, which goes something like this:

>Everybody has somebody.
>None, they say, have I,
>Yet all the lasses smile on me
>When comin' through the rye.

This song is evoked in the mind of Holden by his growing feeling that every human in his life is phony; is presenting to him a contrived façade in order to make a certain impression or to get something from him. He goes from one situation to another, feeling that he is having no sincere or "real" contact with anyone.

As one reads the closing pages of *Catcher*, one is to imagine that the rye field represents the teenage years an everyman's life, when one is akin to a child among many children navigating through a sea of view-obscuring grain stalks. Many teenagers can safely maneuver through the rye; which is to say, they can feel comfortable with their peers, get through school, manage their awakening sexual urges reasonably well, trust a few other human beings enough to be open to them - in short, feel connected. These lucky ones don't approach the brink of the cliff (don't move toward emotional breakdown) and therefore don't need to be caught by a rescuer (a mental health professional). But there are those children, Salinger's parable goes on to include, who lose the path and start running toward the cliff edge without realizing it is there. The catcher in the rye is the psychologist or other mental health professional who sees children (meaning teenagers such as Holden) running unknowingly toward their falls over cliff edges (a metaphor for mental breakdowns) and catches them before they make the fatal drop.

Salinger's book is generally perceived by those who have investigated Salinger's own life to be autobiographical. Was Salinger, in fact, saved from mental breakdown in his adolescence or young adulthood by psychotherapy? That question is a little tricky to answer because Salinger exists as a recluse and has almost continuously since *Catcher* was published in 1951. Salinger does not grant interviews to anyone and, with only a few exceptions, has not in decades. An unauthorized biography, *In Search of J D. Salinger*, written by Ian Hamilton and published in 1988, portrayed the renowned writer of the great book of hope for all teenage boys - *Catcher in the Rye* - as being so alienated from humankind as to be "invisible, all but dead". Hamilton's recounting of Salinger's life was expanded upon by Paul Alexander in another unauthorized biography published in 1999, which includes material found in court documents brought into being by Salinger's divorces and lawsuits.

To Salinger's biographers, *Catcher* appears to be the one trick of a one-trick pony. If Hamilton and Alexander are to be believed, Salinger stopped submitting further writings to publishers only a few years after *Catcher* came off the presses in 1951. The reason Salinger gave for putting an end to his associations with all editors and publishers was, in sum, that they were pigs and he was not about to cast any more of his pearls before them.

According to Alexander, Salinger's relationships with family members and friends were hardly closer than his relationships with people in the literary world. During one marriage, he had a writing shop or office built for him, separated by some distance from the house he had led his wife to believe he would be sharing with her. Soon he was spending most of each twenty-four-hour day alone in his shop, justifying to his wife his withdrawal by claiming that he had to be free of distractions in order to write. Whatever Salinger did with the output of all the days, weeks, and months of "writing" that he claimed to be producing in his shop, is unclear. According to his biographers, there is no evidence that Salinger had ever shared with anyone the decades' worth of literature he has supposedly created since his last published writings of the mid-to-late 1950's. One biographer suggested that Salinger's extensive periods of seclusion in his shop were spent watching television, not in writing.

Is J. D. Salinger's life the life of a person who has been saved from crippling alienation by psychotherapy? I don't see any evidence in Hamilton's or Alexander's biographies to suggest that it is. Salinger himself seems to be, and to have been all of his adult life, just as alienated a human being as Holden Caulfield is before he is "saved". Is the literary character Holden Caulfield an honest and credible example of what really happens in psychotherapy? To that question I would have to answer that in a young person's first sessions, hopes do surge, and even after years of psychotherapy, hope dies hard. That first blush of enthusiasm and joy exists because the novice in psychotherapy has bought a bill of goods. The same bill of goods that Holden Caulfield, as spokesperson for therapy and therapists, is propagating in the last pages of *Catcher*. I see Holden Caulfield as being an honest representation of a troubled teen only up to the point where he makes contact with his mental health mentor. From there, to the end of the book, happenings are as fairy tale in nature as

Cinderella's rescue by the handsome prince.

Where is the "truth" in *Catcher*, the "truth" that has so entranced educators that they have put *Catcher* on high schoolers' reading lists? The truth underlying our (society's) mass embrace of Holden Caulfield is that we are so desperate to believe that mental health can be created, repaired, and maintained by mental health professionals that we will support any tale, any documentary, any study, any report of any kind that tells us that this is so. None of us dares even utter the thought that psychotherapy is largely ineffectual. Stating an idea like that in our society is akin to standing up in a Christian church and declaring that Jesus Christ was sired by a human being, not by God. Bring to mind just how many of us have bought books and watched movies portraying a psychologist, psychiatrist, or psychoanalyst as savior. Bring to mind just how voluminous and steady the flow of those books and movies, from publishers to eager public, has been over the past century. We want - in fact, we demand it by putting our dollars down - for mental health professionals to be portrayed as healers who turn broken people into whole ones.

Society is in denial, mental health professionals are in denial, the media is in denial, and we sufferers of mental anguish who go to therapists, are in denial. We don't want to know the truth. The truth is that folks like Salinger and Holden Caulfield, who are already in deep trouble emotionally by their late teens, are almost never changed for the better by therapy no matter how institution-endorsed or public-endorsed the therapist. The truth about the expected outcome of psychotherapy for them can be found in Salinger's real life saga, in Sylvia Plath's biography (not in *Bell Jar*), in the regression-to-childhood of women like

Marilyn Monroe, and in the excesses and failed relationships characterizing the last years of many public figures who have bought the best psychotherapy money can buy.

GOOD INTENTIONS

High Verbal IQ and Psychotherapy

Based on my own life experience and my observations of the lives of others I have known who have had very high verbal IQs and who also have endured chronic depressive disorders, my belief is that psychotherapy will not only not benefit those of us who fall into this category of depression sufferers; it will be the most frustrating and disappointment-producing undertaking in which we will ever engage. Why am I making such an assertion?

The big picture is that if you are a very intelligent human being, when your therapist is conducting your treatment in a way that yields you no benefit, or worse, is conducting it in a way that arouses fears and defenses in your personality that defeat you and destroy what healthy functioning you possessed when you put yourself in their care, intuitively you will see what's happening, you will recognize why it's happening, and you will try to communicate all the information that you intuitively grasp to your therapist so that you can help them to help you. To me, it makes perfect sense that therapy must operate with this kind of feedback going on constantly for anything positive to come of it.

What we people of high verbal intelligence often fail to intuitively grasp is that most people with whom we try to share our carefully pieced out knowledge and insight are incapable of understanding what we are trying to communicate to them. If psychiatrists, psychologists, and other professionals administering psychotherapy were open to feedback from clients, at least clients would stand a chance that their therapists might glean something from it and use it for client benefit. However, psychotherapists hardly ever recognize that humans who haven't been through formal institutional training might have a natural ability at understanding psychological phenomena much more than they, the professionally trained person, has. Intimate that to your therapist, and he will get even with you for what he perceives as your insolence and presumptuousness in one way or another.

As part of their formal training, professionals have been led to believe that their course work and supervised internships and practice have given them omniscience into the human mind and emotions that no person can possess who hasn't gone through the formal training that they have. Out of all the psychiatrists, psychologists, counselors, and psychiatric nurses into whose offices I have entered over a lifetime, I can think of less than a handful who were open to feedback from me about what, in their therapeutic approach with me, was beneficial to me and what was destructive. Even though a mental health professional's work can't work to the benefit of a client if the professional is closed to input from the client about what work he, the professional, is doing, how he's doing it, and the soundness of rationale behind his procedures, I've never had a therapist who would discuss any of those aspects of my therapy with me. In my opinion, that's why therapy fails with most clients.

This "how presumptuous you the client are to think that you know enough to tell me, a professionally trained person, how I should be doing this work I'm doing on you" attitude toward clients is an attitude my soul (my animal instinct self) has always found to be so profoundly insulting I spent decades reacting to it unconsciously with a "man the battle stations" whole-being tense-up and shut-down. That tense-up and shut-down was so in tune with all natural processes; so healthy, so survival-of-the-fittest characteristic. But, I didn't know that through all the decades I put myself in professionals' offices.

Perhaps verbal intelligence isn't real intelligence after all; perhaps it's pseudo-intelligence because, through all the decades that I put myself through the self-destructive relationships with psychotherapists that I did, I never recognized that my resistance to them was in perfect accordance with nature's best rules of self-preservation. If verbal intelligence were real intelligence, my verbal intelligence should have told me that. On a conscious level, I had been suckered into believing quite the opposite - that there was something horribly, evilly, slothfully wrong with me that I would not let my psychotherapists have complete control over me.

One of my younger sisters sought therapy on an occasion in her life when her teenage children had gotten themselves into more trouble than she felt she had the inner resources to face. When, in their first session together, her therapist began relentlessly focusing upon my sister's childhood, she told him that her childhood had indeed been horrible but what she needed was help coping with her children's here-and-now crises and that talking about her own childhood wasn't going to help her with that a bit. Whereupon, she ended the therapy and didn't seek any more anywhere else.

In her situation, I probably would have become obsessed with what I could say to this therapist to show him that his therapy needed to go in another direction. I probably would have kept going back to him for more sessions out of a need to argue him into admitting the validity of my point of view and the inapplicability of childhood-focus therapy in my case. This is the sort of compulsion which trips us high verbal IQ people up.

My sister's writings suggest to me that she might be dyslexic, and I don't know of anything that she reads that's on a higher level than "bodice busters", yet all her adult life she's had energy for work and for recreation, maintained long-term social and family ties, and gotten herself to work every day in a demanding, stressful, high-paying job from youth to honorable retirement in her fifties with full benefits. Upon retirement from her initial employer, she immediately took a position which gave her opportunity to sample life, a few months at a time, in almost any area of the country which she wished to experience. Experts tell us that moving and changing work environments is extremely stressful, yet my sister seems to take such passages in stride quite easily.

Perhaps the kind of intelligence my sister has, the kind which doesn't bestow verbal skills, the kind you can't measure with IQ tests or scholastic accomplishments, is lacking in many humans, like me, who are able to accrue a long list of great scores on standardized measurements, get degrees from the best universities, but who can't seem to get off the ground at living without repeatedly falling on our faces.

Will psychotherapy enable us not to do that--not to repeatedly fall on our faces, but to unconcernedly maneuver through life's obstacles the way my sister seems to be able, intuitively, to do? No! How could it? Our personalities have resulted from genes, and the way we have reacted to life's slings and arrows has resulted from genes. My sister's and my emotional and mental responses to life experiences and to other humans that we encounter as we pass through life experiences differ for the same reasons that a Missouri mule might stand dead in his tracks and refuse to be moved by command and whipping, while a Kentucky thoroughbred could find the slightest pull on his reins by a trainer or jockey to be incentive enough to make him agreeable to advancing. Is a horse whisperer, the psychotherapist of the equine world, going to be able to change the nature of either? I don't see how they could.

A couple of my late 1960's psychiatrists had me believing that I should suspend all attempts to think for myself and allow them to do my thinking for me. When I perceived that I just was not giving them that compliance that they wanted from me, I hated myself and believed that it was my willfulness that was hopelessly blocking these men - men identified by my society as good by virtue of their choice of professions - from being able to help me. If I would just not foul up what they were trying to achieve with my childish balkiness, these men and society had me believing, they would be able to cure my depression.

When I finally grasped, many years after my stints in therapy with my earliest psychiatrists, how gullible I had been for their performances of omniscience and superiority over me, I mourned over how little I had believed in myself when told by these men what I was and what I wasn't, and over how easily I had let my feelings of self-worth abandon me in my lack of appreciation for myself.

In each relationship with these psychiatrists, I sensed that what they wanted from me was a compliance like that expressed in the words of an old hymn, "Have thine own way, Lord, have thine own way. You are the potter - I am the clay. Mold me and make me after they will while I am waiting, yielded and still". Poor misguided soul that I was, I thought that I actually had the capacity to make myself automatically compliant. This was an expectation as unreasonable and unrealistic as expecting that a feral cat is going to be as amenable to handling as is a domestic cat who has been handled by humans from birth. The expectation of a psychotherapist that any given client should drop all resistance to them if she is serious about wanting to be helped, is about as logical as thinking that a sick wolf will lie still for veterinary treatment just because a dog, the wolf's very close relative, will.

Psychiatrists, possibly more so than other mental health professionals, con themselves into believing that their work emanates from a store within themselves of knowledge and experience that is so vast and mysterious that the like of it is inconceivable to their clients. In some male psychiatrists and psychologists I have known, I have seen the entertainment of a self-image that reminds me of the depiction of high priests as conceived by Moses (speaking for God, of course) and laid upon the Children of Israel.

For those readers who have never ploughed their way through all that Moses said God told him to say, here is the basic word on high priests: The high priest had to be male, of course. Moses' God would never have considered women to be clean enough, righteous enough, wholesome enough, or intelligent enough to even think about being priests. According to Moses' God, women were so basically unwholesome, so natured to tempt men to do evil, and so incapable of handling knowledge in a way that didn't pose a threat to themselves and everybody else, women must not, under any circumstances be allowed to acquire knowledge on their own. Only men could be trusted to handle knowledge responsibly, said Moses' God, and women didn't need any more knowledge than what the men in their lives decided they needed. Certainly, women must not be given any opportunity to learn to read. Men could mentally and spiritually handle reading, but women reading would be an abomination to the Lord.

The reason that I am writing about this issue of women's need to learn by reading and the belief in so many cultures that women should get the information they need from men, not through reading, is that I actually did have a psychiatrist who told me to stop reading literature by psychologists, psychoanalysts, and psychiatrists when I mentioned something I had read very early on in our relationship. I felt pretty sure that he hadn't been instructed to stop reading about therapies when he had undergone his own analysis as he said he had.

Of course I did not stop reading; I had to try to find out what this man's hidden agenda for me was since by that time in my many associations with mental health professionals, I knew he was not going to discuss with me what strategies he was going to be using to maneuver me into going where he wanted me to go. This man was even annoyed when some term that had come up frequently in what I read crept into my vocabulary. Since most of my vocabulary has come from my reading due to my dearth of mentors in childhood, my using psychoanalytic terms in talking was no more unusual for me than to allude to something like Lady Macbeth's washing her hands or Dante's goats having "clotted hinder parts".

This psychiatrist thought that my use of terms like "love object" meant that I was in a delusion that I was in psychoanalysis. I knew that I was aiming for the results that a client hopes to achieve who would commit themselves to treatment under a psychoanalyst, but I wasn't the least bit confused about the fact that this doctor was not a psychoanalyst, and I might be attempting to push myself through resurrection of repressed childhood experiences, but what I was getting from this psychiatrist was not psychoanalysis.

When I begin attempting to communicate arguments to another human being that pertain, in my mind, to a point I wish to make to them - to the conclusion toward which I plan to speak - I find it almost impossible to present my ideas in the uncomplicated straight line way that I sense would have the best chance of being heard by them. Therefore, in this chapter, wherein I wish to influence you to consider the potential dangers posed by psychotherapy to those of high verbal intelligence who place themselves in the care of mental health talk therapy providers, you may have to bring to bear all the skill you possess at following paths of free association breadcrumbs in order to arrive at the logic that exists on the subject in clarity in my mind. I compulsively take up free association when I begin any attempt to share my most critical and mental effort invested ideas with those folks whose respect for my ideas I most want and need. What I want to give to those to whom I communicate is a verbal product that will cut to the chase. What I am able to give them is a stream of consciousness.

This compulsive free association is an iatrogenic artifact of psychiatric treatment into which I put myself in 1967; treatment that began with months of weekly, twice weekly, or more frequent sessions during which my doctor directed me to suspend all verbal self-supervision and to let any thought, feeling, or visualization that popped into my mind pour out immediately in words.

I'd met up with free association in college pouring out of the characters Ben, Catty, Quentin, and Jason Compson, who think unstructuredly away in William Faulkner's *The Sound and the Fury*, so when I'd read (just prior to entering this treatment of which I'm speaking) about how Freud and other psychoanalysts employed free association to impel their clients back into their childhoods, I understood fully the nature of free association thought. When my psychiatrist told me that he practiced psychoanalytically oriented psychotherapy, and when I saw that he was asking me to let my thoughts wander without rein, I recognized the free association of the psychoanalyst's tool kit when I saw it even though my doctor undoubtedly thought I had no understanding of what he was having me do.

Although neither he nor I recognized it, what he was asking me to do in addition to letting my mouth move where it would, was to put my cerebral frontal lobe executive neurons - the neurons that would normally send my thoughts where I consciously wanted my thoughts to go - out of a job. I now recognize this with my more recently acquired neuroscience knowledge, but I knew nothing about neurology at the time this treatment was taking place.

What the doctor wanted from me, at each session, was a stream of consciousness. Dedicated stream of consciousness thinking over long periods of time, I now recognize, causes the brain to pull its main offices out of the brain structures that adapt us to adult life and to drop the center of its operation back into the parts of our brain that functioned automatically by animal instinct throughout our young childhood years, before our brains had fully developed the last and most sophisticated of its cell layers. Psychoanalysts call this regression, but I've never read any material by psychoanalysts or other mental health professionals that has showed recognition of how damaging "regression" is to a brain's continuing ability to operate in a way that is essential for well-thought-out adult functioning.

Being filled with excitement at the prospect of showing this medical authority figure, who had been touted to me as one having great status in a pack of authority figures (that is, the psychiatric teaching staff in a large metropolitan medical school), the great work of which my brain was capable, I enthusiastically sent my frontal lobe CEO into exile, hopelessly oblivious to what limbic system free expression, uncurbed by frontal lobe judgment, can do to a human brain's ability to function in that human's best interests. Desperately wanting to believe that my free association cerebral operations were the best this man had ever seen, desperately needing to think that this psychiatrist was greatly impressed with my ability to see through my transference to him and the free associations that were evoked by my transference to him, I put my mind to work at free association and to thinking about who the doctor represented to me to the exclusion of every other aspect of my life.

When a person we take to be an authority on humans (and society does take it that psychiatrists are authorities on humans) listens to us talk for extended periods of time without ignoring us, censoring or interrupting, as if interested in and accepting every word that comes out of our mouths, that person is shaping the way we think with every word he does not say if we let ourselves fall into the trap of imagining that he's listening to us because he really is intrigued by what we're saying and thus is intrigued by us. As behavior modifications go, a generous quantity and a validating quality in how much a person gets listened to by other humans might possibly be the most powerful behavior and personality modifier known to humankind. This is particularly true if one had, throughout childhood, caregivers who either hardly ever listened or else who listened with a perpetually censuring attitude. I know that, in my own case, it didn't take but a few sessions of this psychiatrist's encouraging my free associations for my personality and behavior to be permanently altered.

I, being (superficially, at least) naïve and trusting of doctors at the time I began treatment with this man, thought that his attentiveness to the verbiage issuing from my mouth, as I sat session after session, meant a lot to him, so I let myself slip into believing what I wanted to believe; that he was very favorably impressed by my work in psychotherapy and thus by me. In a way, I suppose my verbal outpourings did mean a lot to him but not in the way I wanted to believe. I'm sure that he was listening attentively to me in the same way that a linguist might listen to someone whose country of origin he wishes to ascertain by analyzing the speaker's dialect. Another analogy I might bring up of the way in which a psychiatrist listens to a client is the manner in which a speech therapist might listen to a client whom she is treating for stuttering. She's not listening because she's entranced by the content of her client's communications; she's listening for how he's producing targeted speech sounds. (And that lack of interest in what a client is saying is probably why speech therapy for stuttering has rarely helped stutterers.)

It's completely natural to assume, when someone listens attentively to us when we talk, that we are holding that person's attention with our oratorical attractiveness and that our communication acts are creating intellectual or emotional ties between us. Being able to draw positive attention to ourselves with what we speak and the way we speak it, and being able to influence the attitudes of our fellow humans with spoken words to such an extent that they want to help us achieve what we want to achieve, is what having personal power is all about. Having communication power in one's dealings with one's fellow human beings banishes depression. Having no power to change the opinions or feelings of others with communication is the adult equivalent of being an infant whose caregiver will not respond to her crying. In my experience there is no surer precipitant of depression.

As I was devoting all my waking hours in 1967 and 1968 to free association (something my brain's CEO allowed because psychoanalytically oriented literature had led me to believe that was the work that would get me back to childhood where I would find the etiology of my depression and thereupon be freed from it), I was imagining all the while that my psychiatrist was mentally and emotionally right with me - on the same page, so to speak - when I came to sessions and unloaded my regressed mind's current contents. Because the psychiatrist maintained with me a bedside (well, chair-side to be precise) manner that would have elicited positive transference out of a feral cat, I went through all sorts of mental and emotional gymnastics to keep myself from looking at the fact that he and I were not working in a partnership.

I believe my doctor saw himself, me, and my psychotherapy much like my pets' vet sees himself in relationship to my pets and his handling of their health. He's kindly disposed to my pets, but he's not open to their ideas about correct diagnoses and appropriate treatments for them. It's a shame doctors persist in viewing their clients as being unable to offer to them anything valuable or credible as to diagnoses and appropriate treatments. I have seen no evidence that mental health professionals' clients are as clueless and incapable of seeing themselves accurately as the pros want to believe they are. Were mental health professionals such as this doctor of whom I'm speaking, able to shrink their grandiose ideas about their own knowledge and skills down to more realistic dimensions, they might be able to recognize that their clients' heads do contain brains that are roughly on a level of functioning commensurate with their own.

I'm writing this now, but at the time the coup de grâce to my personality was taking place, I was far too brainwashed in far too many of humanity's asinine dictates about what constituted good mental health in a female and what saviors psychiatrists and psychologists were to have the faith in myself to walk out my doctors' doors when they related to me as if they were school principals advising compliance with the wishes of those who were my superiors. When a doctor talked to me as if he were talking to a little girl, I deserted myself instead of turning my back on him. I didn't, at the time, know that any psychotherapist, M.D. or not, male or not, would have to be willing to "lower himself" to working *with* me if anything positive was going to happen in the therapy.

Yes, my instincts kept telling me, psychiatrist after psychiatrist, that nothing useful to me was coming out of all the time I was spending spilling my guts in office after office. Society said psychiatrists eased the pain of people in emotional agony who presented themselves for treatment. I didn't think to question that belief when I failed, with doctor after doctor, to see any reprieve from my depression. Now, I can look back on all that time and money I wasted in my twenties and thirties on psychiatrists, at the awful addictions into which my fear of these useless men's disapproval sent me, and at the loss of ability to relate to my husband and children that resulted from my mushrooming anxiety over being unable to win respect from these therapists, with an understanding about it all

I never had at any time while I was casting away from me everything that makes life worth living ... that would have made my life worth living if only I could have escaped from my imprisonment in depression.

It is true that the psychiatrists to whom I took myself for treatment in the '60s and '70s were completely incompetent to do what they presented themselves to society as being able to do, but they are not to blame for my life's becoming a wasteland. What I must blame is the image I had of myself as someone so inferior to doctors that if I failed to benefit from treatment under them, my failure had to be because I wasn't letting them manage me. For decades I thought that I had been an unmitigated flop at psychotherapy because I hadn't allowed my doctors to save me; because I had been uncooperative, resistant, incompliant. Guilt and shame gnawed at me year after year. The late '60s psychiatrist to whom I kept going back for seven disastrous years because I wanted to "work through the transference", told me in great annoyance one day, "Mrs. Bowden, you're trying to control your treatment, and if you don't stop, I'm not going to see you anymore." Oh, would that I could have been so lucky as to see him keep his word.

By that stage in our relationship, I had already lost so much of my frontal lobe executive functioning and gone so far into limbic system, animal instinct fear and defensiveness that I never would have been able to recoup under the best of circumstances. Continuing in my treatment with this man was simply keeping myself in the worst of circumstances. I had begun treatment with him in the full belief, based on his first meeting description to me of the type of therapy he practiced, that together we would follow the trail that my transference to him created and that we would not turn aside or quit the trek until, at trail's end, my unconscious would give up to me, its overseer, the complete vista of the pain of my earliest years which it was trying to hide. My doctor stopped recognizing me, the overseer (if he had ever recognized the overseer part of my personality), and talked and behaved toward me as if all there was to me was the terrified, agonized child to which my transference to him had returned me.

I never lost sight of my goal. Perhaps I should clarify what "I" means in that sentence. My frontal lobe CEO continued to try to run the company, so to speak, but my psychiatrist became like an affronted stockholder with majority interest who devotes himself to seeing that the CEO never gets the support he needs to carry a plan through to fruition. There was not an hour or day of my life during my years of therapy with this doctor in which I did not keep faith with myself that I would keep searching through the emotional world of my childhood, through the contents of my unconscious, until I found the source of my disabling adult pain.

I trusted that, given the strength of my emotional investment in this therapist - this stand-in and surrogate for my childhood caregivers - there was all the stuff in me that would make it possible for psychoanalytically oriented therapy to succeed. I had full faith in my ability to work through my transference to the therapist. My brain's executive, here-and-now, keep-your-eye-on-the-target supervisory functioning went right on keeping faith through positive transference and negative. My doctor wasn't up to it. Because his assessment of me was so uncomprehending, he couldn't seem to imagine that my transference to him involved anything other than a little girl's Electra complex. The only thing his mind could conceive was that I had the hots for him because of transference and was acting that out because I was in denial ... no, I wasn't just in denial, I was not working, and worse yet, I was not allowing him to direct me to the truth of my erotic attraction to him and thus was keeping him from curing me. Because this man was woefully deficient in insight, he had to project onto me that it was I who was as clueless and misguided as a firefly making sexual advances to a lantern. At least, that is what I think.

I don't want to dump too much blame on this doctor for the iatrogenic problems which my treatment under him piled on top of the emotional and physiological disorders I already lived with when I put myself into a relationship with him. After I finally realized (only a few years ago) that a client has to be the executrix of her treatment - and her doctor has to recognize the necessity of allowing her to be the executrix - I gained an understanding of all that transpired between my '60s psychiatrists and me that I certainly lacked at the time the disaster was going down.

In the last year of my seven year run with this doctor - who I had thought was going to guide me back to my repressed events - he, without sharing his thinking with me, decided that what I needed from him was supportive therapy; that he had to continue to see me because I would fall completely apart without him, and we sank into that classic case of the addict and the enabler, or the destroyer and the destroyee (as they put it in AA and Alanon). But, I'd had no exposure at all to twelve-step programs at that time, so I didn't recognize what had happened to the therapy I had thought I was receiving. Apparently, this doctor was just as ignorant of the dynamics between us as I was. If I had known that he had switched horses on me midstream, I would have escaped my relationship with him years sooner.

A young heterosexual woman's seeking psychotherapy from a man in her age range can't possibly lead to anything but failure, in my opinion. There is one possible exception: If doctor and client find each other so interesting and likeable that they choose to enter into a real relationship that transcends and therefore makes obsolete their paradigmatic professional one - a relationship that the doctor perceives as being with a woman who is his equal - I believe the outcome of the relationship would be good. That is because each would find in the here-and-now a good finish to their childhood unfinished business. Both doctor and client, in such a case, had needs or desires in childhood that couldn't be satisfied at that time; but now, in each other they have a chance to experience more of the good transference from childhood relationships and some neutralization of the bad.

For treatment that employs psychoanalytic principles to work to good effect for the client, the psychiatrist has to give her something that is the equivalent of what she desperately wanted but couldn't get from the controllers of her childhood world. It isn't recovering childhood trauma memory and emotion that helps an adult client, it's getting, in her relationship with her therapist, what she couldn't get way back then when she was in the midst of her anguish and couldn't get a caregiver to extricate her from her misery or to meet her needs. The male psychotherapists I've known, who have wanted to steer me back to my childhood, have been as horses wearing blinders that prevent them from seeing anything except the narrow track straight in front of them. I gather, as I look back on experiences I've had in therapy with two or three of these doctors, that they were convinced beyond a shadow of a doubt that all my years of depression could be traced to my having had a deviant relationship with my father. Such assertions by a therapist are nothing more than means of insulting and intimidating clients and getting away with it.

At various psychiatrists' insistence, I've looked at my childhood relationship with my father and my comfort level in, and outside of, male-female relationships since my childhood, and I'm convinced, if there are no females around anywhere that can affect my relationships with males, I'm comfortable with men just as long as they are not malicious or arrogant in their behavior toward me. With females, it's a whole different story.

What my male therapists often seemed to be focused upon, to the exclusion of all other considerations, was the Electra complex, that female equivalent of the Oedipus complex, the discovery of which has been generally attributed to Freud, whose writings and lectures about the Oedipus complex are probably what made him a giant among his peers. Just to recap what that is all about, according to most psychoanalysts as well as many professionals who study the inner lives of small children, little boys typically go through a stage of psychological development at the age of three, four, and five (with some variations) wherein they entertain emotionally passionate and erotically charged attachments to their moms. The theory goes on to say that a boy experiences untold frustration and disappointment through this period of his life because, while one instinctual part of him wants mom to love him in the way mom loves dad and would like dad to be out of the picture, an equal and opposite part of him doesn't want mom to love him in the same way mom loves dad, because he knows in his little heart he's not up to that kind of relationship (and, besides, dad might just squash him like a bug if he were to manage to supersede dad in mom's affections).

Coexisting with this inner conflict in a boy, between enjoying his feelings for his mother and being terrified of them is the love and admiration the little boy instinctually feels for his dad. He's very uncomfortable seeing in himself a treacherous little usurper when he greatly desires his dad's love and good will. Psychoanalytic theory proposes that the naturally occurring healthy conclusion to this tumultuous developmental stage comes as the boy gains confidence that he will not really become mom's mate but will have a mate when he grows up that will be to him as his mom now seems - he will have, in the future, a relationship of his very own that is like the one he sees dad having with mom. In his unconscious, he sees himself as the person (in the love triangle touching himself, his mom, and his dad) who is the decision maker, who willingly gives up the chance to become mom's chosen consort in order to have a relationship with dad uncomplicated by all the competition-for-mom stuff.

Once the boy's adoration of his mother is transferred to dad and his bond to dad is sufficiently strong to sustain him emotionally and spiritually, almost all the Oedipal erotic desires and fears fade and are forgotten except by the parts of the brain that house instincts in which every feeling that one has ever felt seems to live on with strength and urgency that swell with time instead of diminishing. I believe those feelings and memories go to the limbic system where they join up with the instincts that come hardwired in the human brain - the instincts that have been accruing to humans through millions of years of evolution. The hardwired instincts, together with the alterations and additions that are made to those instincts by our experiences as we interact with the world outside ourselves during our early years all build the part of us we think of as our soul. That's the part of us that unfettered free association roaming will take us to under certain environmental conditions that catalyze that process.

I imagine that every female who arrives at adulthood as a heterosexual, hormonally healthy person went through, in childhood, the Electra complex. The Electra complex is for little girls a mirror of what the Oedipus complex is for little boys. According to those who see evidence that little girls go through a phase during their third, fourth, and fifth years in which they have combined love and erotic feelings for their fathers, these feelings form the platform or foundation upon which adult love/sex relationships will be built. Male psychiatrists who take female clients seem to have a predilection for attributing depression in these women to their having unfinished business from their childhood Electra stage relationships with their fathers still lying in their unconscious and adversely affecting their current ability to healthily relate to males.

A professional relationship between a female client and a male psychotherapist is hardly going to lead to benefit for the client, because male therapists abide by a professional code that tells them they must keep themselves from getting emotionally involved with their clients and must steel themselves against being sexually attracted to them. That's laudable. Where this code is violated, we have psychotherapists using their professional position to attract prey. (In a way, we do anyway, but that's a subject for another chapter.) A psychotherapist who maintains the aloof, uninvolved attitude toward his clients that his profession teaches him he must have, is hardly going to be giving his female clients anything spiritually and emotionally that equates to what they desperately needed in childhood from caregivers and couldn't get; that feeling of being "one of us" in a pack in which a child can bond with an alpha she can trust to protect, support, respect and emphasize with her, as well as love her.

So, sessions of free association may regress a client inexorably back into her childhood emotional turmoil, where she can feel all over again all the agony and defeat she felt then, but unless her therapist recognizes what desperate need of hers was going unmet way back when and is willing to meet that need now, no change is going to take place in the poor client's soul. All that will have been accomplished by this return to the traumas of childhood will be to resurrect the agony and add fresh agony to it.

As the 1990s progressed, I began to come to my senses. Very, very slowly the realization began to creep into my mind that I was presenting myself for treatment to a world of people who didn't have a clue as to what would ease the misery of a depressed woman. The only thing they were doing that was effective at all, as far as I could see, was to write prescriptions that sometimes helped if the woman's depression had been of very recent onset and if, concurrent with the medication, the woman's life circumstances improved a bit. For decades, I had been thinking that for me to fail to benefit from psychotherapy made me some sort of freak. How I could possibly have thought that; how I could have let myself be so conned by mental health professionals' talk about "patients getting well if they kept going to their psychotherapy and taking their prescriptions", can only attribute to pathologically-off self-evaluation criteria.

My psychoanalytically oriented doctor practiced deception with me from the moment I first walked into his office in the summer of 1967 and sat down, until our last communication in the mid-1990s, which was a brief phone conversation. The deception that he practiced was in allowing me to think - in fact, employing numerous strategies to make me believe - that he and I were working on something together.

This psychiatrist wasn't about to work *with* me on anything. He was going to work *on* me, and he expected me to be completely compliant with his working on me. If I accidentally stab myself with a gardening tool, opening up a laceration that gushes blood so voluminously that I can see stitches will be necessary to close the wound, I want a doctor to work on me. Maybe I'd want the doctor to work with me if I saw that he was handling my wound so grossly incompetently that I'd better put my two cents in or else end up with a serious infection.

❖ ❖ ❖

What has made human beings the most successful and intimidating predator on earth isn't fangs or claws, it's language as expressed through vocalized and mouthed sounds. Being able to get someone to listen to you when you try to communicate is the greatest survival trait a human can have. Language and speech developed in humans because high reward accrued to those who could use it to influence peers' perception and interpretation of environmental cues. A child's being able to plead a case to Mom for buying her the new version of Barbie that will change Mom's "no" to "yes" is enough to bring on euphoria in a little girl. Observe a typical parent-child relationship and you can't miss the joy and excitement that show in a child's whole body when he sees that he has reasoned his parent out of a position opposing him and has talked his parent into a position where the parent validates and agrees. If a child has parents who value her, this is a common occurrence and is a cause of considerable exuberance but doesn't have the effect that a mega dose of ecstasy would.

On the other hand, for a child whose caregivers couldn't care less about whether she's happy or not, being able to affect them positively with communication may be so difficult to do that achieving it, on the rare occasions that happens, might bring a release of neurotransmitters in her brain for which she is as unprepared as American Indians were for the effects of alcohol when it was introduced to them by Europeans who had had generations of experience with its daily use. What I'm trying to say is that psychotherapy sessions that follow the Freudian model can be hopelessly addictive. If you suffer depression as the aftermath of childhood neglect and maltreatment, having an authority figure listen to you as if what you have to say is worth listening to may have an effect on you similar to being introduced to cocaine or heroin. I think that is where I got the reinforcement for stream-of-consciousness thinking that turned it into an unshakable behavior. Almost from the first hour of my therapy under this doctor, my capacity for communicating with family members, friends, and acquaintances began to go down the drain.

But (trying to get back onto the theme I launched in the first paragraph), why am I linking high verbal IQ with poor outcome in psychotherapy? May I answer that by asking you to take an inventory of your verbal intelligence assets and your team-player, fit-into-the-pack assets, and compare what you realistically believe your standings on these two disparate cerebral packages may be with what you imagine the standings of most psychotherapists are likely to be in these areas? If you have ever taken standardized tests of intelligence or aptitude, and almost all of us have, please consider the percentile ranks on verbal ability into which your test scores placed you. Out of your scholastic records, draw an overall estimate of all your grades on all humanities courses you have ever taken or independent studies you have pursued, and give some thought to where you might rank if ninety-nine other people and you were given a test for recall and comprehension of all content of all humanities subjects you have ever explored. What are the chances that you will find a psychotherapist that will rank on a level equal to or higher than the level where you are?

Mental health professionals would have us gullible folk believe that their course work and supervised practica lift them into a realm of knowledge and understanding of psychological matters that is beyond the ken of us un-institutionally-trained people. They would have those of us who take ourselves to them for help believe that they can observe us for only one or two meetings, perhaps gather some scores from standardized questionnaire-type tests they give us, and the training that they have undergone enables them, without further ado, to know what our diagnosis is and what treatment is right for us.

If a psychic were to say to us, "I can see inside you and know all your hidden fears and longings", most of us would smile in amusement and roll our eyes. When a mental health professional makes exactly the same assertion to us (although worded quite differently) we take every word seriously. In fact, we are so intimidated by what they tell us about ourselves that we may spend years or even the remainder of our lives with our self-images on the knees, before their pronouncements. I know I have done so. In my first years of treatment, in my teens and twenties, I was so brain-washed into believing that everything about me was an open book to them - a book I was too ignorant to be able to read - that I took every negative picture of me that they presented to me as true and laid down the little good self-image I had to take up the crappy one they told me was me.

When I think of the devastating effects psychiatrists' "shrinking" of our personalities can have on us, I can't help but think of a man I used to converse with occasionally at a church I attended in the 1960s and '70s. He was of late middle age and made his living as a salesman. As a young man, following his acquisition of a bachelors, he had entered a medical school in Chicago with the ambition to become a psychiatrist. At some point in his training, after the man had gone through a period of a psychoanalysis which he was required to complete for his specialty, the administrators of his program informed him that he would not be allowed to continue - that he had personality problems or neuroses that rendered him unqualified for a degree from their school. They had high standards, they said, and allowing an emotionally substandard person such as he to have a degree from their program would jeopardize the reputation which their school and its world-class graduates held.

I remember the man's perpetual whole-body affect well. His movements lacked ease and communicated self-consciousness. When I think of the way he walked, the word "stumpy" is the adjective that my mind associates with his gait. When I revisit his face in my mind's eye, I always see apology and discomfiture. I was listening to a man speak who was still living in a world of humiliating failure even though thirty or more years had passed between the time that the actual failure occurred and the day on which he spoke of it to me. The source of his lifetime of shame had been nothing more than a few words spoken by a few psychiatrists and psychoanalysts. The toxin they had delivered to the man's self-image had passed to him a handicapping condition of the soul. I got a dose of toxin of the same type from psychiatrists before whom I exposed my soul while in my twenties.

If mental health professionals had no power to destroy our lives with what they say and write about us, we could shrug off the comments they make to us and about us as easily as I shrug off being called a sinner by a fundamentalist preacher. We could give thoughtful consideration to the personally-diminishing statements they've delivered to us, assess whether the put-downs were realistic or goofy, and either try to change or else forget all about what they've said. But once a person has taken herself to a mental health professional for help, she loses the freedom to be able to do that. People with mental health credentials issued to them by recognized institutions, even as meaningless a credential as a BA in psychology, are taken by our society to be infallibly correct when they characterize humans who don't have those credentials. Their opinions, no matter how dangerously inaccurate they might be, can mobilize many people in our environment to move against us in a heartbeat and take away from us everything that makes life worthwhile.

People with mental health credentials have the power to destroy your relationships and your livelihood, and they are doing so all around us. They do not see that the slander in which so many of them routinely engage is slander. Many credentialed people, when they find they are hypothesizing to a person who is impressed by their credentials, seem to get so consumed with their power to affect their listener with their words, they blindly rattle off wild analyses of the person in front of them or of anyone in that person's life that they think they can successfully demonize to her or blame for any of her complaints. I guess the payoff for the professionally trained person comes when the person they've counseled thusly turns away from the significant other under whose influence they have previously operated and adopts the pseudo-analyst as the source of all direction in how to think and feel about everyone in her life. I guess the trained person must actually believe that by "exposing the real character" of a significant other - one who, they tell the listener, only pretends to love her so they can use her, he or she is being a Mother Theresa in mental health Calcutta.

Whether a mental health professional is telling a client how mentally ill she is or telling her how mentally ill and unsavory someone that she knows is, the typical professional, in my experience, seems to be unable to admit to themselves, or to anyone else, that their judgment is subjective, and that there is no training, no protocol, no test, or any other process which will ever eliminate subjectivity from their judgment of their client's mental and emotional status. Both the professional and society at large say that since he or she has been institutionally trained and licensed, their judgment with regard to human beings is objective. They say that whatever they think about you is right, and, unless you have equivalent training and licenses, if you don't agree with them, you are wrong.

Arguing against the diagnosis of a mental health professional will be a lost cause, because the professional will interpret your protest against his diagnosis as proof that his diagnosis is correct. You will probably be informed that you are in denial or that your defenses are preventing you from seeing that his diagnosis applies to you. A high verbal IQ will lead you down the garden path when attempting to communicate with mental health professionals. You will think that these pros, of all people on the planet, will surely be able to see the same things in human communications that you intuitively see with no formal training. Because you can recognize truth, falsehood, pretensions, deception, hypocrisy, illogical conclusions, irrelevant material, stereotyping, dogma, and the like, you will assume they can also. If you believe that you can provide a psychotherapist with the reasonable explanation for a particular behavior of yours that he's calling a symptom and that he will say, "Oh, I see ... your behavior was to be expected given your circumstances", just try that.

Whatever diagnostic label is pinned on you by a mental health professional is not a label that is known to only you and your therapist. Don't forget insurance companies, government agencies, and employers' applications and lie detector tests. Even applications for drivers' licenses and gun purchases ask if you have ever been diagnosed with a mental illness. If you are depressed, according to medical codes, you are mentally ill. It makes no sense to me that depression should even come under the heading of mental illness unless it's accompanied by psychosis. Most of us who are depressed are depressed because of unbearable life events; we are frozen in response to fear, in survival terms. Our being frozen occurs because either fighting or fleeing will make our situation even worse than cringing inertly. Fighting, fleeing, and freezing, as appropriate, in response to fear, couldn't be more biologically healthy. How many organisms freeze to escape detection or to avoid exciting aggression in those larger organisms that prey on them? Depression (freezing) is too instinctual among far too many living things to be classified as a mental illness.

But, if you are depressed enough to seek treatment in a typical setting and pay for it through the typical insurers, you will acquire the identity, "mentally ill". As if that's not depressing enough, your therapist will stick a few more labels on you like "bi-polar" or "borderline personality disorder" or "obsessive-compulsive". You will feel as if you've just been told you don't belong with "normal" people anymore. As stigmas go, seeking help from a mental health professional and being therefore classified as "mentally ill" will get you one of the most powerful stigmas there is in our society. When I see ads, letters, and articles sponsored by mental health organizations or authored by psychotherapists in which they proclaim that society must get its view of the "mentally ill" out of the dark ages, I cannot help but remark to myself that were it not for mental health professionals' characterizing everyone who seeks help for emotional complaints as "mentally ill", society might not have a dark ages attitude.

If your therapist is a licensed practitioner, whatever he or she says you are becomes who you are to society, even if they are wrong. Even if your therapist is a delusional, sadistic bully - you don't think such individuals would have a license? - society (your employers and co-workers and maybe even your friends and family members) will believe you are what a therapist says you are. You might assume that you, having a high IQ and thus being able to see in what way a mental health professional errs when he applies symptoms and a diagnosis to you that just don't fit, would be able to open a discussion with the professional, explaining to him why things aren't with you as he says they are.

You might imagine that he would seriously consider your arguments. You might think that your logical and reasonable points would stimulate some thought, on his part, that he might need to take another look at his assessment in light of what you've told him about his misinterpretations. Because you have a high IQ and are therefore fully open to new information flooding in from everywhere and seldom dismiss novel ideas out of hand without even investigating them, you might have the notion that your psychotherapist's brain must surely work the same way. That's what I assumed for many years. After decades of being frustrated in my attempts to communicate ideas to therapists from whom I've sought services, I've come to the conclusion that possibly most of what I've tried to communicate was probably over their heads. Excepting statistics, psychology courses have been the easiest to pass of any courses I've ever taken.

HIGH VERBAL IQ AND PSYCHOTHERAPY

Would course work and practicum really give any human being the ability to observe and listen to another human being for a few minutes to an hour or two, perhaps administer some one-size-fits-all psychological tests, and thereupon make a correct diagnosis of her emotional and mental health? Having been put through the interview, test, and render-diagnosis process many times in my life, I would judge this approach to be worthless to clients. (This makes a lot of money for psychiatrists and psychologists, though.) If medical school course work and practica don't give psychotherapists the wherewithal to bring relief to people who are hurting emotionally, what would adequately prepare those who aspire to help us? I believe that mental health professionals of every variety - psychiatrists, psychologists, counselors, and all others who adhere to the paradigm for treatment that seems to be employed universally - need to chuck the paradigm and build something from scratch that's as far from the fifty-minute-hour concept as they can get.

The fifty-minute-hour concept works beautifully for those seeking to earn a living by presenting themselves to society as healers and offering to sell individuals segments of their time, by appointment, in their offices, during hours convenient for them, as they so choose. Their sense of well-being is enhanced greatly, too, when you, the client, allow them to meet other of their needs at your expense; specifically, their need to be seen by their friends, family and community as one benefitting society. A person might get the impression that the therapists are doing all the giving and the clients are those who are getting.

I believe that if you have a high verbal IQ, you yourself have an intellectual asset that you may never find in a therapist. For now, I can't think of any word more applicable to that verbal asset you probably have most of than creativity. You are an artist with genius in producing thought. Who are you going to find, among therapists, who will recognize and appreciate the value and beauty in your thought work, if you have never published anything of commercial significance, don't have a prestigious professional title like professor or editor, and loathe speaking publicly?

Further, if you have a high verbal IQ, you probably have a natural curiosity that leads you to stick your nose in books and to investigate and research with the kind of passion and relentlessness that surges in the breasts of gold miners when they think they're onto a vein. Before you even take yourself to a therapist, you might already understand more about your psyche, what makes it tick, and what it would take to make it tick better than your prospective psychotherapist will grasp after you've been seeing him or her for years.

During my school years, I took physics, algebra, geometry, chemistry, music theory, physical education, and statistics. I passed all those subjects, even earning an A on my second go-round with statistics. Does that mean I have any skill or competency in putting into practice principles that were presented to me in these courses? I remember hardly anything of these subjects. Even after taking two graduate level courses having to do with evaluating scientific studies and resulting statistical data, I can't remember enough about research design to even be able to tell you what it is I don't know. I have the right to put on my resume that I've had courses in research design at the graduate level, thereby giving anyone who reads my resume the impression that I'm competent to pass judgment, credibly, on scientific studies. Am I?

How many mental health professionals might there be who are just as clueless about the rationale and application of psychological concepts they've studied as I am about the concepts I parroted back to my professors on end-of-course tests on research design? I've known many psychiatrists, psychologists, psychiatric nurses, collegiate psychology instructors and professors, and counselors. Few, if any, have been carrying over understanding of the simplest Psychology 101 concepts to their practices when it comes to the administration of therapy to their clients.

Just to mention one concept which I remember well from Psychology 101, do you recall the rule which says that if one wishes to have a mutually beneficial relationship with another human being, one cannot entertain hidden agendas? Which, of my many, psychiatrists, psychologists, counselors, psychiatric nurses, ever said to me anything like this?:

"I have your file here with all the notes I have made as I've talked with you. I've made a tentative diagnosis in your case, and I've written up a treatment plan which I want to propose to you. If you will take this chair beside me, I will spread the material out on my desk so that you and I can review what I've written about you and your symptoms. If you see, at any time, that I've misunderstood something you've told me, please say so.

"After we've completed a review of my notes and I've corrected any misinterpretations I've attached to what you've told me, I will present to you my proposal for your treatment. After you and I have selected treatment options and details on which we can both agree, I will give you a copy of your treatment plan so that you will never be in doubt as to what we hope to achieve with therapy and how we hope to achieve it. If at any time in the course of your therapy; you become dissatisfied with the plan and want to revise it or chuck it entirely and work with me on devising a new plan, we can do that. Any notes or observations that I make or that I receive from elsewhere pertaining to you will go into this file - and to nowhere else but into this file - and you are welcome to review your file any time you are here for an appointment and request it."

I can only think of one provider who previewed my treatment plan with me in a similar way. A right to this kind of open access to one's personal material is guaranteed for any child receiving special education services through any government program of which I have knowledge. A right to this kind of open access is guaranteed to most employees with respect to the personnel files on them that are maintained by their employers. There is no sound reason why medical people have the right to maintain files on clients that they won't let clients see. It strikes me as absolute stupidity for a psychiatrist in a clinic and his fellow staff members to write notes containing their opinions about a client's character and personality without sharing with that client what they're writing, to post those opinions in a permanent file, and to prevent the client from seeing what's been written about her while readily passing the material around amongst themselves and any insurers.

Any therapist who had any natural intuition or capacity for imagining themselves in the client's chair would sense that these acts - writing down very personal things about a client with whom you work, keeping quiet about those things when with her yet sharing those things with fellow staff members when she's not present, and making plans in advance about what you are going to say to her and how you are going to behave toward her during her therapy sessions - constitute a hidden agenda.

Let us take another snippet from Psychology 101. Remember all that stuff about needs? The need to be able to express yourself and the need to be understood by others when you do? How much is psychotherapy going to help you, if your psychotherapist can't grasp points you try to explain to him or her? I can guarantee that the psychotherapist will not be thinking, "This person is telling me things that are beyond my understanding". I can guarantee to you that he or she will be thinking instead, "This patient has grandiose ideas, unusual thought content, delusions, obsessions", and will be writing in their session notes any one of those words and phrases and others they can think of to convince themselves and anyone who reads their notes that you are a mentally ill person, maybe even psychotic.

What are the chances that it won't make any difference if your psychotherapist is nowhere near the level where you are in natural aptitude for grasp of humanities? The AMA (American Medical Association) and other professional organizations want us to believe that if a psychotherapist has gone through the prescribed number of prescribed courses, undergone the prescribed supervised internship, and has sent in all the required fees and forms for the prescribed state and federal licenses, they're skilled and competent. Further, these organizations want to tell us that the most competent among the competent are those who hold membership in national professional organizations. I know, unequivocally, that none of these things ensure that a psychotherapist will be skilled or competent at doing what he or she presents himself or herself to society as being able to do.

HIGH VERBAL IQ AND PSYCHOTHERAPY

THE LATEST APPROACH TO DEPRESSION IN WOMEN: INSULT, INTIMIDATION, AND ACCUSATION

Coordinator, Psychiatric Training and Services
XXXXX School of Medicine
April 2003
Subject: Your Training Programs for Mental Health Professionals
Dear Coordinator:
An article in the most recent issue of *AARP, The Magazine* reopened wounds that have to do with how your psychiatrists, psychologists, and psychiatric nurses were being trained to treat women suffering from depression in the 1990s. I hope with all my heart that the XXXXX School of Medicine has brought these practices to an end, but if you have, I don't think you've gotten the word out

to former trainees.

Just prior to my coming as a client to your psychiatric out-patient clinic, my daughter-in-law and daughter had conversations in which they apparently decided that neither felt comfortable around me and the only thing that could cause that had to be that I was an incestuous pedophile; that I must have sexually molested my daughter as a child and would do the same with my grandchildren if the family didn't prevent me from having any further contact with them. In one of the final conversations I had with my daughter, she screamed at me, "If you ever try to see my children, I'll slap your teeth down your throat".

As I plan to share with others this letter I am addressing to you, I believe I need to explain what the situation is regarding slander in North Carolina under the law, because I don't believe that the average citizen of this state is aware that institutions of higher learning here are sending their graduates out armed to make accusations against whomever they choose without fear of reprisal. Usually these accusations (manufactured by those who have gone out from state universities prepared to work in health, human services, and education fields) are of child abuse and molestation. Those graduates of your classes and internships seem to know full well that, no matter the horrendousness or falseness of what they are accusing their target human of doing, they will never have to face any consequences when their accusations have destroyed relationships and lives.

Defamation is protected by law in North Carolina under the pretense that it is giving legal protection to freedom of speech. Freedom of speech has nothing to do with the fact that a lying slanderer can concoct any characterization of a person they want to hurt (more often than not that person is a female) and whatever the liar has said is legally taken to be true. The Constitution of the United States is supposed to guarantee that a person in this country be proven guilty, with "due process", by a judge or jury, before they can have their life, liberty and pursuit of happiness taken from them. Even then, the punishment cannot be "cruel and unusual", according to The Constitution.

Here where I live, slanderers, with their accusations of child abuse and molestation, deal out punishments to the people they accuse that are far more cruel and unusual than most punishments handed out in courts to convicted criminals. Slanderers revel in their power to deprive their victims of life, liberty, and the pursuit of happiness. That society and the law collaborate to reward slanderers for torturing their targets, is just icing on the cake for those who rise by lying with malice.

Ask any parent, who has a child who has been led to believe the parent has abused and molested them, how it feels to see their child - with whom they previously have had an open and loving relationship - suddenly turn cold, angry, and suspicious toward them, and that parent will tell you that the pain of this is indescribable. Further, there won't be time limits to this pain - it will be a life sentence because introjections, by a child, of a belief that a parent who they had thought loved them, is really a deceiving predator who has only been pretending, putting on an act of loving them, implants a toxin in the heart and soul of a child that his or her body and brain will never be able to completely excrete. The child is left permanently damaged as well as has been the innocent parent whom the child has been led to believe has done something bad to them that they can't remember.

As those on your staff who teach and train well know, if a child accuses his or her mother of any kind of abuse or molestation, the law says that mother is guilty of whatever it was that her child said of her, and she can, from that moment in time on, be treated by representatives of health care facilities and state agencies as if she has actually been proven to be guilty.

This unconstitutional circumstance all but gifts some among us, particularly those with "good guy" credentials (like RN, MD, or BA in counseling or psychology) with a way to get a lot of admiring attention and elevation in status from maneuvering children (and adults, all of whom were once children) into imagining that they were abused or molested in early childhood and have repressed that memory. Humans are fantastically suggestible - far too suggestible to have their imaginations of what *might* have been done to them by a parent in the past, or what *might* be done to them in the future, carry with such conjectures the weight of factual evidence under the law.

That, I think, is where you, as administrators, instructors, and trainers in the XXXXX School of Medicine come in. I have heard, from a reliable source, that you operate on the theory that women suffering from depression are deceptive, callous users of children, and that it is good practice to unflinchingly accuse them of being such (preferably in front of their children, but anywhere you happen to come across them). Treatment of depressed women (you and other North Carolina institutions of higher learning appear to me to be teaching) should center on talking to depressed women and behaving toward them in as debasing a way as you can contrive to do.

Before my ex-husband's wife, a woman with a degree in psychology (so my children said) had begun telling my daughter that I didn't love her, that I was "only pretending to love her in order to get her to lower her guard so that I could use her in my plan to turn her to prostitution", she had loved me. That my daughter would ingest this sick, delusional tale and vomit it back up to me as true just wouldn't have happened had this woman not presented herself as having a degree in psychology from an in-state university.

When my daughter-in-law, with her brand new psychiatric RN credentials from your school of medicine piled on, demonstrating for my children and their paternal family members how she could do far more damage to me than their psychology-BA-degreed stepmother had been able to do with her fabrications, that was the end of the world for me.

Later, it became more and more clear in my mind that there must be some idea afloat in our state's institutions of higher learning that depression in women is synonymous with the greatest evil that has ever existed in the hearts of humans. Although, it should occur to instructors and students alike that such a theory was precisely the kind Hitler made up about Jews. How on earth could trainers of psychiatrists, psychologists, psychiatric nurses, and other "helping" professionals be teaching such malicious and obviously baseless ideas?

At the time I made an appointment at your clinic, however, I had not made the connection in my mind with the epidemic surrounding us here of life and relationship destroying insinuation, intimidation, and accusation and programs of study at state universities - particularly for us here, yours.

Imagining that a doctor or psychologist or therapist at your clinic could help me find a way to rescue my relationship with my children from the women of my ex-husband's pack (women institutionally trained in psychology and psychiatry) who barely knew me personally but who, for no reason that I could see other than to gain power over gullible minds and to impress each other and my children, had concocted an image of a monster-mother and told my children that was me, I made an appointment at your clinic.

This is where this article, "We're Wired to Connect" in *AARP's* magazine enters the picture. When I anticipated my intake visit at your outpatient clinic, I visualized pouring out to some empathetic mental health professional the agony, the grief, the anger, the overwhelming despair I felt that my daughter could be led to believe such an awful thing about me when I loved her and would have given anything I possessed just to have her love and respect me again. When my daughter was an infant and preschooler, I had been pretty cold, unaffectionate, and critical with her just as my caretakers had been with me, but I had realized I wasn't being the unconditionally loving mother I should be, and I had gone to work diligently on myself to change that. I did change that, totally. Never had I abused my daughter in any way other than by failing to give her the warmth, affection, and understanding that all children need. That is terrible, surely, but it doesn't rank with immorally using or sexually molesting your child.

When I cried out in anguish to the male psychologist who was my first contact at your clinic, that my daughter had accused me of sexually molesting her as a child, he coldly asked, "Well, did you?". I didn't say it out loud, but I certainly puzzled with myself, "If I had molested my daughter, why would I be over here begging you in anguish for help in getting this falsehood - that has been planted in my daughter's mind by something that went on in conversations she had with a woman who has just graduated from your program in psychiatric nursing - undone?"

Next, I was shuffled on to a young male intern dressed in an old, baggy red tee shirt and pants of the same sort, looking as if he'd just come in from harvesting crops or doing construction work. He videotaped an interview with me, went off to confer with superiors, and came back saying they'd diagnosed me with "borderline personality disorder" and that they were going to take an "aggressive treatment approach" with me.

First, this doctor instructed me to journalize - to write for him what I felt was pertinent to my life-long depression. In my usual, totally transparent, wide-open-to-the world way of communicating, I wrote exactly what he told me to. "That's not really what I'm looking for," he told me. Then he turned my appointments with him into a series of interrogations that reminded me of scenes from cop shows where detectives grill a suspect who they know is guilty of a crime but who won't confess.

When he kept inserting the question, "Were you sleeping with your father?" into our discussions - never apropos to anything we were talking about at the time - I took it calmly for awhile. I'd had enough years of psychoanalytically oriented psychotherapy in my twenties in Miami, Florida, to work through my repressed Oedipal stage fears and fantasies. There had been no incestuous relationship between my father and me, and I'd told that to this incest-obsessed intern. I have three sisters, all educated and aware, one an RN, and all of us agree that while my father could be an insensitive brute to his daughters, he had no sexual interest in anyone except our mother, inside the home or out.

Before I go any farther in this account of my experience at your outpatient psychiatric clinic, I would like to bring up the fact that not one of the people who've supposedly had the education and training that enabled them to see that I was a deceiving child abuser and pedophile - and state that to my children as fact - has ever said one word about signs and symptoms in people that would indicate they suffered abuse in early childhood. I'm sure that the reason my children's lifelong good mental health has never been mentioned by my children's stepmother (BA in psychology, according to my children) or my son's wife (RN in psychiatric nursing) or my children (who have so enthusiastically acted upon the horror tales about me that psych-trained people have fed them) or the professionals who conducted interrogations of me at your clinic, has been because none of you have cared at all about whether or not my children suffered abuse in their childhoods. If any of you had, you would have asked after my children's adult functioning in love and in work.

The humiliating, torturously painful accusations and games to which I've been subjected have all been about the pleasure that my accusers have derived from having the freedom to gang up on and emotionally torment another human being who has no power to defend herself that they can see. The added reward for them has been that they could engage in inflicting this level of inhumanly cruel pain on me and get their prestige boosted into the bargain by mythologizing everything they were doing to hurt me as being the good guys saving poor, innocent, abused, molested children from a woman who was a monster.

Richard Dawkins, in his book, *The Selfish Gene*, spent more than a few words talking about those who present themselves to their fellow human beings as "helpers", "saviors", "rescuers", when roles of that type are often sought by people who just want to gain for themselves a certain image and an enhancement to their prestige among the people whose opinion means the most to them. This is all I have seen going on in the hearts and minds of all those who have seemed to me to be absolutely euphoric as they have accosted me in front of each other with the most humiliating and painful things they could think up to say and do to me; just people addicted to getting high off torturing a helpless woman with no defenders.

If the two psych-trained women, who have been the originators of the most outrageous accusations created about me and fed to my children and others, actually cared anything about children, they would have shown concern for their own. I see absolute evidence in each case, that they did not do that.

As to my children: both are college graduates; both have had close friends, mentors, and mates over periods of time that have lasted for years; both have had loving ties with relatives that have endured a lifetime; both have maintained careers for years, and I have never heard that either had problems with supervision or teamwork. I've never heard that either has been a victim of addictions (other than the addiction to hurting me, humiliating me, and making up lies about me) or has had the necessity to take themselves for treatment to any mental health professional. For children who have been as egregiously harmed by their mother in their first years of life as my children have been made to believe they have been, they surely are in fantastically great shape emotionally.

Returning to my visits at the XXXXX School of Medicine's psychiatric clinic ...

When the intern kept trying to force me to give him what it looked obvious to me he so badly wanted from me - a tale that my father and I had had an incestuous relationship - I endured his tiresome campaign without much protest because I know how badly a young intern must want to impress his superiors. But when he asked, "Was your father sleeping with your sister?" and my older sister was eight when I was three, the dehumanization of me and my family that this man was practicing with his "therapy" suddenly registered. His "therapy" was nothing more than repeated insults to me and my family of such magnitude that society reserves them for the most scorned among us.

His insistence on continuing to cram "sleeping with your father" down my throat after I had told him that I knew, from having had previous psychoanalytic therapy, that my father had nothing to do with my developing depression in early childhood - in fact, was the only saving relationship with a caregiver I had had in childhood - his insistent inferences that my father molested his daughters wasn't therapy; the man was communicating to me, over and over, that the scrupulously upright Presbyterian Scots-Irish Virginia family from which my father (and thus

I and my sisters) had sprung was not one with which to be comfortable and proud, but was rather one of shameful degeneracy. "What in the world is wrong with everybody that everybody is absolutely obsessed with incest?" exploded from my mouth.

Later, at home, I decided that since my profession was communication, and since my national test scores for licensure in my profession had proved I was pretty near the top of the heap, it was up to me to inform him that we were not communicating and to try to get through to him why we were not. I called. As soon as I told him that his discrediting of everything I wrote or said was preventing any communication from taking place between us that would be of benefit to me, he countered with, "You've been lying to me".

That utterance cleared up for me why every response he made to anything I tried to relate to him was completely irrelevant to what I'd said, a non sequitur, nonsensical given my circumstances. "All right", I told him, "if you don't believe what I've told you, maybe I can get the psychiatrist with whom I worked in Miami to tell you what I've told you; I worked through my Electra complex, and there was no sexual molestation or sexually inappropriate anything practiced on me in my childhood. I don't think any child has ever been any more shielded from all carnal knowledge than I was throughout my childhood. Incest runs in families, and it absolutely did not run in mine, or I or one of my sisters would have discovered it somewhere along the way."

To my great surprise, my Miami psychiatrist was still in practice at the same location where he had practiced when I had been a client of his twenty plus years before.

To my even greater surprise, his name and phone number were listed with the phone company, and when I called his number, he answered. As I've said, creating self-doubt in a client is a forte among psychiatrists, so my XXXXX psychiatrist intern, who had told me he was implementing a treatment plan for me approved by superiors, had created doubt in my mind that I really had worked through my Electra complex in Miami. When I had finished that work, my psychiatrist had never said to me, "You have successfully worked through your Electra conflicts". I just felt confident I had because of having read so much about how psychoanalysis proceeds and having compared my own experience with what I'd read.

But, as I said, the intern at XXXXX had created self-doubt in me, had confused me, left me in need of validation from someone I trusted to know more about Oedipal and Electra conflicts than those psychiatrists at XXXXX School of Medicine who were having this intern shove "You had an incestuous relationship with your father as a child, and you're lying about it" down my throat.

When I asked my psychiatrist of years before, "I worked through my Electra stage, didn't I?" his affirmative reply was very, very comforting. I had been almost certain, for many years, that my father played the least part in my miseries of any relative whose life had touched mine during my childhood, but I had never before received any validation of that self-assessment from any mental health professional. Now the interning psychiatrist at XXXXX Medical School was telling me I was lying to him when I said I'd worked through my father-daughter issues with a psychiatrist in Miami in my twenties. I asked my former doctor if I could give the psychiatric intern at the

XXXXX clinic his name and phone number. He had no objection to that, and I did so.

Your treatment team's next move was to greet me on my following appointment there with a roomful of males; doctors in white coats and others (probably whoever they could dig up at the spur of the moment, I suppose). I knew that certain Health and Human Services regulations stated that I couldn't be separated out from other women and put into a room with a group of male-only interrogators, so I demanded that another woman be present. It wasn't that I cared that much about their isolating me with a group consisting of males only. I simply felt that these men were too pleased with themselves at devising a game in which they thought they'd have me trapped into being intimidated by a power pack of men.

The woman who came seemed to be very annoyed that she'd been drawn into my appointment, and I don't recall that she contributed anything except for exhibiting great impatience to be out of there. One man and another questioned me; all appearing to want to prove I'd been affected in some injurious and lasting way by my relationship with my father. At the end, whatever it was my treatment team had hoped to accomplish with their "aggressive treatment", no one bothered to divulge to me. What I'd come there for - some help with the injustice that had been done to me by allegations of a defamatory nature, related to my children as if they had been fact - had been completely ignored, and instead of offering me any help, it looked to me as if the whole treatment team had been concentrated on how they were going to make me face that I was a predator by wringing out of me an admission that my father had been one. How disgusting!

I'd come to your clinic trying to get some answers as to what had happened in her psychiatric RN training at XXXXX that had led my daughter-in-law to presume that she had the right to step into my relationships with my children, influence them to turn all my communication with them over to her (just as my children's stepmother had persuaded my ex to do much earlier in my children's lives), and to begin the same kind of planning of family events my ex's wife had consistently undertaken so that my children could show in their behavior toward me how clearly that wanted their shunning of me to be seen by everyone. Is this kind of animal-pack game-playing actually being modeled by trainers of those who are going to be coming out into our communities as therapists? I can't help but get the impression that your trainers are modeling the behavior of wolf-pack alphas to the omegas they run off as being the behavior you want to see your trainees and interns show to depressed women.

After this, I have no idea why I would ever go back to your outpatient clinic again, but I was lacking enough in good sense to do that. Still longing to have a relationship with my children, I came one more time. This time, I got a new young male intern whose supervisor instructed him to get from me the name of the doctor who was prescribing Wellbutrin for me. By this time, I wouldn't have trusted your people with info of where I was getting my electricity and water, much less the name of a doctor who was actually and empathetically trying to help me. I respectfully and politely declined to provide the name of the prescribing physician.

The intern left to confer with his superior then came back. "You are not being honest with us", he said. By this time, I'd had enough of accusations of my being of low character from my ex's wife, my daughter-in-law, my daughter, my son, and your previous treatment team to really be fed up with things being said to me salted with words associated with deception and untrustworthiness.

When the intern returned with the statement his superior had sent him to make to me regarding my failure to give him the name of my provider of Wellbutrin, "You're not being honest...", I replied completely honestly, "I'm being totally honest with you. I'm not going to tell you!" Back the intern went for more consultation with his superior.

Into the room a woman swept with a folder in hand. She extended her hand to me as physicians generally do when they enter a room where they meet a client, but when I reached out to take her extended hand she pulled it back hastily and walked briskly past me to seat herself at a desk in the corner where she bowed her head over her folder as if reading and kept her back to me. She began some stern, authoritarian statement like, "We can't help you if you are not going to be honest with us". I said, "No, I guess not", got up from my chair and left your clinic without more ado.

Is this the state-of-the-art approach to depression in women now? Talk and behave toward them so coldly and crudely they just don't come back?

Dawkins and the Genes that Rule the World

Throughout the first two-thirds of my life, I had the notion that human beings were, by nature, good, and that the only reason some did bad things was because of life experiences that had put them on the wrong path. I envisioned humans as all having an underlying operating system that predisposed them to want to do unto others as they would have others do unto them. People who did bad things, I imagined, were people who just needed good therapists like the Menninger Brothers, the Fromm's, the Freud's, or the Jung's of this world to help them rid themselves of their veneer of badness. Then, in the early 1980s, a psychology professor of mine at William and Mary recommended a book to me, *The Selfish Gene*, by zoologist Richard Dawkins (copyrighted in 1976 but derived from earlier publications of his own and dozens of other scientists writing throughout the mid decades of the 1900s) that over time came to change my concept of the human psyche. After reading *The Selfish Gene*, doubt began very slowly to creep into my mind about the motivations of people in my life that I had hitherto regarded as paragons of altruism.

It seems to be generally accepted now by most biologists, zoologists, and other scientifically oriented researchers that humans are, unless sociologically programmed to continually resist their core instincts, the most vicious, bloodthirsty predators that have ever inhabited this planet. At the present time, there is no doubt in my mind whatsoever that their view is correct. This belief represents an almost 180-degree turn from the Pollyannaish, infantile concept of humans which I held prior to my encountering Dawkins' theories. Without rereading the book, I will attempt to paraphrase some of the notions I acquired from it that lodged in the back of my mind and which began to cause me to reassess what goes on in human relationships - most especially what had gone on in mine.

Dawkins believes, as the name of his book implies, that the genes of humans, as in all other organisms, are driven to survive and to produce as many copies of themselves as possible by fair means or foul. He reminds the reader of the path by which humans have gained dominion over almost every other living thing on earth. Humans who have eschewed peaceful coexistence with other of earth's inhabitants and who have relentlessly engaged in complete annihilation of competitors have been the humans who have flourished. Humans have wiped out whole species, practiced infanticide and genocide, and, not uncommonly, killed and eaten not only their fellow men but their own children.

Humans have displayed addiction to violent conquest of lands belonging to others of their species, following orders to kill every man, woman, and child (after raping the women and humiliating the men) so that they could take over their dwellings, fruiting crops, and fertile land, and assuring themselves and each other that God - or Allah, or whoever - had given them all that wealth they'd taken, and that those of their species they had just wiped out weren't fit to live.

From every millennium of history, we see evidence that physically torturing and psychologically humiliating other people has been one of the most animating and euphoria producing things that humans want to do, to be seen doing, and to be audience to other people doing. Those of us who grew up Christian were led to believe we don't do things like that. Laying aside the blarney about how we had to do that to those we did it to because someone had to punish those evil people who would have corrupted the righteous if they'd been left unmolested, Christians have been as gung-ho about torturing, humiliating, and stealing from their fellow beings as any religion ever was.

As animals go, we humans are really a sorry lot. While wolves, lions, and most carnivores attack and kill for food, humans attack and subjugate or destroy other living things because the act delivers a satisfaction to them that has nothing to do with filling the stomach.

Dawkins concludes his book with the proposal that those humans who have met and survived evolution's trials have done so, primarily, not because they have been unexcelled among animals in viciousness, but because they have developed the ability to trick those upon which they think to prey into letting down their guards. The survival trait that beats all others, says Dawkins, is the instinct to successfully deceive. The more a predatory animal, such as a human, can deceive his intended subject into thinking, prior to his incursion, that he's harmless - surely even a friend - the easier his task of preying will be. The ultimate in successful deception genes, Dawkins says, is the gene that moves the predator to attempt to disguise himself as benefactor, not foe, and then to be taken in by his own disguise.

Deception and self-deception work symbiotically with viciousness and ruthlessness to assure a human's success in this life. If I can covet, steal, slander, fornicate irresponsibly and murder while passing myself off as a great guy or gal through smiles, charm, praise and acts of generosity and self-sacrifice, then I can get a whole lot more opportunities to covet, steal, slander, fornicate and murder than if I employ no cover-up for my vicious, predatory activities. With my "I'm a good person" nametag on (metaphorically speaking) I can convince the skeptical and suspicious to lower their guards and allow themselves to be vulnerable to my using them for my purposes.

However, if I do not also have the trait of self-deception, then my deceptions won't be nearly as effective as with it.

Lacking self-deception, I won't have the complete confidence and faith in my own goodness to carry off presenting myself as altruistic when I am predatory. Whether we are aware of it or not, in our interactions with other living things, we are giving off communications on many levels continuously whether we are speaking or silent. Most of us are largely unaware on a conscious level, at any given moment of our interactions with another human being, what a great impact each of us is having on the other through communications that are extraneous to words being spoken. Without self-deception, my deceptions will be conscious to me, and I will betray myself to you through many of the same bodily signals that allow a lie detector to identify a liar who knows he is lying.

As survival traits go, it's great to have a gene that moves one to put on Granny's gown and nightcap, climb into her bed, and pull the covers up to one's eyeballs, if one is a wolf hoping to deceive Little Red Riding Hood into letting down defenses. However, like Red, prey can be quite clever at recognizing deception and at maneuvering a predator into giving himself away. If the wolf, having donned Granny's nightclothes and having scrunched down under the covers in Granny's bed, had suddenly been consumed with the delusion that he really was Granny, he might have pulled the whole deception thing off. Thinking himself to actually be Granny, he wouldn't have responded to Red's "Granny, what big teeth you have!" with "All the better to eat you with", or jumped out of bed while Red's suspicions were not fully allayed.

Had Big Bad Wolf been a human instead of a wolf, even the initial thought to eat Red would have come into his mind in a disguised and self-deceiving form. It seems to be nature's way, in human minds, to perceive ourselves as performing some beneficial and charitable service for our victims when our instincts begin to propel us toward using them in ways that may well leave them worse off than they were before we bestowed on them our help. When a predator is in the grips of a delusion that he or she is not a predator but rather a good Samaritan and is charismatic enough and verbally gifted enough to begin to convince the victim and observers that the delusion is not a delusion but is the truth, the predator will succeed.

Dawkins' theories about the pervasiveness of avariciousness and self-deception in humans and all the ills that genetic inheritance causes for humanity seem so obviously sound to me today that I have difficulty understanding how I could have been so blind to what was going on in the world as to imagine that humans are instinctually good, altruistic, kind-hearted and humane, and respectful of their fellow human beings' needs. I now see that childlike impression that persisted in me for so long as stemming from that same evolutionary trait of self-deception of which I'm speaking - but not the self-deception of the sort practiced by alphas, rather, the Stockholm syndrome kind; the self-deception of those who can look at a deceiving/ self-deceiving user and see there a protector/ savior who loves her (or him).

That strange and unfortunate trait - the self-deception trait that we label "gullibility" - leads members of a pack that are lower ranking, or without rank, to defer and to invest their energies into attempting to ingratiate themselves with the power-wielding alpha in a pack of which they want to be a part. Often the alpha who holds the power in a human pack does so by showing they can hurt and humiliate their fellows more severely than any other member of their pack can. It is a lucky human who didn't grow up in a family where this was the image of what a good leader or parent is.

Most of us grew up in families, schools, churches, and communities where the person whose good opinion and support we most desperately wanted was the person whose bad opinion we most feared. Perhaps that is why so many of us turn our backs on those who really care about us but who appear to be powerless, and give all our support to deceiving self-deceivers like Hitler, church elders who declare women to be witches, guys who treat girls badly, Joseph McCarthy types, the bully who shames the special-ed kids, and women who destroy other women's lives by accusing them of abusing children.

In my attempts to explain Dawkins' theories in as brief a way as possible, I've made it seem that human deception/self- deception has been a tool mostly used in war or getting rid of indigenous peoples whose land and wealth we wanted, but the stage on which the use of deception and self-deception has its real impact on societies is in the family.

Alphas of families and those family members who have family alpha support are treated better in the world outside the family than those members who have no support from an alpha-type relative. The power path leads up and out from family.

Too often, a person who has their eye on a position of leadership in their family, begins their effort to rise by demonizing someone else in the family, painting that person as either too weak, too incompetent, or too lacking in intelligence to lead. The ruthless among us up the ante of their campaign to control family members' hearts and minds by selecting some family member who won't be able to hurt them back, someone they can use as a scapegoat, and they begin to depict that family member as one who poses a threat to other family members. There are all kinds of variations on this theme about which the alpha, aspiring to influence and control, can spin mythology.

No matter how many times we have been through history classes, watched documentaries on TV, and read historical accounts and memoirs by survivors (about the leader who has fired up a multitude of people to see him as a god by claiming that he alone can save them from an evil plot being developed by such-and-such that only he can see), the next time someone comes along who resurrects that same old fear and suspicion engendering ploy, from family level all the way up to president, we fall for their fairy tale as if humans had never been tricked with defamation of the powerless before.

The creator of the delusion (the delusion that evil individuals pretending to be good are covertly plotting to gain by using innocents in a way that will harm them) is completely sucked into believing the fictitious narrative their own mind has concocted and stated to others, it seems; although, I cannot even visualize how someone could be that deaf and blind to themselves. This comes about through a personality defense and offense, which some humans possess a lot of (alpha types) and others little (omega types), projection.

That is the sort of use to which human beings put deception - never seeing it as callous use of the gullible or harmful use of the innocents whom they represent themselves as standing up for.

No matter how many examples we have seen of the gullible and innocents being used by deceivers in their lust for prestige and influence over the minds of others, when the same thing is happening in the here and now, in our own families and local institutions, we seem to be as clueless to what's happening and as accommodating to the perpetrators as any used populations ever were.

Hitler was actually worshipped by masses as a result of his projecting onto Jews the plotting to destroy a whole culture when it was he who was plotting to destroy a whole culture. There were no masses saluting him and shouting his name when his end came, but all his victims were just as dead and his worshippers' country was in ruins. Roman emperors wowed thousands of spectators with the torture and burning of Christians, who, they claimed, were plotting to overthrow the Roman empire. Arousing Romans to fear and hate Christians was a deception used by Roman rulers to divert public attention away from how poorly they were performing as rulers. Church ministers and elders in Old Salem found ways to hint to teenage girls of their congregations that little old ladies of the community were casting spells on them, whereupon these girls, who had been called to serve as witnesses in trials of these ladies for witchcraft, gave their ministers and elders exactly what those authority figures wanted from those girls - testimony that the ladies across the room from them were putting spells on them. Some girls were actually fainting due to their suggestibility to what they'd been told had been done to them by these innocent women.

It seems amazing to me that we have passed the year 2000, and we still have not arisen from the level of ignorance, and the level of lust for seeing powerless people hurt and humiliated, on which we were hundreds and thousands of years ago. Maybe there is something in the human psyche regarding our view of leadership and alphas that simply has not evolved and has stagnated at the point where it was when we were chimpanzees falling for an alpha male's tricking us into thinking there were enemies waiting for us in the bushes that only he could see and protect us against.

Dawkins, in his book, does not define and illustrate the working of self-deception in a human being with respect to whether the presence or absence of its working would be concurrent with the presence or absence of depression. My conclusion that depression results from a breakdown in the functioning of the gene of self-deception comes from observation of personalities in my extended family. Self-deception is easy to come by if one's beliefs about oneself are supported by other members in one's own wolf pack, whether that wolf pack be human family, school, church, or social group. Self-deception, I believe, cannot survive as a viable survival-of-the-fittest trait unless it is bought, early on in life and consistently over time, by a family member who will validate the self-deceptive person's lies as being truths and allow themselves to be used by providing support of those lies as truths.

Dawkins speaks about those who enter helping professions such as are spread across medical and religious fields. Our society has elevated so many members of these "savior" vocations to almost deity-like status and has idealized away doubts about them because it has served our purpose to believe that there are people to whom we can turn for help who are there for us as a result of altruistic motivations. There is no such thing as purely altruistic motivation, Dawkins states. The "savior" who is sure that he is working under the overriding guidance of altruism deceives himself, and because he has deceived himself as to his real motivations, he is effective at deceiving those upon whom he seeks to bestow his "salvation."

When I read Dawkins' book, what I came away with

was the idea that those of us who occupy positions that are seen as being in the helper professions - psychiatrist, psychologist, counselor, nurse, teacher, etc. - need to look within ourselves to make sure that we are really helping those we tell ourselves we are helping. Too many of us "helpers", Dawkins suggests, train for a "helper" profession because of the prestige we would get out of being seen by our fellow human beings as "good" and as authorities on what goes on inside personalities that the common man - those not trained in institutions of higher learning as we have been - wouldn't know how to spot.

The problem has been that all those "helpers" who Dawkins hoped would look within themselves for their own self-deception, have, instead, turned this good intention into an instrument for evil (at least they have, in my experience, in the area where I live) by accusing individuals who are powerless and disadvantaged pack-wise of having the traits of deception, self-deception, and predatory use of other humans. What Dawkins and his colleagues intended to be a wake-up call to doctors, mental health professionals, and educators - to alert them to the fact that they needed to look within themselves to make sure they hadn't entered the field they were in solely for the purpose of enhancing their own images - suddenly got turned into accusation inspiring material to use to intimidate, terrify, and slander the vulnerable among us.

All at once, a person's desire to practice social courtesies was recharacterized as deceit; an act whereby the practitioner of good manners was "just pretending" in order to get us to "lower our guard". The projecting accusers began to take over the whole social fabric, so that all a person had to do to become labeled as a sexual degenerate, a child abuser and molester, an illegal substance user and dealer, a racist, an Islamist, was to get oneself into a relatively powerless position: living alone, needing help of some kind, showing signs of suffering from depression or some other kind of "difference", being of other than local blood.

"Helpers", claiming to see deceivers and predation in anyone who showed some weakness that left them unable to defend themselves against defamation, became the psychological terrorists of our time and place here.

I am sure that all those students in state colleges, universities, and medical schools, studying and training to go out in society and hold positions as mental health professionals diagnosing and treating those to whom they can apply some label described in their *Diagnostic and Statistical Manual* of mental health anomalies, learn what I have outlined as Dawkins' survival-of-the-fittest theory.

Apparently what they are not learning is that they, not individuals bearing DSM labels, are the deceiving self-deceivers who use the powerless and innocent. It is mental health professionals who are looked up to as authority figures, alphas, leaders, in our families, schools, communities, and other pack constellations. It is alphas who are the deceiving self-deceivers in any predatory pack; and humans, probably more than any other predator, form packs for the attainment of protection and power. Those of us who bear the weight of having been diagnosed with some condition described in the DSM aren't alphas, we are not leaders of anything; we don't even have enough deceptive skills to get included in packs, much less have influence in one.

The public hears and sees stories about women who

murder their own children, and in those stories, always, the homicidal mothers are described as suffering from depression. Mothers who kill their children are suffering from insanity, and depression, by itself, does not put a woman into a state of insanity. Depression probably will coexist with any state of insanity because insanity surely would interfere with getting social needs met. But the defamatory view of depression, as being a condition which *makes* a woman a danger to her children, is no more sound an idea that any of those other inhuman mythologies that alphas in leadership positions have dreamed up and broadcast as truths that mandated them and their followers to commit genocide, enslave rather than indenture, burn women at the stake, and the like.

This idea that seems to have become rampant among those who have had classes or training in this state's institutions of higher learning in the last few decades - that depressed women are plotters of harmful uses of their children, meanwhile deceiving their children and others into being unaware of their plots by feigning love and concern for their children - is projection of the contents of the minds of the instructors, trainers, students, and trainees onto people who are not nearly as likely as they to ever use children in trying to implant aggrandized images of themselves in the minds of others.

What possible reward could a depressed mother get for deceiving herself into thinking she is helping and protecting uncared for, harmed children when she really feels no love for them and is harboring ideas for how she can maliciously use them? A depressed mother would get no reward whatsoever for doing that. The only woman or man who would get a reward for being in such a delusion of self would be one who will see a way he or she can use such a myth to get themselves seen by an audience as someone to look up to, someone to support and work for. That is the individual who gets a reward. For a depressed mother to get any benefit out of portraying herself as being the savior of her own children, she would have to claim she was saving them from the ill treatment and harm they have suffered from someone. How is that going to buy an enhanced opinion of her?

❖ ❖ ❖

Postscript:

Regarding Dawkins and his theory that the gene for self-deception is the most successful of all survival-of-the-fittest traits a human can inherit ... it has taken me a few decades to see my error in buying this theory. I can now see my error in judgment in equating becoming a winner — an alpha — with surviving. The number of deceiving self-deceivers at any one time on our planet seems to me to be miniscule in comparison with all those hordes of humans who are believing in and following the words of the deceiving self-deceivers. The consumers far outnumber the vendors.

Experiences of the past decades have finally gotten through to me and shown me that there are relatively few of us who practice deceiving (lying, slandering, fabricating, falsely accusing, advancing grandiose misrepresentation of ourselves, and disseminating other fraudulent communications) and many, many drinking the Kool-Aid.

Humans, en masse, it now seems obvious to me, are exuding evidence of possessing the trait of gullibility. The survival-of-the-fittest trait that exists in most humans (and the trait that has been, therefore, the most successful for survivability) has been the trait for being irresistibly drawn to the deceiving self-deceiver and the alternative reality he or she is selling.

Dawkins lays the blame for all the miseries human beings inflict on one another on the doorstep of deceiving self-deceivers. I think Dawkins couldn't see the forest for the trees. If it were not for all the humans wired to want to be deceived, deceiving self-deceivers' spouting of defamatory inciting rhetoric wouldn't do any harm to anyone. It is the support afforded to deceiving self-deceiving alphas by gullibles that accomplishes success for wolves in sheep's clothing.

It seems to me quite probable that at the time of my conception I had both the gene outfitting me to be gullible to the words of deceiving self-deceivers and the gene propelling me to manufacture positive images of myself with which to nourish my self-image and to win the good opinion of other humans. However, I think that alpha gene was of little use given the environment with which I had to cope as a child. Probably, the genes for practicing deception and for being gullible to deception are complementary - that is, it seems likely that the alpha gene would only come to the foreground in your personality when there are those around you gullible to your sales pitches.

If your fabrications are less attractive than fabrications of another member of your pack who wants you out of the way, your deceiver gene, being of no use to you, would fall back in the survival-of-the-fittest scheme of things. What would now be of use to you would be for you to support the deceiver whose skills had deposed you. It would profit you to be gullible so that you could really support your enemy. If you were only pretending to love and support him, you would run the terrible risk of inadvertently giving yourself away.

A human would have to fall back to being a gullible right-hand man if he/she wanted to remain in the pack. Humans, being so pack dependent, would surely switch the gullibility gene to the foreground.

A reward for gullibility is dished out by nature randomly, and random reward is the most powerful motivator there is - at least that is what Psych 101 told me.

When a con artist is able to make you believe that they are good and great (a person whose words must be right, you think, else they surely couldn't speak and act as confidently as they do), you feel (if you have an instinct to be gullible) that you will be up there with them, knowing yourself to be good and great along with them, if you help them with what they are trying to achieve. You repeat to yourself the justification the con artist has given you to stifle any cognitive dissonance your intelligent civilized brain has bestowed on you.

The immediate gratification you get - which may or may not morph into something horribly unpleasant over time - is a self-image; an image that gives one that "I'm valued, I'm included, I'm trusted" status that humans have to feel in order for their lives to have quality.

The more gullible for a con a subordinate is, the faster she'll move to get to the side of her leader, and the whole pack is thus on their way to either acquiring their necessities or else being led to slaughter. Predatory packs seem to have been successful through the strategy of following a leader more often than they've met with failure. So, the combination of deceiving, clinched by self-deception, coupled with gullibility in subordinates, seems to be a paradigm unbeatable.

Off and on over the years, I have felt sure that we can find out a lot more about ourselves watching wolf and primate documentaries on *Animal Planet* and *National Geographic Channel* than in typing our great-grandfather's name into Worldwide Web search launches. I am not thinking that as I add a few lines to an essay I began around 2004.

On this particular day, I am thinking that millions of humans (of which I am one) operate under something that has more driving force within us than canine pack instincts. The concept of "Do unto others as you would have them do unto you", has proven to influence us more often and more determinedly over our lifetimes (we can now see as we reflect upon it) than the instincts bequeathed to us by our furry forebears. In my case, I don't think that could be due to genetic inheritance since neither my children nor my granddaughters seem to me to be self-restricted in what they do by any such concept. That leads me to believe that, just as J. K. Rowling has inferred in her *Harry Potter* books, the inheritance any human receives is neither an inheritance useful to wolves nor an inheritance useful to humanistic humans, but the capacity to be either.

That is, selfish genes (either deceiver/self-deceiver or its complement gene, gullibility) may not rule the world after all and may not be what insures our survivability in the long run.

DAWKINS AND THE GENES THAT RULE THE WORLD

In the Beginning

"Ruth Leitch with daughters Leah and newborn Coraya"

IN THE BEGINNING

When I caught this picture of Mother, Leah, and me in a family publication a cousin of mine sends out every year to all our kith and kin, I burst out laughing. I had never seen the photo before - Mother hadn't had any photos of me as a newborn in her collection. Every time I look at this, I can't help but shake my head at the predictability of where Leah positioned herself for the photographic commemoration of my arrival in the family. As if the picture wasn't worth a thousand words at showing me how easily Leah could make me disappear, the caption my cousin or some aunt or uncle had placed under the picture just had to spell out a few more ...

It was I, Emmy, whom Mother was holding, not Coraya, my little sister, who was born four and a half years later when Leah was nine.

How I wish I could here begin describing to you (without creating fiction) how extraordinary a baby I was; how I had memories all the way back to my first year of life and being breast-fed by my mother. I don't, and I don't remember anything of my potty-training or of having potty accidents, although I suspect that's where my troubles began; not because Mother was heavy-handed in her potty-training methods — I never saw her to be so with my younger sisters - but because Leah would have taken my potty-training over, and Mother would have let her.

The only way I have of gauging how old I was when I began remembering events is that my third birthday fell on an Easter Sunday, an event of such low probability that one convergence of my birthday with Easter Sunday will be the only one I will ever see. It was spectacularly memorable. The reason that it was spectacularly memorable is that Leah made a huge fuss over me that day (in a positive rather than negative way), even going so far as to take me with her to the home of three playmates of hers where she and those girls feted me with an Easter egg hunt. For Leah to voluntarily invest so much of her time in me, to let me participate in her play with her friends, and to influence them to treat me kindly instead of disdainfully, made my third birthday a day of such joyousness and self-image pigging-out I could never forget it.

Other significant events around this time are harder for me to place in proper time context and in chronological order.

One event was the first to which free association led me when I began psychoanalytically oriented psychotherapy in my late twenties. That I associated my way "freely" to this experience is suspect, since for months prior to my focus on this memory, I had been reading psychoanalysis-inspired literature and, from what I read, had gathered that in my relationship with my father at ages three through six lay the repressed material that I must bring from its hiding place in my unconscious into my conscious awareness in order to achieve success in my treatment for depression.

One evening, as Mother and Daddy were weeding our vegetable garden, I decided there would be more exciting things I could be doing at the barn than watching my parents chop in dirt between little plants with hoes. Successfully keeping a low profile, I left the family's company and headed up the hill for the cistern beside the barn from which Daddy drew up water for our farm animals. I had frequently stood by observing as Daddy took the lid off the cistern access and lowered into the hole a bucket that had a very long rope attached. After Daddy had played the rope out until most of it had disappeared into the chasm, he would wait a minute or two, then begin hauling the rope back, hand over hand, much more slowly than he had allowed the rope to drop. Finally, what would emerge from the cistern opening would be a bucket full of water.

A trait with which I know I had to have been born, is a trait that compels me to gain understanding of what I don't understand. Where all other females in my family, and many of the males, are content with faith, I'm driven to doubt what authority figures tell me should never be doubted. I will comprehend or bust what those around me are content to leave un-comprehended. Unfortunately, this trait has led me relentlessly to experience that which my fellow human beings have sense enough to avoid experiencing.

Why the disappearance of a long stretch of rope with a bucket on the end, into a dark hole into which I could not see, and the reappearance of the stretch of rope and its bucket shortly afterward with the bucket now full of water, was a progression of events always controlled by my father that I had an overwhelming desire to control myself, I can't say. What explanation could there be for such a level of "everybody's warnings and consequences be damned - I will do whatever I decide I need to do to find out what's behind this mystery" attitude?

Getting the cistern opening's cover off was tough. It was pretty heavy, but finally I got it to one side. I stared down into the hole expecting to see water but saw nothing but black. I got the bucket and, playing out the rope as I had seen Daddy do, let the bucket down into the cistern. With gratification, I felt through the rope the bucket becoming heavier. Ah, I was succeeding in getting water into the bucket - the whole purpose of the operation of Daddy's that I was recreating. Next step … haul the water up. There, my visualizations of accomplishment came to an abrupt end. I couldn't get the bucket back up. I pulled, I strained with everything I had in my little body. The bucket did not even begin to come to me. "I can't give up and let this bucket go", I thought. "If I drop this rope, Daddy's bucket and this rope will be gone forever down in this cistern. He'll be so angry with me, he might spank me hard enough to knock the bottom half of my body out from under my chest and arms and head."

Time was dragging on and I wasn't cognizant of the fact that I could merely hold the rope - that I did not have to keep pulling up with all my might - to prevent the bucket from sinking away forever. Believing that if I couldn't overpower the bucket - which I could see I couldn't - the bucket would pull me down into the cistern where both it and I would be lying on the bottom, irretrievable, forever, I began screaming with all the strength my struggle with the rope and bucket had left me.

Mother, Daddy, and Leah looked up. Daddy was the fastest at throwing his hoe to the ground and heading for me. He ran faster than I ever saw him run before or after and was where I was within a few seconds although it was a long way from the garden to the barn with a gate to open along the way. I have no idea what happened to the bucket. I don't remember Daddy's giving a rip about his bucket. My memory says that the instant Daddy reached me, he had me by an arm and was spanking me with such force it was as if he couldn't put enough strength in his blows to adequately punish me.

As you can see, there was in that brief drama involving Daddy and me, the love/fear-hate dyad that brings repression to automatically intervene to stifle one emotion or the other, according to Freudian psychoanalytic theory. If our primitive instincts ascertain that we need to keep loving a person because our survival is dependent upon that person's feeling motivated to take care of us, then repression will come to our aid by keeping fear-hate for that person out of our awareness, regardless of what he or she does to hurt us. Repression behaved as expected in this situation where Daddy paddled me unmercifully. What I repressed was a fear I felt at that time that Daddy was going to kill me.

Why would a little girl of two or three imagine her father might actually kill her just because he spanks her in the same circumstance where any parent - given that society and that era - would have spanked a child? I'm sure all very young children entertain such unconscious fear and repress that fear when caretakers punish them physically while very angry. Why? A child of two or three or four doesn't have rational insight into what a person who has control over her may or may not do. What controls her assessment of her fellow humans' feelings and intentions is instinct, and that instinct has evolved over millions of years of relationships of parents to their children.

Only two or three thousand years ago, parents were cutting their own children's throats (or giving them to priests to do it) and offering them as sacrifices to gods. Within the last few thousand years, when cities have been under siege and food has run out, some mothers have eaten their own babies. Why would not a child's instincts tell her to always be a little afraid a parent might kill her? How old is a child before she is intellectually aware that parents have higher human powers exercising control over them who won't let them kill their own children at will? I don't know the answer to that, but I do know that when Daddy paddled me at the cistern, I didn't know he wasn't free to kill me if that's what he wanted to do. Best practices for me, through all my childhood, regardless of what Daddy did? Love him and have little or no consciousness of fearing and hating him.

Across the road from the property on which we lived-property that belonged to an aunt-by-marriage of my father's - was the home of a sweet little old lady who collected figurines of all sorts, and who had them displayed on shelves that lined every wall and window. One day Mother decided to visit her and took me with her. I had seen a few of the figurines from outside this neighbor's house - the ones on the shelves filling her windows - but I had never been inside and seen the full gallery. It was breathtaking, awe-inspiring, heart-stopping.

These little replicas were more marvelous to me than any of Leah's wonderful playthings, and Leah had a lot of playthings that made me yearn for possessions like them of my own. Leah had a big dollhouse with tiny furnishings for every room. She had a set of child-size kitchen appliances - appliances with doors that opened and closed just like real ones, a stove with faux oven, a refrigerator with shelves, and a cabinet-with-sink replica. Leah had paper dolls - lots and lots of paper dolls and lots of beautiful clothes and accessories for each one, all in a little pink cardboard suitcase covered with fleurs-de-lis. There were Rita Hayworth, Betty Grable, Lucille Ball, Cary Grant,

IN THE BEGINNING

Clark Gable, and so many more - all the most famous stars along with little paper copies of the beautiful clothes they had worn in their most popular films. Vivien Leigh was there with her green drapery dress from *Gone with the Wind*.

Since none of the family adults alive during my childhood seemed inclined to make gifts to children of such desirable playthings (if any at all), my guess is that Daddy's mother had given them to Leah. This grandmother died two months before I was born. The only grandmother I ever knew was the (expletive deleted) grandmother that I think of as the mother of all mean-spiritedness.

But, returning to our neighbor's captivating figurines, the one with which I fell more hopelessly in love than I did for all the rest was a dog. Our family had a dog, a female, a female who regularly produced big litters of pups and nurtured them devotedly, who was mostly German shepherd - one whom somebody had unimaginatively named Shep. Seeing Shep tenderly clean her pups and nurse them was probably what filled my heart with love for her, and perhaps that is why our neighbor's ceramic dog was the figurine after which I lusted the most. I can't imagine I would have asked for the dog - I'm sure I would have been taught even before the age of three not to be so forward, but the sweet woman offered the dog to me. I accepted that dog from her with a feeling that I had never had in my hands anything so precious, so beyond my wildest hope of ever possessing.

Once back in our apartment with my treasure, Mother began one of her refrains of the character with which I was so familiar: "You're going to drop that and break it. You need to put that somewhere and leave it alone. If you carry it around, it will just get broken."

Even only having lived with Mother two or three years, I'm sure I'd heard so many warnings from her of the dire consequences that were going to befall me if I didn't do so-and-so or if I did do so-and-so that this particular warning was just another to ignore. Mother never took any action to control me. She verbally harangued me for wanting to do almost everything I wanted to do, and after I had done anything I wanted to do, she usually verbally harangued me for doing it. But she never physically moved to prevent me from doing anything she'd told me not to do, nor did she ever move to propel me to do what she told me to do. Where Mother had acquired the notion that all children (except for those who are so hopelessly evil their parents should turn their backs on them) will heed any admonition from their mothers the moment the words fall from their mothers' mouths, I don't know.

Knowing that Mother would rant but would never take effective action to enforce anything she said, I took my ceramic doggy and went outside to pedal around on my Kiddie Kar with it. As Mother had predicted, I couldn't hold the figurine securely while also holding and turned the handles of my Kiddie Kar. The doggy fell to the concrete sidewalk underneath me and shattered. Horrified, unbelieving, screaming with the pain of awareness of the irreplaceable nature of the treasure I'd just lost, I ran around the house, in at the back door, and up the stairs to Mother. I sobbed out my heartsickness to her.

Surely, I must have known that she would do and say what she did and said. She stood glaring at me as my tale of what had happened gushed out of me. "I told you not to carry that around," she said with heat. Then she turned her back to me and busied herself with some bit of work, making it clear that time in my therapy session with her was up.

There came a second event in my early childhood - I'm not sure what my age was when it happened - in which my ignoring of my mother's admonitions combined with my captaining of my Kiddie Kar to again produce an experience having lasting memorability. It must have been winter because this time I was riding my Kiddie Kar on the landing in front of our second-floor apartment. Mother had warned me sternly not to wheel anywhere near the heads of the stairs.

I soon was sitting on my Kiddie Kar very near the top step at one of the stairwells, looking down the stairs and considering possibilities. "I wonder what would happen if I just let my front wheel ease over the edge of the top only a tiny bit." Mother had told me the consequence of getting too close to the head of the stairs would be dire, but that got translated in my mind into "Emmy, if Mother said I must not pedal anywhere near the tops of these stairs, then we [you and I, Kiddie Kar] have to investigate to see what experiencing this consequence would feel like" whereupon I eased the front wheel over the edge just a tad.

That threw the center of gravity of the Kiddie Kar with me on top of it off, and we catapulted off the landing into the ride of our lives. The Kiddie Kar and I took turns bouncing off steps, the banister, and the wall. First, I would be on top and the Kiddie Kar under me, then we'd cartwheel and the Kiddie Kar would be in the air while my body became the thing slamming into stair treads. As adrenaline rushes go, I think I hit my all-time life's high there. The house was one of those Victorian monstrosities where the ceilings are twenty feet above the floors, so I had plenty of time to "investigate what experiencing consequences would feel like" before my Kiddie Kar and I were caught by a floor flying up to meet us.

I don't remember ever seeing my beloved Kiddie Kar again after that. It might have been smashed beyond use in the fall - it probably was already ancient when I inherited it. Perhaps the Kiddie Kar was okay, perhaps I pedaled around on it as before and just can't remember that because my memory wasn't so good for quite a while after my vertical whirly-gig shake-up.

In the eighties, when I came to the subject of closed-head injury in one of my university neurology courses, I began to wonder about this childhood fall and to think about my decades of depression and disappointingly low performance in many areas where peers, who supposedly had far lower IQs than I, were succeeding with ease. I asked Mother to tell me what she remembered about it.

"I was terribly worried about you," she said, her face revealing the concern she had felt, as memory of the incident came back to her. "You were unconscious for a while, and at first I thought you might be dead. I saw a child die once after being hit in the temple by a doorknob, so I was terrified when I saw you lying there, not moving." The image that Mother's words brought into my mind - an image of my mother bending over a little-child me, panicky with concern for my life - was one that overtook me unawares, an image I didn't want to dwell on for long.

You see, whereas in my relationship with my father it was fear-hatred that my instincts called up repression to stifle, in my relationship with my mother, love for her became the emotion my instincts began to take steps to crush at a time so early in my life they must have started their work even before my memory became operational. I feel that I had in my life, right from the beginning, an overseer - a personal manager after the manner of God allowing or disallowing Adam and Eve to exist in the Garden of Eden - one I feared so much I would abandon to her whatever there was of mine she wanted, including any claim I had to the love of just about anyone, but principally the love of my mother.

There is nothing abnormal about a firstborn's feeling jealousy toward a younger sibling; especially when she's had her mother all to herself for five years. But, doesn't our society expect parents to protect the younger from the older and to teach the older that taking her jealousy out on the younger in the form of abuse will not be allowed? Daddy was ready to step up to the plate on that responsibility. He was an ogre in many respects, but seeing amusement and entertainment in an older child's shaming and physically abusing a younger one was not one of his character pathologies. That seems to me to be a predilection of Mother's and her family members — mainly those of the North Carolina Quaker mitochondria.

Mother never was one to keep a conversation going for long, and though in my forties with years of psychotherapy behind me, I unconsciously held too much of a grudge to put forth even minimal effort to keep her talking, so the bit of information I've quoted regarding my childhood fall is all I found out about the extent of injury I sustained. I don't remember anything of the day of my dramatic tumble after seeing that the floor rushing up was about to smack me.

In trying to find out if this childhood accident might have left me with permanent brain damage severe enough to have caused the cognitive, personality, and emotional deficits that have so bedeviled me, I have encountered nothing but frustration. An MRI of my head shows some unremarkable slices at the very top of my brain. As the image slices get closer to the eyes, the brain midline begins to curve. One cerebral hemisphere begins to bulge a bit at the front, while the other bulges at the rear. As more of the eye sockets become visible, so does more lopsidedness of brain and bone. Horizontal slices beginning just under the eye sockets show bones so skewed and volumes and shapes so lacking in left-right symmetry, I would think any neurologist or technician trained to assess MRIs would come upon these slices, jump back a bit, and say, "Wow! What a mess!" None ever has. The verdict of one and all has been that there is no pathology. Clinical exams by neurologists have gotten me only big bills and the same opinion: "Nothing wrong here."

Finally, I had to accept that unless a scan of my brain and supporting structures showed some abnormality so obvious it could be spotted by an untrained person from across a room, the opinion of any medical professional would always be, "Nothing wrong here." Even if a licensed medical person did confirm my own identification and diagnostic labeling of my neurological deficits, it's highly unlikely that he or she would have any sensible ideas on what to do to enable me to have a better quality of life. But that consideration is moot because the medical professionals who are licensed to make diagnoses of neurological deficits see nothing wrong with my deviated midline, skewed bones, and unequal ventricles and lobes.

Then, too, there is the fact that having a severely deviated septum, lopsided skull, and unequal-sized and unequal-shaped lobes and hemispheres may not result from injury; those things may result from genetics or from some deficiency in Mother's diet or health status while she was gestating me. Trying to find answers to "Why?" has taken up a lot of my time but hasn't done much for my sense of well-being, except to keep me occupied through many a day I might otherwise have wasted on trying relentlessly but in vain to find something to eat, drink, take, or do that might lift my spirits a bit.

Finally, there is the effect on a child's brain development of lack of stimulation or over-stimulation from her environment. I'm not licensed or credentialed to state with authority that childhood relationships or lack of relationships will cause a child's brain to develop differently than children's brains do develop under ideal conditions. However, Dr. Lise Eliot, author of *What's Going on in There?* (Bantam, 1999), does seem to me to be well-credentialed to comment authoritatively on that, and I believe she has. Dr. Eliot subtitles her book *How the Brain and Mind Develop in the First Five Years of Life*. As I move through the pages wherein neuroscientist Eliot explores her subject from every possible angle, I find confirmation and expansion of ideas I began to acquire about children's development in the 1960s as I consumed my first books by psychoanalysts.

Just so I could have a university document formally validating my notion that I do know something about how a human psyche develops, I took advantage of an offer in the 1990s by the North Carolina Department of Public Instruction to get free courses in birth-to-kindergarten child development sufficient to add a bachelor's equivalency in that subject to the master's I already held in a communication science. So perhaps I shouldn't say that I'm not credentialed in Dr. Eliot's area of expertise. Let us say that, so far, my many years of independent study and research have passed under the world's radar.

Given our current knowledge of neurology, how can I believe anything other than that development of certain structures, neuronal pathways, and chemical outputs would be stunted in a developing brain deprived of positive social and cognitive stimulation, leaving the child with unusually large ventricles and unusually diminished volume in brain tissue in specific areas. Along with deprivation of social and cognitive stimulation, expose the child daily over years of time to fear and misery from which she has little refuge other than fantasy and stories in books, and certain brain structures, pathways, and chemicals will overgrow. The resulting brain can very well look like mine, I surmise.

What I'm trying to say (in case my point in bringing up my brain seems vague) is that, in my own case, my decades of research and study leave me with no doubt that my depression is a physical illness. Just as a diabetic is ill because of insulin insufficiency or a stroke victim is ill because of having had his brain's blood circulation interrupted, just so must a depressed person be physically ill whose depression had onset in childhood. I wish mental health professionals would stop calling depression a mental illness. It makes no sense at all to me to call depression a "mental illness" any more than it would make sense to call a thyroid imbalance a "mental illness" or aphasia a "mental illness". Labeling a depressed person "mentally ill" is the ultimate in stigmatizing her (or him), stereotyping her, and taking away her pride and dignity. If those who treat depression could visualize their clients' illness as it really is, a physical illness, I believe they would alter their attitudes and their approaches infinitely for the better.

❖ ❖ ❖

When the next photograph was made, I have no idea. The picture-taking event is not one that got stored in my memory banks. I include it here because looking at it makes me feel good. There is an expression on my face in this photo that tells me life was good — that I had a significant other in my life who unconditionally loved me and whom I loved in return. I don't know who that could have been if it wasn't Mother.

For much of the time before my fourth year while Leah was at school, or when, for some other reason, Leah was not with Mother and me, Mother didn't have to be rejecting me to save Leah from the pain of jealousy, and I didn't have to be suppressing and repressing my love for Mother in order to keep Leah from seeing it and attacking my presumptuousness in thinking that my mother was just as much mine as hers. I could relax, let go, and feel for Mother whatever emotion spontaneously came to me — including love. Gazing at this picture, I can see in the way my hair has been attractively top-knotted and braided and in the expression of peaceful happiness on my face that, for this little time at least, I probably was very much in love with my mother.

IN THE BEGINNING

Those Little Things I Don't Want to Remember

In early childhood, I did have a few relationships which Leah was not given the right to own and manage. Neither my father nor his older sister Emmelia would allow Leah to determine how they would feel about me or behave toward me. My recollection is that the same was true of other adults and children who were of Daddy's Valley-of-Virginia roots and traditions and his family's Scots-Irish Presbyterian religion - for the most part. As long as my father, Aunt Emmelia, or some child or adult of Father's kin, culture, or Presbyterian background was present, I was usually (but not always) safe from Leah's drives to get people to perceive me as someone undeserving of any human warmth. Unfortunately, Mother was not born of that Jeffersonian, Virginian, Scots-Irish Presbyterian ilk. I'd characterize Mother and her family members as support-the-biggest-bully sorts. Nonetheless, Mother could not be influenced to treat her infants badly, no matter how unwanted or unloved a new baby might have been by some other family member. Until her baby could feed herself, walk, talk, and was potty-trained sufficiently to be out of diapers, Mom was as compassionate and caring a mother as the average child is apt to come by. If that hadn't been the case, I don't believe I could ever have developed the love for my mother at one, two, or three that morphed into torture at four and failure in work, parenting, and intimate relationships forever after.

Once a child could walk, talk, and no longer needed to be diapered, Mother's family tradition held that if she (or he) tried thereafter to get attention from adults she should be refused it and treated as if she didn't exist. Children had to be taught that expecting adults to interact with them (or talk with them, touch them affectionately, respond to questions, or provide services or things requested) would spoil them. In Mother's eyes there wasn't anything more morally abhorrent than a spoiled child and the parent or other adult who spoiled her. I had enough exposure to Mother's mother to see where she got that starve-them stinginess of spirit.

I have only brief memories of a few times of symbiosis with Mother which must have occurred before I reached that age when Mother thought it was time that I be on my own, and that I deal with whatever slings and arrows came my way the best way I could. It is much more painful to recall these episodes of closeness with Mother than it is to hate her. Hating someone who once loved you but who stopped loving you while you still desperately needed them is actually of some comfort.

While the United States was at war with Germany and Japan (through most of my preschool years) Daddy worked at what we called "the powder plant" at Pearisburg. For our little family, the war was an economic blessing beyond any we were ever able to again enjoy. Daddy was severely disabled by narcolepsy, but this did not prevent his being able to do the work required of him at the plant, and with workers needed so badly at home for the war effort, Daddy's problem was one his employers and fellow workers could easily overlook. We had money, while this job was available to Daddy, for basic necessities, and even for some minor luxuries like train and auto trips.

Aunt Emmelia and her husband lived a hundred miles from us in Lexington, but even with the primitive condition of roads at the time and with the decrepit condition of vehicles available to Daddy, we managed to visit back and forth often. The first trip there that I remember was in a Model A Ford truck. I don't recall Leah's presence, but I'm supposing that she sat in the middle and Mother sat next to the window with me on her lap. Mother's allowing me to sit in her lap was something I can't imagine her doing had I been much past two. However it was that I happened to be there — whether due to lack of space on the seat or to Mother's accommodating my desire to see out the window, she was not resenting holding me nor was Leah. If either of those emotional conditions had been present, I believe I would have been unable to concentrate to the extent that I was on what I was observing out the window.

What fascinated me during the trip and kept it from fading from my memory was the moon. The sky was brilliantly clear and the moon was full. I had thought that the moon was a heavenly body that was over our house in Dublin, and that if we left Dublin behind, we would also leave the moon behind. I had no idea that the moon was far above the whole earth. (Well, I suppose I had no concept of the whole earth either.) Here we were getting closer and closer to Lexington — a long, long way from home to me — and the moon was making the trip with us. As we moved along, mile after mile on the highway, the moon kept right with us in the sky, going the same speed as our truck, whether we slowed for towns or speeded up in open countryside.

It seems to me that we often went by train to visit Mother's parents and siblings in Radford. I only remember one of those visits, but my impression is that the train trips back and forth to Radford were ones we took frequently. In the ride which registered strongly enough in my memory to lodge there, I'm guessing that, again, I was on Mother's lap. Had I not been, I don't believe I would have been able to see out the window. What a sight came to my eyes on this particular day as the train began its crossing of New River. The river was in flood stage of such extremes that the water, which was usually far, far below us as we crossed the trestle, was almost up to the tracks. The flood was the color of yellow-brown clay, swirling and frothing, and so close to us it looked to me as if it could almost get to the wheels of our train car.

Thinking about these trips the three of us took to Radford and back, and visualizing sitting on my mother's lap, with my mother's accepting that placidly, and with Leah's not being perturbed by it one way or another, gives me a strange, strange feeling. It's hard for me to believe that it ever could have happened — that Mother would let me sit on her lap and that Leah wouldn't punish me for it — but I know that my mother didn't always hate me. I can remember when she didn't seem to.

One time during the war, for some reason that I can't recall, Daddy took Leah by train to Richmond ... I think. They were gone overnight, so Mother came to Leah's and my bedroom, which was down a hallway from our apartment proper, to sleep there so I wouldn't be alone and afraid. Just as Mother was about to turn out the lights, the town's air raid siren went off, indicating that blackout was required. We had drills like this fairly often as the powder plant at Pearisburg was not so far away and could, conceivably, had been a target for German bombers. I think Mother and I talked about this as we settled down in the dark in our beds. Mother didn't talk to me in this conversational way when Leah was with us, so this little interlude of camaraderie between us was a very special and very unusual thing.

Once, when I was very sick - so sick Mother put me in the bed in the main room of our apartment where she could hear me from the kitchen - Mother actually called a doctor to come and see me. To ease my chest congestion, she would lift me up enough so that I could swallow and give me spoonfuls of sugar dissolved in lamp oil. When I think of this, I cry. Touching me was something my Mother never did unless there was no way to get around it.

LITTLE THINGS I DON'T WANT TO REMEMBER

Milepost Four on the Long and Winding Road

If I were asked by a researcher to locate my lifelong base happiness level at some inch mark on a foot ruler, I believe I'd have to hand that ruler back and ask for one that showed centimeters and millimeters. Perhaps a generous estimate would only get my base happiness level to one or two millimeters on the scale; but, there was one five-month-long block of time in my childhood in which, day after day, God was in his heaven, all was right with the world, and I was a perpetually exuberant, joy-filled child.

That was the summer and early fall following my fourth birthday, in which Leah and I went to stay with Aunt Emmelia at Lexington. Aunt E's husband had died a year or so before after a stroke and lengthy illness, and I believe she was dealing with the loss by surrounding herself with people in whom she could invest her attention and energy as she had in her husband during his last months of life. That may have been the reason she chose to keep Leah and me with her for such an unusually long stay that year and to shower us with the paradisal attention and affection she did. During this wonderful summer of love, Aunt Emmelia, whose namesake I was, called me "Precious" and constantly showed me with smiles and hugs that in her eyes I was charming, delightful, and yummy to cuddle. Leah voluntarily and happily played the role of my nanny, or teacher, or substitute mom, or agreeable playmate instead of running me off, expressing revulsion for me, or slapping me about liberally.

Except for these five months, my experiences of childhood joy were so brief they flashed by almost before I had a chance to glean from them the gratification for which I longed, and they occurred so infrequently months or even years might pass between the little respites. I'll try to give you a summation of the general state of things, although attempting to describe misery, while maintaining organization and coherence in the writing of it, is something I don't seem to be able to do very well. Something about concentration on painful experience seems to "mess up my mind" and cause me to fall into rambling and repetition. However, I'll do the best I can to give here an overview:

Leah despised the sight of me from the day I was born, wanted Mother and Daddy to take me back where I came from, and loved repeating the tale in my presence (if anyone was there to be her audience) of how she had told Mother and Daddy to do just that. Mother (and to a certain extent the rest of the family) yielded ownership of me to Leah before I was even potty trained in the same way that plantation owners of the Old South used to make gifts to each of their own children of the child of one of their slaves for the little white "master" or "mistress" to use in any despotic way he or she pleased.

Mom had a baby, totally unbeknownst to me, while Leah and I were packed off at Aunt Emmelia's for a five-month stay when I was four and Leah was nine. We were yanked out of the paradise of Aunt Emmelia's world and brought home to hell when the baby was only two weeks old and Mother was in deep postpartum depression. Why was Mother so depressed? There were so many contributing factors I hardly know where to begin, but I'll start with Daddy's attitude.

Daddy was gung-ho about producing offspring ... male offspring. He viewed female babies with all the enthusiasm he felt when he saw that nut grass had sprouted up overnight in a corn row he'd just weeded the day before. He looked upon his repeated reproductive disappointments at planting in Mom what he knew had to be valuable male-producing seeds only to see Mom do something with them that she shouldn't have so that they didn't produce the plants they should have.

Many years passed before Daddy finally became aware that it is the father's input that determines the sex of his offspring, not the mother's - too late to save Mother from what Daddy emotionally put her through each time she bore yet another female child. Up to the time of which I'm writing, what Mother had presented to Daddy, including Leah's and my newborn sis, were three daughters and a stillborn.

No one in the family has ever mentioned the fact that

there was a stillborn — even Leah had no knowledge there had ever been one until I told her so recently — so I have no idea what its gender might have been; but, considering how unfailingly bad Dad's luck always was, I'm sure the stillborn baby must have been that son for which he perpetually longed. I discovered the stillborn's existence well into my own adulthood when I happened to notice a line of tiny print on my own birth certificate which read: "Number of children of this mother (At time of this birth and including this child) (A) Born alive and now living 2 (B) Born alive but now dead 0 (C) Stillborn 1".

As if each of their new progeny's arrival didn't bring enough disappointment to sour Dad's disposition and depress Mom, there was an erotic poverty — and thus a substrate of chronic silent hostility — in Mom's and Dad's relationship that affected me as if the hostility were radiation penetrating my body and working in union with other toxic elements coming into me from my environment to mutate my soul from a carefree and joyous thing into a somber and uncertain one.

Other children's parents slept in the same bed with each other. The fact that mine stopped sleeping together around the time of Little Sis's birth or not too long thereafter was very disquieting and sad to me. Other women didn't shrink from all physical and emotional closeness with their husbands as my mother did from my father, nor did they behave toward their husbands as if they were habitual violators of their dignities and ought, therefore, to be ashamed of themselves. Even as a child with no more knowledge of mating than I had seen in movies of that era of the *State Fair* sort, even never hearing a word spoken by my mother or father that even touched upon their physical relationship with each other, I think my father's unrequited longing for physical and emotional love and my mother's absolute distaste for both was clear to me.

Besides the reproductive problem introduced into Daddy's expectations of Mom by her aversion to having him touch her or look upon her with desire, Mom was not physically or emotionally fit enough to have been bearing children in the first place. Neither was Daddy, but I'll tackle diagnosing Mom's disabilities first.

Mom had fairly severe lordosis and kyphosis of the spine with some additional displacement of the upper spine laterally. No one in the family knew it at the time — I only began to see it when my daughter was diagnosed with scoliosis — but these orthopedic abnormalities were components of a heritable syndrome that expressed itself in whole system deficits; a syndrome severe enough to cause Mother's physical, mental, and emotional functioning to deteriorate, when she was under stress, to the point that she was incapable of performing activities of daily living that wives and mothers must if they are to keep their households from falling into chaos and their children going pathetically neglected.

As if being a victim of that syndrome (whatever it is — I have yet to find the medical name for it despite my years of independent research and presentations of myself to doctors) were not enough to disqualify her from being an adequate caregiver for children, Mother had had her thyroid surgically removed as a young woman after developing a goiter. She received no follow-up treatment afterward, so I can't help but think that she probably existed in a chronic state of hypothyroidism.

As for Daddy's fitness for parenting, he had contracted a near-fatal illness at the age of four — I'm assuming it was Economo's (lethargic) encephalitis although no one in the family ever called it that — which he surprised his family and physician by surviving, but which left him with permanent brain damage, the evidence of which was most visible in his "sleeping sickness". Narcolepsy was a medical diagnosis which hadn't been applied to his condition at the time, and the misnomer "sleeping sickness" was the term Daddy's older sister (our Aunt E), a nurse, always used to refer to his disabling disorder. It has been much harder for me to sort out the etiology of some very unfortunate personality traits of Daddy's, than it has been for all who knew Daddy to recognize that his glaringly inopportune sleep attacks were a brain residual of his childhood illness.

Daddy had a lack of empathy for the feelings of living things in his care that fell back to the degree of human civilization we think of as Neanderthal ... more than a lack of empathy — an outright contempt. Daddy's mother and older sister had felt he should never marry or beget children because his "sleeping sickness" left him incapable of earning a living adequate to support a family. I acknowledge that that was sound advice on their part, and I wish he had taken it. But, more damaging to his family's health and happiness than his narcolepsy was the compulsion that seemed to drive him to say and do things to us which couldn't bring any other outcome than to enrage us and cause us to hate him. His demand always was that we keep stifled completely the hurt and the hatred he often purposely set out to arouse in us.

Mother was a woman so natural-instinct-deadened that

she was able to react to Daddy's incensing slaps at femininity as dully as if he were merely stating that the weather was bad. We girls weren't emotionally that zombie-like. I could sense during the awful episodes he provoked between himself and one or the other of us children that he secretly hoped we would be unable to keep a lid on our anger so that he could then justifiably judge us insubordinate and therefore deserving of correction. That correction was always a vicious spanking.

Mother's boycotting of the sharing of a bed with Daddy from Little Sis' birth onward was apparently felt by Daddy to be such an injustice that he had sufficient cause to violate conventions of conjugal privacy and lay his problem before a powerful ally who would help him fight for his coital rights. He must have divulged the news of his banishment from Mother's bed and her abhorrence of the thought of making more babies with him to our landlady, Miss Willie, who besides being our landlady also happened to be the widow of one of Daddy's uncles. Aunt Willie, feeling an obligation to stand up for her nephew's rights (even if he was only her nephew by marriage) didn't shrink from what she saw as her Blue-Stocking-Presbyterian responsibility for getting Mother straightened out as to what a wife's relationship to her husband morally demanded of her, but came up from her first floor domain to inform Mother that she should be obediently meeting Daddy's requests for sex and joyfully bearing every baby that resulted.

How I managed to grasp and comprehend the content in all the spoken and unspoken communication about Mother's and Daddy's relationship that was going on among adults around me when I was four, I have no idea. The word sex was never uttered by any adult I knew then or at any other time in my childhood that I can recall. (Discovering that a child had come by some knowledge of copulation and its frequent result, extrusion of an offspring through a birth canal — even if it was only knowledge of the mating or birth of pets or farm animals — horrified adults with whom I was acquainted.) Perhaps it was later in life that I unconsciously applied adult-gained knowledge to conversations I overheard or events I witnessed with no comprehension in early childhood.

Now seems like a good time to take a bit of an excursion away from life as usual in Aunt Willie's decaying three-story mansion in a tiny town in Pulaski County on Virginia's western plateau, in the year following Little Sis' birth, and wallow awhile in memories of the silver-spoon life Leah and I had so recently been slurping up in that Great Valley repository of First-Families-of-Virginia culture, Rockbridge County.

ROOTS, RELIGION AND DEPRESSION

MILEPOST FOUR ON THE LONG AND WINDING ROAD

Go Ye Unto All the Earth

At the close of the last chapter, I said I would be going, in the next, to the subject of heaven at Aunt Emmelia's. However, my reason for writing is not only to satisfy my own needs — needs to relive past pleasures and prattle on about old wounds — but also to share experience, strength, and hope about the type of life-destroying depression in females which mental health professionals, as a whole, are treating in ways that I'm convinced exacerbate rather than relieve.

Just in case there might be depressed women or mental health professionals who ever read what I'm writing today, I feel I need to interrupt my thread on the subject of my preschool brain development long enough to insert a message which I believe is the most important message I will ever repeat in anything I might write. The message is this:

If you are a depressed woman with children dependent upon you for their care, do not undertake any therapy the objective of which is to put you in touch with your "inner child". Also, if you are heterosexual, steer clear of one-to-one therapy with a male psychoanalyst, psychiatrist, psychologist, social worker, or any other male therapist, counselor, or minister as assiduously as you would avoid an area where you knew there to be a cloud of toxic gas or deadly radiation. Well ... perhaps seeking the counsel of a homosexual male won't harm you and your marriage irrevocably.

Don't allow any mental health professional to influence you to pursue the subject of whether or not you have repressed into your unconscious some past experience of being abused or sexually molested. Is there a human in any sort of psychic discomfort these days in the United States who isn't being pressured by a therapist, a friend, a teacher, or someone to believe that she (or he) must have been incestuously victimized in childhood by a parent, or someone enabled by a parent, and that the experience was just so painful for them that they repressed all memory of it? To me, doing this to another human — that is telling them or implying to them that they must have had an incestuous relationship with a parent in childhood — is the most dehumanizing and insulting communication one human could convey to another. What's the difference between that and calling a man an MF?

Even if this "your father practiced incest on you and you repressed it" were a true version of events; in the first place, repression is not an unhealthy thing which makes humans mentally ill. Repression is a very healthy, survival-of-the-fittest, evolved instinct that works better to keep a human functioning at their best than anything a therapist can give them. Recovering memories of being incestuously assaulted in childhood isn't curative. Repressed traumatic memories are better left right where they lie, if one compares the result of doing that with the result of a therapist's or self-appointed analyst's suggesting to a client, family member, or acquaintance that an innocent caregiver of theirs surely must be an untrustworthy, deceiving predator who has molested them.

Secondly, I'm convinced that most memories of sexual molestation that therapists think they are so competently leading their clients to recover, either didn't actually happen or else were not the monumentally significant events in clients' lives that therapists want to make them out to be. Any person who has studied and understood human psycho-sexual development knows that human children, from birth onward, have erotic feelings and fantasies about first one then another of their caregivers, siblings, and playmates.

As years go by, these erotic feelings and fantasies, which form the nuclei of preparatory memories gain infusions of new material from additional experience, so that when we ladies marry, our experiences of copulation with our husbands get superimposed over memories and feelings from our childhoods of our fathers or other males for whom we had intense feelings as children. In memories stored in the unconscious, there are no separators to keep what we do and feel as adults out of what we did and felt as children. Don't take my word for that. Read Freud. He probably did much more harm than good with his psychoanalyses, but that wasn't because he didn't grasp how things work in the unconscious.

Carnal knowledge in children is hardly evidence that they have been sexually molested. Children's seeking carnal knowledge and absorbing it from all kinds of perfectly wholesome events and relationships in their lives is something not only normal, but a process necessary to being able to have healthy sexual relationships as adults. Don't take my word for it. Explore psychoanalytic literature. Those people who believe that children's minds would be devoid of explicit erotic visual images, and that they would entertain no fantasies about attracting adults unless they had been sexually preyed upon, are simply grossly ignorant of human sexual development.

Where the unconscious and recovery of repressed memories are concerned, we humans are far too vulnerable to suggestion to put our faith in anything any therapist wants to imply to us is in our unconscious. Neither should we trust any therapist's judgment about whether or not any particular sort of repressed material has any bearing on our current dysfunctionalities and unhappiness. Allowing ourselves to be led by a therapist (or anyone else) to think that we were abused or sexually molested in childhood by a family member with whom we've always consciously thought we had a pretty good relationship, will hurt rather than help our mental health.

During those years when we are responsible for the care of children, the best thing we can do for ourselves, our children, and our relationships with our partners in our child rearing endeavors, is to avoid reactivating any of our own inner child's repressed, frustrated longings and unfinished business. That will be hard enough to do, due to the empathetic reaction that will be aroused in us by our children's daily struggles to deal successfully with their environment, without having some therapist try to put us back into our own childhoods intentionally.

If we suspect that we have an inner child who needs to resolve unfinished business, the time to do it is not during the years when we are needed by our external children to help them make it through their developmental stages satisfactorily. What we need to do during those years is anything we can to make our own lives more enjoyable and less stressful. (Psychotherapy always did the opposite of making life less stressful for me.) I wish that when I first became a mother there had been some godmother-type woman, some mentor in my life, to give me the advice I was given as a newcomer to twelve-step programs when I was introduced to my first in the late 1970s.

The advice, altered to fit a new mother's circumstances, is this: if you possibly can, delay making any life-altering decisions until that future time when your children no longer need parenting to keep them afloat. (Psychoanalytically oriented therapy is life-altering. Don't even consider undertaking it while a child needs you.) Keep your life simple. Avoid stressors like geographic relocations and job or mate changes.

If at all possible, avoid putting yourself and your children in the company of those who have little admiration for your mothering practices (might your husband's mother, perchance, be one of those?) and put yourself and your children, instead, in the company of those upon whom you can count to support and validate your approach to parenting.

One of the greatest assets you can possess throughout the years when childcare will be your responsibility is a mate or partner who feels that his alliance with you is more important than any other alliance he might have — certainly too important to relegate to a lower status than an alliance with a child or children or with some member of his birth family. For the members of the extended families of each of you to also feel that children's honoring of both parents enhances the children's lives just as much as it enhances the life of each parent, is icing on your cake.

In both my ex-husband's and my birth families, principal players have worked to undermine children's love and natural idealization of their mothers. As I see it, those family members who have done that — in all cases they have been female — have done so because they wanted the children to transfer all those elevating feelings away from their mothers and onto them. The behavior, to me, resembles a behavior in a species of wasp where a worker female in the colony is driven by genes for dominance to unseat the reigning queen and take her place. She begins stealing the queen's pheromones and spreading them over herself until all the worker wasps in her nest come to believe that it is she who is the queen, and the legitimate queen, an intruder. They all begin to serve the usurper with the honor and devotion they have been affording to the real queen, and cease tending the real queen who dies without their care.

That may be a little extreme as an analogy for what I've observed in mine and my ex-husband's families. However, in both our families, I see the consequences in each case of the demotion of the mother in the children's eyes as tragic for the emotional health of the mother and for one or more of her children.

ROOTS, RELIGION AND DEPRESSION

GO YE UNTO ALL THE EARTH

First Families of Virginia and Scarlet O'Haras

While Leah and I spent our five months at Aunt Emmelia's, we were both the darlings of her and her many friends. A childless couple, whom we were allowed to address familiarly as Aunt Marge and Uncle Sam, rented the top floor of Aunt E's house and seemed to love our visits up to see them. These were only two of the many adults among our Lexington contacts who found Leah's and my company a pleasure. Aunt E had a host of friends and relatives in and around town, who, like her, were securely positioned in the region's upper class because their ancestors had invented themselves as the upper class there two centuries before. These people owned beautiful houses filled with beautiful things located on beautifully landscaped and tended sites (just as Aunt E's house was) where leisure and recreation

- not work - filled most days.

While house guests at Aunt E's, we might go to her friend's, Miss Jenny's, for lunch, where we would be served food we had never had a chance to taste before by a uniformed butler in a dining room with an amazingly high ceiling all bordered with bas-relief leaves, flowers, and filigree. We might go to Brushy Mountain to visit the estate of our great uncle and aunt, Codrington and Ann Lancaster, and be allowed into Uncle Codrington's carefully tended orchard, which he was wealthy enough to grow for hobby, unlike our father who had to grow what he grew for subsistence. The plums Uncle Codrington grew were far sweeter and juicier than the prune plums we had back home. Furthermore, we were given permission to eat all we wanted. Back home, Daddy's fruit was forbidden fruit for his children because he wanted it all canned or made into preserves that he could enjoy during the winter.

Often while staying in Lexington, we would stop in the Main Street store where Aunt E bought her groceries and ask the owner to pick out for us a guaranteed-to-be-ripe watermelon. He would kneel amidst the melons and select one from which he would carefully cut a small square and withdraw the resulting plug. Aunt E would examine and sample. If she found it insufficiently red and sweet, the grocer would select another for her and plug again until she had a melon to her satisfaction.

When Aunt E invited one or another of her friends to share dinner with us, evening meals that were always good at her house under any circumstances became something special. We all dressed up as if we were preparing to go out to an exclusive restaurant. Those living in and around Lexington who were descendants of the first European landowners in the area did, when I was a child visiting there (and I think they still do), afford each other a level of honor, courtesy, and deferential treatment that I have never experienced anywhere else.

Four females' dressing to the nines for each other, when the three of us who issued the invitation and the guest we invited saw each other almost every day anyway, was typical of the social customs by which people of old Valley of Virginia Scots-Irish and English society honored each other. Those little acts by which we said to each other, "You are special, and you are a person of status and importance, so I speak and behave toward you commensurately" - those little civilities made being female so nice.

The meal would not be in the kitchen, where we ate when there were only Aunt E, Leah, and I, but in the formal dining room. Back home, when Mother worked, she wanted no help, and she could hardly tolerate there even being another human in the kitchen with her when she was preparing a meal. Sharing her work with her daughters was not something Mother ever did unless their participation in her project was forced upon her by Daddy. Aunt E was the opposite. When she worked in the kitchen, whatever the task, she enlisted everyone's help who was present and efficiently orchestrated who did what. Aunt E's cooking a meal, serving it, and cleaning up afterward became an occasion for all of us to engage in pleasurable socializing and bonding.

Seated in the light-circle from a chandelier set with bulbs that glowed like candles, our meal attractively arrayed around a fresh flower centerpiece on the table that we girls had set with linen napkins and heirloom silver and china, surrounded by Lancaster Family antiques on thick-piled freshly vacuumed carpets, home was out of sight and out of mind for me. Yes, consciously I remembered that I had a mother and that Aunt E was not it, but I was very young, my mind very malleable, and I think that unconsciously I developed a firm belief that I belonged to Aunt E much more than to my mother.

Aunt E loved to take walks after dinner, and as the scenery and walking paths were pleasing in every direction from her house, we had no routine but ambled along with a completely flexible attitude about our destination. Aunt E was a socially self-confident extrovert, secure in her knowledge that, given her pedigree, her name would be known and respected by most who were indigenous to the town and surrounding land. Quite frequently as we were on our evening walks, we would be hailed by families from their lawns where they sat enjoying the Garden of Eden ambience that summer dusks usually brought in Lexington. We would be invited to sit and chat and usually did until well after dark and Aunt E judged it to be high time that I be in bed. Walking home in the dark in 1944 in Lexington, from any point to which we might roam, was nothing to evoke unease, even in females.

Often our walks would take us from Aunt E's house to the boundaries of the estate Sunnyside which had once been our Lancaster family's plantation. Leah, who had been given the middle name Lancaster, would fantasize aloud about how she would someday marry a man who would enable her to become mistress of a mansion of the grandeur of Sunnyside; and she and I (with Aunt E's encouragement) would give leave to our self-images to swell to grandiose levels as to who we were and what kind of men would be good enough to deserve being our husbands one day.

Of course, there would be so many men asking us for our hands in marriage (since, like Scarlet O'Hara, we would have more going for us than any other females) we would be able to pick and choose, and we would wisely choose only the very best of the lot - men desirable in every way but principally in having lots of money and being eager to spend it on us. We saw ourselves being treated throughout our future lives, by everyone with whom we would have contact, somewhat as royals in England are treated by those who aren't royals but wish they were. Aunt E affirmed to us what Daddy often stated; that we were descended from nobility, and that our lofty lineage made us better than most of those among whom we lived.

This idea introduced considerable cognitive dissonance into my head in subsequent years as it became more and more apparent to me that my personal circumstances weren't as good as other children's I knew, rather than being better. However, at four, I loved these myths about our family's superiority and was only too happy to accept them as reality. Nor did I have any trouble catching onto the fact that what Aunt E expected of me then, and for all the future years of my life, was that I prove myself, in everything that I was and in everything that I did, better than others. Of course, Aunt E also expected the same of Leah, and here I must digress for a moment and give you a sneak peek at the future I couldn't foresee at that point.

The reason Aunt E's expectations became like a lead shroud for me, while for Leah they were like adrenaline and serotonin producing challenges in a game which she was confident of winning, was that Leah either had the right stuff to be what impressed Aunt E in a female, or else

Leah sincerely thought she did even when there seemed to be pretty clear evidence to me that she didn't. Self-deception is a wonderful thing. Leah had it and still has it, the last time I checked. I didn't, don't, and seem to be obstinate in my refusal to try to get it. To me, Leah always has been so adept at deluding herself that she does have all the right stuff that her admiration for herself seems to infect everyone around her — so much so that I've often sensed a belief exuding from people as they have listened to Leah talk that they felt themselves to be in the presence of greatness.

In sum, Leah had the right stuff to become what Aunt E was constantly demanding we become. What I had the right stuff to become was the kind of woman with whom I've always felt a kinship — the nose-in-a-book, reflective, nerdy sort — but that kind of woman was not what Aunt E had in mind. In fact, Aunt E had no light in her eyes for that sort of woman at all.

Returning to my discourse on Sunnyside ... despite the fact that our great grandparents Lancaster had owned the property only a few years around the time of the Civil War before they lost it through bank foreclosure, that brief era of wealth and prestige in one generation of our ancestry provided Leah and me with what impressed us as tangible justification for thinking of ourselves as exceptional beings, entitled to bask in the aura which ownership of Sunnyside had cast on our great-grandparents and their children.

We were of the elite, we were told by Aunt E, having the blue blood in our veins that others did not have — certainly none of those people we knew back home in our rural, uncultured environment. As an aside, I must comment that after being made aware of this phenomenon of "blue blood", for a good while thereafter I couldn't understand why, when I happened to cut myself or have a nosebleed, it was red blood that came out — not blue. Where was the certain proof — blood issuing from my body that was of the color blue — that I was of the class of Aunt E and her world and not of the class of all those inferiors of whom it was so pitiful, so common, to be a part?

At Aunt E's everything was clean and polished, or freshly painted, or evenly mowed and raked, or thoroughly weeded, or permeated with the scent of flowers and willows, or backed up by the sounds of mourning dove calls and the water of the creek at the foot of the yard rippling along over pebbles and rushing between stones. Opening her sturdy front door with its big black metal knocker, one entered a foyer never looking any way other than as if it had just been meticulously furbished for the arrival of very important company. Always, there was a slight hint of rose sachet in the air; a smell so sensually satisfying to me that by itself it almost had the power to quench thirst.

Aunt E, unlike Mother, had all the energy she needed to do anything she wanted, whether work or play, and the total self-assurance and absence of self-doubt necessary to shoulder, without shrinking, the position of matriarch and CEO of everything and everybody within her world. I was her namesake. That was one of several circumstances that caused me to imagine myself as being hers rather than Mother's. In the five months that we spent at Aunt E's house in '44, I got used to her environment. Life back home faded, and I began to take life in urban Rockbridge

County for granted. I got used to bathing each night, going to bed with a clean body in clean pajamas in crisp, commercially laundered and ironed sheets, plaque and residues from the day's meals brushed from my teeth.

I got used to my hair being clean, brushed, and cut to a length that made it easy for me to keep that way. I got used to looking down at my feet and seeing feminine shoes that had been bought for me because those were the ones I liked rather than being bought for me — as Daddy was wont to sadistically do — because I found the shoes so ugly and masculine the thought of how I would look to people with them on my feet brought tears to my eyes. I got used to feeling quite proud of myself; proud that I made my own bed every morning with the neat hospital corners Aunt E had wanted me to use, proud that I could set a table with the napkins, spoons, forks, and knives all in their proper places. I got used to being called "Precious" and being cuddled, and being taught cute little recitations or songs to sing for the entertainment of company.

When I regaled Aunt E's and her friends with ...
After the ball was over,
Sally took out her glass eye,
Put her false teeth in the tumbler,
Uncorked a bottle of rye,
Put her false leg in the corner,
Hung her false hair on the line,
The rest of Sally went bye-bye,
After the ball...

Aunt E would laugh until tears came to her eyes, and her friends' reactions were the reactions I saw in the adults in Shirley Temple films when she sang. I was unmitigatedly pleased with myself, and I didn't think to go find a place to hide from Leah before allowing myself to luxuriate in such a self-image.

I completely forgot that in my regular home, the home to which I would be returning before long, Leah and Mother expected me to defer to whatever Leah wanted, and what Leah had always wanted was for me to receive no love or praise (or anything else good) from anyone. I made the mistake — there at Aunt E's in the summer of '44 — of forgetting to exercise constant vigilance over my feelings so that self-loving energy wouldn't leak out of me to offend Leah and ignite the fires of her hatred for me. I lost awareness that it wasn't safe for me to let go of constant self-suppression around Leah and to behave with spontaneity and joy; that for me to do so was to her a transgression against her so egregious it had to be stopped by any means.

The panic attacks had not yet begun that sent waves of fear sweeping over me each time I became aware that I was giving a performance that was mesmerizing an audience of my fellow human beings. Neither had the attacks of shame or guilt that later began to torment me day and night for weeks following occasions wherein I saw that some act of mine had caused someone to see me in a negative light or to feel dislike for me.

Not every four-year-old would be able to memorize both words and melody of little ditties like Aunt E's version of "After the Ball", and I find it sad that once I was away from Aunt E's protection, Leah made me pay so dearly for every moment of attention my performances had gotten me at Aunt E's that I was left with performance anxiety — stage fright — so severe I never have been able to make it through any public performance of a solo since that summer without falling apart.

Children absorb the emotions of others almost as through the skin, so I must have realized that Leah was, even in Lexington, jealous of me. But, I didn't understand that Leah would soon be free again to exercise unfettered control over me just as she had before we'd come to Aunt E's, and that she would wreak vengeance on me for every moment of envy or jealousy good attention paid to me was arousing in her. I suspect that back home she had been used to being allowed the freedom by Mother to intimidate me into keeping to the background and foregoing any claim to Mother's attention if that's the way she wanted it. I suspect she felt it was her right to terrify me into shrinking back and remaining mute when third parties were present since Mother never interfered with her doing that.

Leah must have felt that she was being subjected to great injustice by Aunt E at being deprived of the right to keep me making of myself a part of the woodwork. Perhaps that was one of the reasons why, once we were back home, her treatment of me became, overnight, so virulently hostile. She was making up for five months of being denied what she felt was her right — her right to exercise power and control over me. What gave rise in her to this imagination she had (and has to this day, I think) that it was her moral right to own me; that owning me gave her the moral authority to do anything with me she pleased, and that interference from anyone in her business of keeping me humble and silent in her presence was an offense against her? Well ... inheritance from the institution of slavery comes to my mind.

All my life I've been stuck with this nagging feeling that in that summer at Aunt E's, I did something to influence Aunt E to use or abuse Leah in some way; that I was responsible for a major trespass by Aunt E against Leah for which I fully deserved the punishment she dished out to me and the shunning I got from Mother once we were back home. In my unconscious, I equate people's loving me with my having done something shameful to get that love or that it is shameful on my part to respond with feelings of fullness and satisfaction to someone's love for me. I really don't know why or even exactly when I took this load of guilt onto myself and deduced that there's something wrong with allowing myself to fill up inside or to bask in love's glow upon being loved by someone. But, there it is.

Apparently I remain terrified, six decades later, of letting that great self-image that grew in me that summer grow in me again. I'm aware that I nurture a deeply embedded sense that if only I had made myself stay joyless, self-suppressed, and miserable throughout those five months at Aunt E's, being plunked back into Mother's world at the end of that time wouldn't have altered the development of a wrinkle in my cortex, nor would I have done the horribly self-destructive things I've done in adulthood in my desperation to recapture the energy and happiness I felt that summer.

Unless I'm remembering only what it serves my own interests to remember, I can't believe that Leah was not getting her social and emotional needs met while we were living with Aunt E, and that she therefore was driven by attention deprivation to experience pain any time adults paid any good attention to me. Aunt Marge and Uncle Sam were part of the household and seemed to adore Leah. Someone from among Aunt E's friends and relatives visited us every day or else we went to visit them. They were mostly childless or else their children were grown, and I can't recall one who didn't seem to thoroughly enjoy having Leah around. There were many children in the neighborhood and Leah never lacked for peer companionship.

I do not recall feeling emotional emanations from Leah that bespoke resentment over being conscripted by Aunt E to fulfill the role of being my nanny. Aunt E, having grown up, as I said, in a culture where servants took care of moneyed people's children, was programmed to turn over my everyday routine care and minding to somebody, and Leah was there and fully capable of handling the job. Maybe Leah did resent having to function as my caretaker, and maybe I did pick up on it but knew that Leah didn't dare abuse me in that environment. Maybe I gloated over the fact that Leah was prevented there from indulging her hostility toward me.

At Aunt E's, where Leah played with her friends, I went. If Leah wanted to walk across town to Cousin Maud's house to watch her make beaten biscuits, cheese sticks, or angel food cake for customers of her catering business, I walked with her. If Leah or I wanted to go to a movie, Aunt E previewed the movie alone to make sure it contained no content unsuitable for children, and if it was bland enough to pass her censorship, sent me off with Leah to see it. When Leah made plans with her middle school friends to go Halloween trick-or-treating, those plans included me. When, squatting on the rock wall that surrounded Aunt E's lily pond, I leaned too far over the edge to see what the goldfish were doing and fell in, it was Leah who pulled me out, possibly saving my life.

When it was time for me to make my bed in the morning, put my pajamas away and get dressed, Leah helped me if I needed help. At night, when it was time to take my bath, brush my teeth, put away my day clothes, get into my night clothes, and kneel and say my prayers, Leah led the way. When I wouldn't drink my eight-ounce glasses of full-fat-content pasteurized milk because the taste and greasiness of it were ghastly to me compared to my familiar skimmed milk at Mother's table (and still wouldn't drink it even after being spanked by Aunt E) Aunt E looked to Leah for a solution.

Ever-up-to-any-task Leah conceived the idea of pouring the milk, a little at a time, into a shot glass which I could empty quickly thereby eliminating for me the despair of taking a mouthful of the hated milk from a tall, full container and seeing hardly a change in the amount remaining. I thereafter drank my milk under Leah's tutelage, and I think she was rather proud of the competency she had displayed to Aunt E (and to Aunt E's circle, in which Leah's solution became known) in getting me to do something an adult couldn't. In Aunt E's environment, Leah got recognition and appreciation for her skills in good-heartedly managing my care, whereas in Mother's domain, and in the absence of Daddy or Aunt Willie, it was treating me cruelly that seemed to satisfy.

FIRST FAMILIES OF VIRGINIA AND SCARLET O'HARAS

Loss and the Waste Land

Our time in Lexington behind us, Leah's fast slide into hatefulness toward me began, I think, with her realization once back home that she got no reward whatsoever from Mother for attending to my needs or displaying any generosity of spirit toward me. Mother hated seeing children my age get attention from anybody unless they were so ill they might be in danger of dying. Daddy was half asleep so much of the time he was indoors that he hardly noticed what was going on between Leah and me. Besides, he never wanted to give Leah her due for being precocious anyway, even during his most alert moments. Daddy's self-esteem was an open wound that he tried, by many means, to shield from the salting of seeing that Leah could show him to be inferior to her in any contest of intelligence or judgment.

In order of impact, I probably should have listed basic human nature as the first cause behind Leah's turning overnight from being my protective nanny to being my self-image destroyer as soon as she was out from under the control of adults who expected from her a high degree of civilization and humanity in behavior. A story common to most of mankind's earliest myths, regardless of the region from which the tale has come down to us, is one of siblings killing siblings. In Judeo-Christian myth, the first child born of human parents, Cain, was so filled with jealousy when he saw that Abel, the second-born, had made an offering to God that pleased God more than his, Cain killed him. If it were not common for siblings to hate each other, this story would not have evoked such feeling in human hearts that it was ordered prior to all other myths in the world's best-selling book, the Bible, after the myth of mankind's expulsion from Eden.

Perhaps on the first night or two back home, Leah kept up my nightly teeth-brushing and prayers rituals, but no adult noticed or cared whether she did or not. Thereafter, instead of leading me through cleanliness and grooming activities, she switched to shaming me for failing to maintain those habits on my own and to expressing to anyone and everyone what revulsion I caused her to have to endure due to my failure to keep myself clean and groomed. Mother found that much more satisfying than she found any display of good will toward me by Leah. Now Mother was seeing me being treated the way she unconsciously wanted to see children, dogs, and cats be treated.

Leah's need to keep up appearances was also suffering from other encroachments besides my slovenliness. One was Aunt Willie's run-down, had-been-of-a-house, with its yard of weeds and unkempt grass and plantings, with its sagging rusted fencing running along the frontage, with its piles of pigeon droppings and stacks of ancient newspapers accompanying the rotting columns on the porches, and with a plethora of sheds, barns, garages, and outhouses sprinkled around haphazardly, unpainted, all bulging with rusted and dry-rotted junk, most of which probably hadn't been touched in years.

It wasn't the disrepair, decay, or mountains of clutter filling every space of Aunt Willie's house and outbuildings that got me down. Weird as it may seem, I loved all that. To me, her house and property was a wonderland. I miss it and dream about it to this day. How sad I feel that it all inexorably became so rotted and worthless that when she died, her heir had every structure and its contents bulldozed down and covered with earth, making of several acres a very attractive hill which was quickly snapped up by a buyer who had a beautiful home erected on the site in no time. In my dreams, the house still stands and is not beyond redemption.

Exploring Aunt Willie's buildings and their to-the-ceilings collections of junk entertained and occupied me through many a day when my lack of companions and toys, and my awareness that Mom didn't want me to bother her, might have otherwise seemed like a day in exile from my species. It was just being in our apartment, in Mom's domain, that was all gloom and doom for me. Leah, on the other hand, felt perfectly comfortable and welcome in Mom's space - she was about the only living being Mom ever did seem to really want with her in her space - but hated living at Aunt Willie's because she felt ashamed of the bad impression she was sure the appearance of the place made on those people whom she wanted to impress favorably.

The house and grounds must have been magnificent in the early 1900s, which is when they were first built, I suppose, but Aunt Willie never spent any money or time on maintaining her properties anywhere, whether they were her rent-producing properties or her main residence there in Pulaski County. Along with her other gross neglects of maintenance, she had let all the pipes freeze for the running water and heat some years before my time and had never had them repaired. So, we had a monstrosity of a furnace in the basement going unused that could have kept the whole fourteen-room house warm in the coldest weather ... if there had been intact water pipes to and from the furnace and the radiators throughout the house. Some coal-burning potbellied stoves had been installed in a few rooms, so we weren't entirely without heat in the winter.

We had a kitchen with a sink, but the pipes that had once brought water up to it no longer did. I can't remember whether or not we could pour waste water down the drain, but I believe we could, at least, do that. We had a bathroom with commode, bathtub, and basin, and I believe that there, too, pipes may have been adequate to carry waste water out of the house to the cesspool at the back of one garden; but with no running water with which to flush a toilet, wash hands, or take a bath, and with every drop of water the family used in our apartment having to be hand-pumped at the cistern outside the back of the house and carried up two flights of stairs, it made sense to use bathroom fixtures as little as possible and to take one's potty needs outside to an outhouse rather than deposit something into a toilet that would require a lot of water to flush away.

The ceilings of Aunt Willie's house were high and brownish with age and residues from coal smoke. The walls were likewise dingy all the way down to the stand-in for wainscot, which was nothing more than an area around the base of the rooms, up to a level above where fingerprints might be made, painted an exceedingly dark green.

The floors weren't of the meticulously finished and waxed-until-they-shone variety. They might have been of high quality wood, but they had had so many buckets of water, coal, and ashes carried over them, and had been tread upon by so many shoes that had come in from the garden caked with mud or come in from the barnyard caked with manure, that any gleam the wood had once had was long gone. The central areas of the floors in our apartment were covered in cheap linoleum, which was hardly ever clean either.

Leah had been in her element at Aunt E's. Back home, Daddy almost immediately presented Leah with an element into which she had not wanted to be again plunged. I'm sure that I had seen my father spank Leah before we left in the spring to go to Aunt E's, but somehow the more negative aspects of life with Mother and Daddy had fled my memory almost in the short time it took for Aunt E to transport us the hundred miles from our home to hers.

At Aunt E's, equal-to-any-adult, proud Leah didn't exist under the constant threat of anyone's destroying her pride and dignity by spanking her. She was, after all, nine years old going on eighteen. But, Daddy wasn't into tolerating in his children any hint of lack of respect, and Leah didn't see anything in Daddy to respect. She had acquired

Aunt E's attitude about men — if they're not immaculately groomed white-collar professionals who make a lot of money and treat women like knights of King Arthur's court treated their ladies, then they're nothing. Leah, also in imitation of Aunt E, didn't concern herself much with what it might do to Daddy's self-esteem to be seen as just a pathetic substitute for what he should have been as a man. Leah's and Aunt E's attitude toward him aroused a rage in Daddy he often could not contain. Adults becoming enraged at other adults, regardless of the provocation, was considered bestial or evidential of mental defectiveness in the culture in which Daddy was reared, but spanking, betraying, and humiliating one's children wasn't.

When I saw my older sister, whom I thought of as an adult having equal status with other adults, being viciously spanked by our father almost on the day we returned home, I felt Leah's hurt and humiliation as if it were coming in waves into my own body. In my Electra state of emotional and psychosexual development, I had some deep impression of Leah's being Uncle Sam's love — the adored-one of that knightly gentleman who treated his wife like a queen — our Uncle Sam who lived with Aunt Marge upstairs at Aunt E's house. This belief was not one of which I was consciously aware. Consciously, I knew that Aunt Marge was Uncle Sam's wife and his love, and that's the way it would always be. But, Leah, in her spoken-aloud fantasies, had said that when she married someday it would be to someone just like Uncle Sam. In my unconscious, that sureness that someday Leah would be marrying a man who would not be the spiritual equivalent of our father, but who would instead be the spiritual equivalent of Uncle Sam, was a premonition or foretelling of the future in which I had faith as firm as if God had given me the word. All the time that we had been staying with Aunt E, I was sure that I would marry an Uncle Sam too.

In no time after we were back home in Pulaski County, I saw my life beginning to turn in a direction away from where I had thought it must go and turn in a direction that panicked and horrified me. In the presence of Aunt E's sick obsession (if anyone saw it at the time as being the sick obsession it was, I'm not aware of it) with making of us girls little Scarlet O'Haras, I had come to envision my life and Leah's as being lived for one purpose only - to make boys fall in love with us and men like Uncle Sam want to marry us. I was sure that if I just watched how Aunt E and Leah behaved around males and inviolably mimicked that behavior when I was around males, I would be irresistible to any boy I might want to captivate, at the age of four and forever.

This expectation I had of myself — this expectation with which Aunt E infected my psyche with her incessant instruction in how I should get boys to "fall head over heels in love with me" — began to produce illness in me from the moment she commenced drilling the obsession into my head. The little boys of my age in Aunt E's neighborhood who joined Leah and me for play became immediately to me, not playmates with whom to relax and feel comfortable, but males I thought I had been given a mandate to attract in an erotic way.

Lest what I'm saying be misconstrued, let me clarify that Aunt E was not suggesting at all that I strive for any physical erotic contact with males, then or at any time before I would marry. What she was visualizing was precisely the picture of Scarlet O'Hara that Margaret Mitchell painted for readers in the opening pages of *Gone With the Wind*; a look-but-don't-touch, knock-'em-dead beauty who charmed and teased and led males on as one would lead a hungry horse by enticing him with a carrot that one never allows the horse to quite get his lips around. Part of my strategy was supposed to be that I would never succumb to feeling any passion myself or engage in anything physical until it came time to reward my rich husband for making me a Mrs. Rich Person.

As it is not usually in nature's design for a whole pack of four-year-old boys to be smitten by one four-year-old girl and pursue her as Scarlet O'Hara's suitors pursued her in *Gone with the Wind*, I was doomed to fail at what I gathered Aunt E expected of me. I did not inspire the reaction in any of my little male playmates that Aunt E had led me to believe I was supposed to evoke.

However, back home in Pulaski County, in short order, it became apparent to both me and Leah that Daddy wasn't too happy with Leah but seemed to be quite satisfied with me. I got picked up and cuddled by him; Leah got yelled at and spanked. Here I was, all at once, in a terrifying trap with no way out. What did Daddy's affection toward me mean? My God! Was I so irresistibly attractive I had enticed Daddy to me romantically without meaning to? I didn't want a man like Daddy for a husband, but it appeared to me that was the prize I had won. Nor was this a situation where I could turn the prize down and say, "Thanks, I'm flattered that you've chosen me above Leah and Mother [Mother wasn't having much to do with Daddy just then], but I'll hold out for what Leah's holding out for."

There wasn't another human in the household at the time who could even tolerate my company, much less welcome it. Aunt Willie was in Florida for the winter, so I couldn't find human solace by going down to visit with her. Given a choice between Daddy's company, a choice which kept my innards in a wringer for all sorts of reasons, and hanging around two females and a baby, socially on the outside looking in, I usually opted for Daddy's company even though that increased Leah's and Mother's hostility toward me considerably.

With Daddy attacking Leah's self-image and Leah having had her emotional support and self-esteem snatched away from her, she wasn't about to share any of the little she had left with me. Mother existed day to day as if in a foreign country. She plodded slowly through her household and farm tasks as if none of us were there. She attended to the baby conscientiously and lovingly enough, but for the rest of us she had no eyes or ears, and touching any of us voluntarily would have been to her the equivalent of exposing herself to contamination.

Leah had a life-saving strategy for dealing with Mom's ignoring her. She would stand by Mom in the kitchen and talk to her at length without regard to the fact that there wasn't a two-way conversation going on there and that the positive responses she imagined she was receiving from Mom were mostly that - imagined. However, the expression I saw on Mother's face during these long sessions told me that Mother was being entertained by Leah's monologues and found them welcome.

I wasn't able to imagine I was receiving positive responses when I talked to Mom. First of all, I couldn't see that I had anything to talk to her about that would entertain her. Leah could bring home news from school, or talk about things she had read in books, or relate what her music teacher had said to her. Leah was very independent and self- sufficient. Her chit-chat wasn't about things she needed from Mother or about things she wanted Mother to do for her.

Some need of mine was about the only thing that drove me to attempt to communicate with Mother at all. She had given me attention without resenting having to do that before Aunt E had taken us in the spring to stay with her in Lexington. She had let me sit on her lap when we had taken train rides to see her family in Radford. She had let me sit on her lap while she read to me, and she had read to me often. In short, she had owned me as her child and had taken good care of me, not avoiding touching me, but touching me with the ease with which most mothers do touch their young children.

When Aunt E, Leah, and I had gotten out of our car after the long drive from Lexington to Pulaski County and had entered the room where Mother and the baby were, Mother's face said it all. It was as if we were not her children, but Aunt E's, and that Aunt E was bringing her spoiled-rotten children there and dumping them on her.

Welcoming smiles and hugs from Mom after the long time we had been away from her? I don't remember any. I think she sat in her chair and looked at the floor. Maybe that's not the way it was at all. Maybe I just want to remember it that way because doing so will ease my conscience over the ill-will I thereafter bore her for not behaving toward me as if I were the little goddess Aunt E had led me to believe I was. And that was the point when Mother's and my relationship changed for me from being bonded

Mother and child to being Mother and this bad, unclean, spoiled child of Daddy's and Aunt E's whom they had forced upon her and who was her resented burden.

Like an unwanted parasite, I tried to attach myself to Leah and make her maintain toward me the position of indulgent nanny just as she consistently had in Lexington. The incentive she had had at Aunt E's to look after me was gone. The quality in Leah that most antagonized Daddy was the giftedness that made her more knowledgeable and competently aggressive about leading others than he. He had no desire to increase her self-assurance by exhibiting admiration for the way in which she managed me. Unlike Mother, Daddy didn't want Leah to assume that she owned me like a chattel and could therefore do anything with me she wanted. Unlike Mother, Daddy had no desire to give me away to somebody — anybody — so that he wouldn't have to pay any attention to me.

Mother's admiration for Leah, on the other hand, seemed to increase in direct proportion to how hateful and domineering Leah was to me. Early one morning not long after we had been back in Pulaski County, Mother went out to milk the cow for Daddy as was her custom when he had left for work before daylight. What started Leah's jeering and sneering at me, I don't recall. Usually her attacks would come when she caught me exhibiting confidence in myself or in something I had said or done, so I suppose what set Leah off that morning was that I had communicated to her in one way or another that she was not my boss. Her heckling of me progressed until I found myself trapped against a wall with Leah holding a teakettle of steaming water over me that she had snatched from the kitchen range.

I was frightened with a fear made all the more terrifying by the fact that I didn't hate Leah — I loved her. Leah was the most significant of all my significant others because she was accessible to me (even if she didn't want to be) when no other caretaker figures were. She was the surrogate mother with whom I had felt so secure for so many months, suddenly transformed into someone who hated me so much that seeing me hysterical with fear delighted her. For five months she had been constrained, strait-jacketed, denied her God-given right to do or say to me whatever she wanted. Now she had her freedom again, and she was reveling in it and gloating, just as I had reveled in my freedom from fear of her at Aunt E's; my freedom to speak and act spontaneously and to feel good about myself without having to worry, with every word and action, about what Leah was going to do or say to me to stamp out my self-love.

It all took place as if torturing and being tortured were a game we were playing; a game like the innocuous fun games Leah had mentored me in at Aunt E's. I attempted to jump out under her arm to run from her. In so doing, I bumped her elbow and got a cascade of scalding water down my chest. Oh, I felt so sorry for myself, and I visualized myself in the role of the injured party as I would play it when Mother returned from the barn. She would be horrified with Leah for what she had done to me. She would treat the burn on my chest with some sort of medicine that would relieve the pain as she tenderly spread it over my red skin. She would tell Leah in no uncertain terms that her behavior was totally unacceptable. She would comfort me and sympathize with my plight.

As soon as Mother entered the door, I ran to her sobbing out my woeful tale, trying to show her the scald marks on my chest. If she looked at me or my scald marks, I don't remember it. I think she continued right past me to the kitchen with her milk saying "You nasty stinking things. You worry the life out of me ".

Leah was triumphant. She had regained her position of having whatever degree of power over me she wanted — a position she considered as rightfully hers as I'm sure owners of slaves thought was theirs where their relationships with their slaves were concerned. Not only had she reduced me to a trembling, screaming, powerless nothing, but she hadn't had to face any consequences for it. In fact, maybe Mother was secretly very satisfied to see this spoiled child of Aunt E's and Daddy's put in her place.

Our positions, the interlocking positions of the three of us, were firmly established, never to change thereafter. Our lines in the drama that went on until Mother's death, when I was fifty-eight, were always some variation on Leah's theme: "Oh, look Mother at how amazing and special I am and how well I reflect on you as a result", Leah says, using whatever words are relevant to her success of the day and the important person whom she has impressed along with achieving this success.

Then, becoming aware that I am on the scene, Leah switches to addressing me (for the edification of our listening Mother, "But then, there's Emmy over there who just makes us all look bad, and who is jealous of me because I'm so superior to her in every way".

Given Leah's reinstatement in Mother's domain, an environment in which she was free to bully me in just about any way that unsupervised stronger children often do bully weaker ones, I quickly perceived Daddy as my only hope.

I had dreamed of being a princess, just like Leah, who would one day marry a prince like Uncle Sam and live in a world exactly like the exclusive Monroe Park where Aunt E lived in Lexington; of being a good, clean, wholesome, totally desirable, and feminine woman, smiled upon by everyone. Now, it seemed to me, Leah was standing in the kitchen with Mother every afternoon after school, sneering at me, expressing unbearable revulsion over something I'd said or done, expressing disgust over how bad a person I was.

And what was I doing — what had I done - that made me so unforgivably unwholesome that my mother and sister considered it their duty to collaborate to block me from accessing enjoyable human companionship - or if they couldn't block me, to berate or shame me for pursuing it? I've pondered this question my whole life. What did I do at the age of two, or three, or four, that was so awful that I had to be kept away from all socialization?

I can't think of anything a three- or four- or five-year-old could do to deserve social isolation. What could I have done that could have caused Mother to consider it appropriate for Leah to dehumanize me so painfully in front of her family members - my maternal family members — that I ceased making any effort to try to relate to any of them. I don't think there are any possibilities I haven't mulled. Did I wet or soil my pants somewhere I shouldn't have? Probably, but is that reason to shun and shame a child forever after? While I was at Aunt E's, I had really gotten the hots for the neighbor boy my age who was bold enough to pee in the creek. Did Leah tell Mother and Daddy about that, and did they think it evidence of such depravity in me that I had to be isolated from other children else I might behave shamefully? I don't know.

I've finally, in my old age, laid the blame for the childhood shaming and shunning that rendered me incapable of ever being able, as an adult, to sustain relationships in love and work, to roots and religion. I think that the tradition of dehumanizing slaves, coming down to Leah through Aunt E's and Daddy's family, and the Quaker tradition of "disowning" coming down to Mother through her mitochondrial line, combined and found full expression in the way Leah (a female driven to be "Mistress of the Plantation") treated me and in Mother's and her clan's support of Leah's identification of me as the "one among us" who is so bad and sinful the good members of the pack must disown her.

If Leah and I were to meet and converse today, fifteen minutes into the conversation Leah would be employing every trick of facial expression, body word choice, tone of voice, reference, name-dropping — any strategy an expert dehumanizer can contrive — to show me up as being pathetically inferior to her. I'm sure she has no idea that she automatically falls into working to diminish me in my own eyes and everybody else's any time we have anything to do with each other.

In my life I've spent many an hour watching and listening as Leah has socialized exuberantly with Mother and her relatives (or Mother and any number of her and Leah's common acquaintances) while I observed knowing that should I make any attempt to enter into the camaraderie, Leah would instantly have a look for me and a remark about me that would have everyone glaring at me as if I had just revealed myself to be mentally defective or unclean or subhuman in some way.

    I have never been able to shake off the terror Leah aroused in me when she would demonstrate to me, as she seemed to me to be invariably able to do, that she could, any time she wanted, influence anyone who was about to accept me warmly to withdraw their acceptance and express contempt and hostility for me instead. My bewilderment and sense of helplessness and hopelessness as I watched people unfailingly succumb to Leah's power to mold their opinion of me into whatever she wanted it to be, left a mass of quivering jelly where my self-confidence should have been. I've never found any closure for this; the most torturing, frightening, and puzzling aspect of my relationship with Leah.

    I never remember any occasion where Mother told Leah she couldn't have friends come to visit and play or that she couldn't go to playmates' houses to play. Where Mother's permissions were concerned, for every social pleasure Mother invariably denied me, Leah had permission unconditionally granted. In fact, for a couple of birthdays of mine, Leah decided to play hostess (a chance to see herself in Aunt E's identity, I imagine) and throw birthday parties for me. She invited the children she wanted to invite, and, the event being Leah's desire, Mother didn't say one word about my playing with the children Leah had invited. If Mother had caught me trying to instigate play with those same children on my own, she would have harangued me as you might expect a modern mother to harangue a child she had caught smoking pot.

    Even after I started school at six-and-a-half, Mother would not let me play with other children, not even with my cousins. When Mother's clan gathered, Leah played outside with our cousins while Mother made me sit inside with my hands folded in my lap. There never was any time when Leah was discouraged by Mother from laying claim to the undivided attention of everyone in any group in which she chose to hold court. I, on the other hand, had to keep myself so invisible in order to avoid arousing in Leah an instant action to humiliate me in front of everyone, that my cousins don't even know who I am.

By the time I was eight or nine, I knew Mother would say no to anything I asked to do, so I stopped asking. Then, if I really wanted to do something in the way of socializing and thought I could do it without Mother's finding out, I did it. But at four, five, and six, I wasn't yet to the stage where I'd just given up completely on my mother's and my relationship and had decided that whatever she didn't want me to do was bound to be fun and something it would feel very good to do.

As a child, I had a world of ideas about why Leah hated me, why she wanted everyone else to hate me, and why Mother kept validating Leah for expressing her hatred of me and conscripting our cousins and her friends to do the same. I had won praise and love from Aunt E, and I had won that through some kind of inherent badness, I figured. I didn't deserve any such affection and attention as Aunt E had heaped on me, I figured, therefore, I must have used some morally rotten means of getting it. If that weren't disgustingly bad enough, now I was going to Daddy for affection and attention and he was giving it to me. My getting my self-esteem bolstered by attention from other humans — that was bad and that was the reason Leah felt a moral mandate to step up to the plate and mete out to me the harsh and cold treatment she knew Mother wanted to see me getting from Daddy and Aunt E, I figured.

You are no doubt thinking to yourself, "Now what mother on this planet hates a little four-year-old child and thinks that little four-year-old child has committed a sin so immoral and disgusting it merits disownment just because some adult has generously shown that little child physical affection, has put time and effort into bringing the child enjoyment, and has applauded the child's nature and accomplishments?". My mother — that's what mother! My poor mother! I was disgusting and bad for attracting physical affection and good attention from Daddy and Aunt E to myself, and they were morally deficient as human beings for giving physical affection and positive attention to a little child who was old enough to walk and talk.

That I had been given a considerable amount of loving attention and physical affection from Aunt E while in Lexington and had let that positive treatment bring me joy and great self-esteem was a depravity so egregious in my mother's eyes that her emotions were aroused against me just hearing about it from Leah. It was almost impossible for any of us (husband or children) to get Mother emotionally involved with us, so when Leah found that she could open Mother's heart and mind to her with the good old "ain't it awful" gambit focused on Aunt E's or Daddy's treating me in the affectionate way Mother abhorred, Leah mined it for all it was worth.

I was bad and disgusting because I'd gotten praise and affection from Aunt E by telling Aunt E things about Leah that caused Aunt E to be angry with Leah and to treat her badly. I was bad and disgusting because I told

Daddy things about Leah that caused him to feel ill will toward her and that influenced him to treat her cruelly and unjustly. That was Leah's refrain to Mother and anybody else she judged to be a child or adult she could influence. Sixty years later, it's easy for me to see that this was "projection" in pure form; that it was *Leah* who was, everywhere, telling anyone to whom she had a chance to speak that I was telling people things about her that would influence Aunt E and Daddy to think ill of her and treat her badly.

Now, when it's far too late to do me any good to have the knowledge, I know that I wasn't saying or doing anything at all, anywhere, to bring down anybody's ill will on Leah. It was Leah who was doing that to me. Unfortunately for my future life, I let what Leah told others about me in my presence, what Leah told me about me one-to-one and in company, and the way she talked and behaved toward me around people whenever she sensed that displaying scorn and revulsion for me would impress them, to form my self-image — my permanent self-image. When I was four, "projection" was something a machine did at a movie theater, not an evolved survival strategy whereby a person gains support and adulation of masses of her fellowmen by astutely finding someone whom she can successfully market to them as a person deserving of their scorn and disgust.

I saw my dream of what my life was predestined to be float away from me like the yard waste that Aunt Emmelia threw into the rapids of the creek at the foot of her yard. I had a book of Mother Goose nursery rhymes with a picture of three men in a tub spinning down a creek just like the creek at Aunt Emmelia's. Mother read the words for me, and I dreamed about those three men in the tub being run off by the people in their village and being made to get in that tub where the roiling waters of the stream carried them away, never to enjoy the running of their businesses or the patronage or camaraderie of their neighbors again.

> Rub a dub dub
> Three men in a tub,
> And who do you think they be?
> The Butcher, the Baker,
> The Candlestick Maker,
> Throw them out.
> Knaves all three.

They were bad like I was bad, and being banished was the just desserts of bad people.

I was also caught in a briar patch where the more frantically you try to escape, the more thorns you run into that hook you and hold you there. I began to follow Daddy like a devoted pet. I waited in the yard for him to come home from work. I ran errands for him such as walking through the pasture to stand at the fence across the highway from the store where Daddy bought his Prince Albert pipe tobacco. Daddy would have already called the storekeeper to tell her that I would come to the fence, so she would be watching for me and would walk across the highway to hand me Daddy's tobacco when I arrived at my spot.

I went to the neighbor's orchard with him when they offered him apples to make cider and apple butter and helped him gather the apples that had fallen to the ground. I went with him to cornfields and kept him company while he hacked the stalks off just above the ground and placed them in shocks where the ears of corn would dry. When they were dry, back to the cornfield I went with Daddy to keep him company while he pulled the ears off the stalks. When he took the ears to a mill where they would be ground into feed for our livestock, I went along.

Daddy talked to me a lot. I listened and didn't talk unless he asked me a question, which he didn't do very often. This was the kind of relationship with which both Daddy and Aunt E were happy. They wanted attentive, looking and listening companions — not talking ones who put them in listening positions. Mother was a listener who spoke only when remaining mute would have been impolite in as far as adult society's sensibilities were concerned. That was the kind of companion Daddy wanted, and I'm sure that is why Daddy's and Mother's relationship was never, ever a confrontational one.

Leah was a talker whose chatter could draw attention away from Daddy's or Aunt E's words anytime she opened her mouth, and who would have the spotlight by whatever means it took her to get it. That insatiable drive she had, the drive to be the person getting the most attention in every venue, when Daddy or Aunt E expected her to move downstage any time they came onstage, incensed them against her terribly. Often, when I was alone with either Daddy or Aunt E, they would express to me how much they disliked her talkativeness.

Leah had me convinced, even when I was only a preschooler, that she was far more intelligent, knowledgeable, insightful, and good than either Daddy or Aunt E, so when they confided their dislike of Leah to me behind her back, and I, in turn, related to them some analysis of my person Leah had laid on my doorstep that had deflated my ego so badly I couldn't get it off my mind, I acquired yet another view of myself to add to the store of self-loathing with which my psyche already bulged — I was a treacherous traitor to my sister when I should have been fighting Daddy and Aunt E in defense of her. I can see, now that I'm old and have twenty-twenty hindsight, that Stockholm syndrome must have been firmly embedded in me.

If Daddy wasn't away at his job, I was with him, and all the while, I felt horrible about it. Whatever I might be focused upon consciously, underneath it all shame and guilt were always trying to erupt into my awareness and spoil my peace of mind or my enjoyment of the moment. I was bugged without letup by my conscience because I thought that instead of being with someone who liked me — in this case Daddy — I should be in the house with Leah and Mother, letting Leah tell me how bad and disgusting I was while she screwed her nose up (for Mother's viewing appreciation) as if blocking disgusting sights and odors. My conscience told me, anytime I couldn't keep my conscience beaten off, that Leah had me sized up right, and that anyone who saw me as a good child and liked me was a gullible ignoramus, too stupid and too lacking in awareness of reality to see past my conning ways.

Please forgive my insertion here of a chronologically out-of-place comment, but I want to say to you my reader, that I was fifty-eight or fifty-nine years old before I ever realized that this sizing up of me, by Leah, was projection. I wouldn't have ever entertained a doubt about the accuracy of Leah's analysis of my childhood character as being conning and treacherous, if she hadn't, in one conversation with her which I couldn't avoid, begun describing one of our nephews as being a con artist of such fantastic intelligence and charm that he knew just how to deceive anyone into giving him anything he wanted from them and into helping him achieve any ends he wanted to achieve.

In the midst of what Leah was saying, Epiphany arrived. I suddenly became aware that Leah's description of our nephew — a young man earning his living as a truck driver, who had struggled with such ADHD and LD throughout his life that I'm not sure he even made it all the way through high school, a young man who had suffered through more disadvantaged a childhood than most of us even glimpse — wasn't a description of our nephew. Leah was describing herself perfectly. With Leah's projection of her own character and modus operandi being cast on someone other than myself, I was able to allow myself to consider the possibility that Leah might be capable of projecting to a pathological degree without recognizing that she's doing so. Whatever Leah projects onto me or ever has projected onto me, I soak up with a faith as unquestioning as a fundamentalist Christian's faith that Jesus was born of a virgin and arose from the dead.

If Daddy or Aunt E or some adult of like values (that is, some adult who would have been left cold at seeing an older, much larger child abuse a little one) was present, Leah wouldn't slap me, wouldn't sneer and dwell verbally on my repulsiveness, and wouldn't dare drive me off. She'd save the reprimands, the hissing, the slapping, and the shaming for my omissions and commissions until Mother or some blood relative of Mother's were the only other humans present. Leah could forecast public opinion with ne'er a slip-up, so she never made the mistake of abusing me in front of someone who wouldn't admire her for it. Or, perhaps the situation was that's what I thought, rightly or wrongly.

My conscience wanted to tell me that any time Leah sneered at me in disgust, told me how bad I was, told me how shameful something I had done was, or slapped me, she was only doing what Mother wanted someone to do to me due to my being such a bad child and such an "aggravating nuisance". (That was one of several aliases for "Emmy" by which Mother addressed me when she addressed me at all.) Due to my being such a bad child and such an "aggravating nuisance to her", Mother existed in the desire that I would magically disappear from her life (I thought). When Leah expressed revulsion for me or slapped me, she was only communicating to me openly what Mother felt for me but wasn't able to act upon due to her fragile health and the consumption of every measure of energy and time she could muster in her necessity to deal with the load of work that Daddy and I piled upon her, Leah believed. What Leah believed about Mother, Daddy, herself, and me always seemed to become what everybody else believed emphatically almost before her assessments were fully out of her mouth.

That Daddy and I continually loaded Mother down with our selfish demands upon her time and energy in blatant disregard of her limitations in energy and her physical fragility, was a belief that Leah took great satisfaction in impressing upon me and in spreading to as many of Mother's kin as she happened across. She, Leah, was the only caring person in the household where Mother's welfare was concerned (those of us gathered, as we listened to Leah). Mother's only refuge and help against us two selfish, self-centered users (Daddy and me) was Leah, according to Leah.

By expressing hostility toward me until I relinquished the space I was occupying within Mother's space (a domain where my siblings' presence was no burden to mother - just mine), Leah was helping Mother get what she most wanted (Leah said) — to be free of me. I believed that was what Mother wanted anytime I was with her. I lived in pursuit of ways to blot out awareness of that from my mind. This was the trauma I repressed throughout my existence until I had arrived at a point, in my late fifties, where every grand dream and every addiction in which I had sought escape had brought me such failures and humiliations I couldn't find any more hope in any of them. I had repressed, throughout my life, the full impact of being scorned and disliked by the closest sharers in the world of my mitochondria — the pack mates of mine for whom neither my father nor anyone else in the world ever was or ever could be an adequate substitute.

Isn't this the real cause of childhood-onset, intractable depression in women; the fact that our mitochondrially closest kin have cut us adrift spiritually even if not tangibly? Isn't it that we have been unable to hold our space in a nest where we could obtain maternal nurturance and live-and-let-live coexistence with siblings?

LOSS AND THE WASTE LAND

The Pain We Can't Face

When I had left Aunt Willie's in the spring with Leah to go to Aunt E's, none of these undercurrents had seemed to exist at home - or perhaps they had, and I had felt secure enough in my relationship with Mother that they just wafted past me. I was painfully aware now that the relationship with Mother that I'd just taken for granted would be waiting for me when I got home had flown. Why didn't she care anything about me anymore? How was I going to get back that something between us that had once been there but that was now gone? I had to make her care about me again. I got a lunch bag out of a cabinet, found something to eat to put in it, and announced to her that I was running away from home. I walked out to the pasture and then to the fence at the end of the pasture, looking back as I walked at the house from which she would be coming to bring me home. But Mother wasn't coming.

I set my lunch down and mooed at the cow and calf on the other side of the fence. Then I pretended for some time that I was the cow's calf. That was gratifying for a while, then time quickly started to drag. Mom was nowhere to be seen even though I stayed there for what seemed like hours. Finally I understood that Mother was not coming after me.

In Lexington, Aunt E would have been on my trail immediately had I wandered out of her yard alone. I had been valued as a precious thing there, but I wasn't precious to my mother, I could see. I guessed that a chicken loose from its pen might have been worth her while to retrieve because of its value as a producer of eggs and the danger that it might be killed by dogs. I knew that when cows got out of a fenced pasture, anybody and everybody rushed out of the house to get them back in. I guessed I wasn't worth much if Mother didn't care enough about where I might be running away from home to bother to look.

At the first of the winter of '44-'45, I tried to hold on to the pride I had had in myself in Lexington, but slowly I fell into daydreaming about being clean and grownup instead of doing anything to be that way. As long as I didn't "pester the life out of her", Mother didn't notice anything I did, unless it was something I'd done because I was a "nasty stinking thing" who "never minded a word she said", who "pig-headedly persisted in doing what she had told me not to do" and who "had to mess up and destroy everything" I touched. Nothing I was or did was praiseworthy to her, and everything I said or did was a source of sneering and ridicule from Leah, so I abandoned my dream of having the love or respect of either of them, and looked for any activity or any place where I could feel good if only for a few moments.

The complete absence from my life, for the next two to three years, of other children in my age range, after having playmates day after day for months in the summer of '44, was a loss and an unrelenting torture that I did not repress as I did the greater tortures of my ouster from a place in the hearts of Leah and Mother. Consciously, my longing to play with other children eclipsed all other longings. Nothing was left of the relationships I had had with my same-age playmates in Lexington except for the person who had functioned as our babysitter while we joyously played the hours away at Aunt E's creek - Leah. Leah was the only thing in my world that could be a thread connecting me to the lost joy of playing with other children. I needed Leah desperately. Leah had no desire to continue playing nursemaid to me when there would be no reward for her from anyone for doing so.

I wanted so frantically to play with other children again, there wasn't any kind of shame or pain with which Leah could assault me that would deter me from attempting to attach myself to her. If Leah wanted to play with her paper dolls all by herself without me, I had to leave her alone; but the next day, I would go to the place where she kept them and play with them as I had seen her do. Mother would tell me harshly to leave Leah's things alone and would call me all the things she usually called me if she called me anything at all, but my desire to be one with Leah was far stronger than Mother's admonitions to stay away from her and leave her things alone.

Leah was allowed to have playmates visit her or go to

visit them. Upon the first occasion, when we were newly back, when a classmate of Leah's came to play with her, I was so frantic to get on my coat and shoes and get outside with Leah and the other child I pulled my shoes onto the wrong feet and laced them up in a frenzy, all the while hearing Mother tell me that I could not go out in the yard where they were and bother them. I was practically insane with the loneliness of being in that apartment all day, every day, being neither talked to nor looked at while Mother played with the baby and took care of her. The notion in my head that I could play with Leah and her friend if only I could get my clothes on and get out there made me deaf and blind to any other thought.

I scrambled down the stairs as fast as I dared and ran up to where Leah and her friend were standing, even though Leah frowned at the sight of me. Then Leah caught sight of my shoes and began to howl with laughter. With Leah pointing at my feet and telling me how stupid I was, her companion began to point at me, shrieking with laughter too. I got behind a tree and tried to hide my feet from them. I can't even remember getting myself out from behind the tree and back into the house. Probably I don't want to.

After Little Sis' birth in '44, I was never again safe from Leah's modeling for third parties how to feel revulsion and contempt for me. There was always something about me to point out and laugh at, always something shameful I'd done to tell about while looking at me with a sneering face, always something I'd said that showed how pathetically stupid I was. Nevertheless, my psyche kept sending me back to Leah, every time harboring that breathless anticipation that I'd find again the Leah of my five months of heaven in Lexington; the Leah who had been my friend instead of my most feared enemy, the Leah who had been my facilitator for all things fun, my idol, the Leah who was the most interesting and exciting human I knew out of all the humans I knew.

Quite unfortunately for me, my attempt to find help for my depression by putting myself into psychoanalytically oriented therapy in 1967, had, by 1968, got this old routine I'd endlessly repeated in my relationship with Leah refueled, revved up, and unleashed; this time in what I thought was a hunt for a husband "I could love". All I can think as I look back on this is, "Emmy, you poor thing". I hadn't a clue I was trying to relive my relationship with Leah and make it come out some way other than being scorned. My doctor was far less insightful about the whole thing than I, although he kept insisting he knew exactly what my "acting out" was all about. May God grant his mercy to all us poor women who have ever put our faith in a male psychiatrist.

It is very hard to accept that the dominant female of your pack is never going to open the spiritual door to your pack for you again. Even when I was an adult of college age, when Leah sat down at the piano in the presence of her fiancé, Mother, and our sisters, and asked me if I would like to sing, I took the bait. Of course, in no time, a note issued from my mouth which gave Leah justification to look at me with the exaggerated "Oooo, that was terrible" look on her face that she has always managed to work into her performance anytime she has had an audience and I've been present.

Even when I realized that my having a mutually respectful relationship with Leah would never happen, I couldn't see that I was unconsciously trying to recreate my very brief childhood time of good relationship with Leah in an adult relationship with a male mate and experience that good time lasting for the rest of our lives.

As a child I behaved very much like a woman who stays on and on with a man who abuses her, thinking that she can do or say something that will open his eyes to her worth with the result that he will stop abusing her and start respecting her So, I endlessly nourished the dream of becoming something that would be so admirable, so perfect, that Leah would talk to me and behave toward me the way I saw her talking and behaving toward people she respected; toward people she considered to be on her level. Of course (I fantasized), if I did something admirable enough or married somebody wealthy enough to turn Leah's attitude toward me around, all the rest of the family's attitudes would follow.

It has taken me a few decades to wake up, but I have now smelled the coffee and can see that neither Leah nor any of the men and women upon whom I have cast her identity are people with whom I should be trying to strike up relationships. Happily, I have arrived in wisdom at least to a point where I can see that as invariably successful as Leah has been at showing me up to others as being pathetically inferior to her, the fact that she is driven to enlighten me and others as to how small I am is a pretty sad thing.

Throughout the years when I imagined that I could go where Leah was and somehow come away from the contact with a salvageable self-image, I had many an opportunity to learn otherwise. People who have never seen either of us before quickly learn from the way that Leah talks and behaves toward me, how to regard me. The first time I ever saw my cousin Tommy, who was older than I but younger than Leah, he had come to our grandparents' house in Radford for a family reunion and had brought his cat with him. As children do about pets, I wanted to see his cat and pet her. He was about to invite me to do so when Leah quickly intervened. I was too little and stupid to know how to pet a cat, she told Cousin Tommy, her face screwed into lines of disgust and scorn. Immediately Cousin Tommy's attitude turned from willingness to accept my approach to virulent hostility. No, I could not touch his cat, and he had better not catch me trying to.

Stunned and overwhelmed with terror at what I had just witnessed Leah accomplish with my cousin's attitude toward me, I retreated into the house. I hadn't yet grasped that Mother would never stand up for me against anyone, but most particularly, she would never ask of Leah that she treat me humanely. I hadn't yet learned that when Leah hurt me, if I went to Mother thinking I would be comforted, I would get a reprimand because I had "bothered" Leah. On this occasion, my crying over how Leah and Cousin Tommy had treated me inspired Mother to make me stay inside the house, where I could not "bother" Leah and Tommy.

THE PAIN WE CAN'T FACE

Forget Freud and Give Us Cesar Millan

Sigmund Freud had brilliant insights into what makes human beings tick, but the quotation of his which most of us remember is not a pearl of wisdom but a question. *Barlett's* puts it this way:

"The great question ... which I have not been able to answer, despite my thirty years of research into the feminine soul, is 'What does a woman want?'"

I've no idea what women en masse want. Undoubtedly women's wants differ widely according to the situations and environments in which they are immersed. What I think I can address with some credulity is what young depressed mothers with small children want. Whether they know it or not, one thing they want is a Cesar Millan (aka *The Dog Whisperer*) to come to their houses and show them how to get their children into calm, submissive states. Like dog owners profiled on National Geographic Channel's *The Dog Whisperer* show, they wish their charges would do what they want them to, and they wish their charges would stop doing all those things that drive them up the wall.

Sometimes, Cesar has to convince a dog owner's significant other that he has to become a pack leader too — that by maintaining a "this-dog-is-hers" attitude and declining to try to work with the dog himself, he is actually contributing to the dog's behavior problems. Depressed mothers also often face situations where husbands take it for granted that they bear no responsibility for making order out of household chaos. A mate could help a depressed spouse a lot by validating her rules, boundaries, and limitations for the kids and helping her to enforce them. If only there were psychotherapists who would try to pull in help from their depressed clients' significant others in the same way that Cesar pulls in family member help for his dog-owning customers.

But, that's hardly the kind of help young depressed mothers with small children are able to find or obtain. What I've often observed is that the more depressed young mothers get, the more their husbands detach and retreat into a denial of their responsibility to support their wives. So, young depressed mothers do the only thing they know to do; they take themselves to mental health professionals for psychotherapy and medication. That's what Andrea Yates did.

In my own experience, the professionals whose "help" I found as a young mother (three out of four) focused attention on *MY* insides only; communicating the message to me that my depression was due to there being something seriously wrong going on in my psyche that I was not admitting to, and that if I would face it, I'd get better. (This is the sort of "help" Freud originated. Freud himself called his profession one of those in which "one can be quite sure of unsatisfying results". Why are so many mental health professionals still thinking in Freud's box?) While it was certainly true that PTSD (post-traumatic stress syndrome) was going on in my psyche, these pros' notion that they knew what that toxic element in my psyche was, and that they were going to "help" me by maneuvering me into seeing it, was nuts.

Fortunately, the first clinic where I sought help for depression in the year after the birth of my second child followed an approach that had nothing in common with the psychotherapeutic model I've just described in the preceding paragraph. There, I did see significant relief from my depression as soon as I began receiving therapy. A psychiatrist oversaw my treatment, but my visits with him were pleasant check-ins where he neither pried nor implied that I was holding some unwholesome stuff within me that he was going to make me face. This psychiatrist, the clinic director, respectfully inquired of me, in my two or three brief meetings with him, how I was feeling and whether my therapies were helping me to obtain more fulfillment in my relationships with my husband and children. Respect of staff for clients, from the director down, was the environment I encountered in every visit to this medical facility.

There, once a week, I had a session with a psychologist. Instead of zooming in on my personality with an attitude that my misery was a personal illness in which no other member of my household played a part, this psychologist immediately concentrated on how he might help me obtain more calm, submissive behavior from my children, and fewer frustrations. He never, at any time, took it upon himself to imply there was something "wrong" with me. His hints and suggestions for obtaining behaviors from my children that would lessen my stress never conveyed the message that I was a poor parent — merely that I was a client who was his peer; one to whom he was imparting some tricks-of-the-trade in parenting that I might not have come by.

In addition to my session each week with the psychologist, I spent one morning each week in an arts/crafts lab where other clients and I could chat while we occupied our hands with making whatever we chose out of whatever materials we saw that struck our fancies. The coordinator who managed the materials and who helped us with our projects was not a mental health professional, and she made no effort to fill the role of one but made it clear that her training was solely in art and her duties were limited to helping us achieve artistically, not psychologically.

These mornings of arts/crafts respites from the daily grind, where we clients could chat with each other freely about anything bothering us, were far more ameliorative than any formal group therapy sessions I've ever attended. No therapist was there to judge "what was wrong with us" with every word that came out of our mouths or to supervise style or content in the communications among us. These opportunities to socialize with other ladies who, like me, weren't functioning at 100 percent, were just what I needed to satisfy my intense need for companionship while allowing me to escape having to deal with a mental health professional's assuming the right to manage my speech and emotions, as those do who have "therapy" groups.

Upon my psychologist's suggestion, I arranged with my husband to again start doing things alone with him. On the day of my first child's birth, over two years earlier, I had lost that most emotionally sustaining force of all forces that I'd had in my life in several years – time alone with my husband.

My husband hadn't seemed to be bothered at all when our first-born baby's colic abruptly put an end to our habit of communing together in the back yard while he grilled steaks. When baby's demands on me ended my having midnight meals with my husband when he got home from work and ended my playing scrabble afterward with him until dawn, I never saw one shadow of disappointment cross his face. There were no more afternoon delights. The disappearance from my life of these wonderful after-lunch hours of romance and erotica with my husband had been a devastating loss to me. If my husband missed our former carefree, relaxed indulgence in sexual pleasures one whit, I never perceived so much as a hint of it. I picked up a feeling, in my husband, that he now saw the primary relationship of each of us as being with our child, not with each other. That was profoundly depressing to me.

But, as I said: now, at my psychologist's urgings, my husband and I found a babysitter and started trying to reconnect as a couple. We began by going to a local baseball game together. I'm not really enthusiastic about any sports, but having my husband all to myself for an entire evening made that minor league ball game a very satisfying date. We continued to put effort into trying to find a little of what once had been. The effort paid off. We started making love again, my spirits lifted, I thought I had conquered depression. Then my husband received notice he was being transferred from our mid-west city to New York State, to a higher position within his organization. I thought I'd take my new and improved mental health right along with me when we moved. I hadn't been in New York two months before I was on my way to total emotional melt down.

When I realized, in New York, that the good emotional health I'd achieved where we'd just been living had not only vanished, but that I was as down as I had ever been, I looked upon the treatment I'd received as a dismal failure — judging it to be so because it hadn't cured me, once and for all, of depression. I don't see it in that light at all now. My assessment of that treatment model now is that it was, by far, the most insightful and effective treatment for depression I have ever received anywhere from any mental health professional or in any facility. I didn't appreciate its effectiveness at the time, because I had been taken in by the myth that mental illnesses like depression are cured by mental health professionals. I have been exceedingly slow in divesting myself of that delusion.

Psychotherapy I've had which has adhered to the model of focusing upon the client's personality has never been anything other than an abysmal failure for me.

Before I even married and had children, I'd had "help" for my psyche troubles when I was trundled off to see my first psychiatrist at age nineteen, three months before the end of my second year in college. My childlike belief that I would find surcease to my pain in that psychiatrist's office was so pitifully naïve, I look upon that experience as one of an innocent minor being led on and used by an adult con artist.

Once every week I walked miles to and from bus stations to catch buses that took me many miles to and from the town where my psychiatrist's office was. There were no psychiatrists in the town where my college was located. Each week I cried my way through fifty minutes thinking at the end of my fifty-minute hour, "Well, he didn't do anything to help me this week. I don't know when he's going to start helping me, but surely he will, because psychiatrists help people who are in emotional pain. There's no doubt they do, because everybody says they do.

"If I'm not helped by his treatments it will be all my fault; it will be because I didn't do what I was supposed to. I don't know what I'm supposed to do, but I'm supposed to know what I'm supposed to do, so if I don't do it, it's my fault if I don't get well." For three months I waited for that relief - the relief from depression the psychiatric treatment was going to give me — to come.

Then, the end of the school year arrived. My emotional status had deteriorated over the three months during which I'd been receiving treatment until I was existing in as complete social isolation as Holden Caulfield was on his approach to the denouement of *Catcher in the Rye*. I'd moved out of the room I'd shared all year with two roommates, found a room vacant because its occupants had finished their exams early and gone home, and holed up there like a humiliated person trying to hide from the people in front of whom she's shamed herself. Then I received in my mail the bill from my psychiatrist for his services. That's all it took to tip my scales down to perceiving suicide as my only out. As you can see, the attempt

I made didn't succeed.

At that time in my life, and for decades to come, fear gnawed at me day after day and week after week following the end of every failed therapy. Some damnable chemical would keep sending surges of shame through me making my heart pound and my stomach and guts heave. Often shame would wake me out of deep sleep. (I still have those surges of shame occasionally and I suppose what awakens me is a sudden, large release of stomach acid.) My damnably brainwashed little conscience (the one that believed a psychiatrist had to be right about me, whatever he said) wouldn't shut up long enough to allow me any peace. It would spam me with the message that my doctor had done everything just right in my treatment, and that it was I who was guilty of having done or not done something that had caused us both to fail.

While in these destructive therapies, before I would become so dysfunctional that even self-doubting-me could see I had to escape them, I would be so preoccupied with rehearsing what I might say to the doctor at my next appointment or what I had said to him in my last, I didn't have the presence of mind to be able to take care of children. I might be compulsively sifting through mountains of things past, wondering which, of all the subjects there, was the one my psychiatrist was expecting me to bring him. My mental exertion was Herculean. Then, when my next appointment came round, I'd offer the material that I thought was relevant to my depression to the psychiatrist, only to meet with his feedback that what I was giving him really had nothing to do with my depression, wasn't what he was looking for; that he wanted me to be thinking in another direction.

How many depressed women must there be, who, like me, believe the kind of crap these credentialed, licensed, misguided folk feed us, and go on and on (as I did) hitting ourselves over the head because we think it's our own fault that we're not getting better in therapy?

Depressed mothers with young children can be helped considerably, I think, but not through the therapeutic strategies to which they're usually subjected. I've recounted one model of treatment with which I've had experience that brought relief and improved functioning to me almost from my first exposure to it. Not only I, but my husband and children benefited from that treatment paradigm as well, due to the fact that as my pain was eased and as my needs were met, I had more to give to those dependent upon me.

I don't know what paradigms prevail in other regions, but here the one-to-one office visit with a psychotherapist, concentrated upon what's wrong with the "patient", is the only approach offered. I know of no facility that offers a program anything like the one so beneficial to me, where the aim of staff was to work toward helping me to get my environment modified to be less stressful and more needs-fulfilling to me personally. If mental health professionals would drop the whole fifty-minute-hour concept, (including the twenty- or thirty-minute fifty-minute-hour) that's so convenient and profitable for them and stop insisting upon relating to their clients as if their clients were medical "patients", I think a giant leap for depressed womankind would have been made.

Humans are just as much pack-dependent predatory animals as are dogs. Many scientists are saying we humans are even more pack-dependent than canines or any other animal. Mental health professionals and their clients may howl with laughter at this suggestion, but I think mental health pros and clients could gain useful insight into how to make their relationships with each other bilaterally beneficial in addition to being unilaterally remunerative for the therapist by visiting *The Dog Whisperer* programs on their TVs and studying how Cesar Millan relates to his human clients and their pet stand-ins for children.

Cesar states with no equivocation that he counsels his human clients in psychology. If only mental health professionals could see their relationships with their clients as Cesar sees his relationships with his human clients. Cesar doesn't have a subordinate make an appointment with the dog-owner to come, alone, to his office at such a time on such a date to be seen by him, Cesar Millan, in his capacity as "El Jefe". That would be what a psychiatrist would do. The Dog Whisperer goes to his client's territory, which is a much more courageous (and respectful) thing to do. Cesar interacts with his clients in all ways that we expect people to interact with each other in relationships that have some relevance to the real world. He laughs at clients' jokes. Mental health professionals I've known hold themselves so aloof from their clients they will not even bend to do their clients that small courtesy.

❖ ❖ ❖

In my chapter "In the Beginning", I revealed attitudes I had about my mother's authority as a three-year-old that probably would earn me a diagnosis in today's world of Childhood Oppositional Defiant Disorder. I wonder how many women, already prone to depression, fall deeper into it when they see behaviors in their children they can't tolerate but don't know how to stop. One could compare my mother's and my relationship to the relationship a pet owner has with a pet whose behaviors are driving her to distraction.

I think Cesar Millan would say that the reason the pet has developed such problem behaviors is that the pet is a pack-dependent, pack-leader-needing animal whose pack leader refuses to lead. I wonder how many women there are, who, like the pet owners with whom The Dog Whisperer typically works, and like my depressed mother, don't realize that peace, cooperative behavior, and mutual respect can come into a relationship with a child when the person more competent to lead — the mother — accepts her responsibility to do so.

As many times as my mother told me that she'd never have any peace as long as I was under the same roof with her, it seems clear to me that my ODD must have contributed significantly to her depression. Her depression contributed monumentally to my ODD. I imagine this scenario is very common in households of depressed women.

Most adults who were faced with the responsibility of managing my behavior found me to be quite compliant with their wishes. Why, as soon as Mother told me not to do something, did I compulsively go straightaway and do it? What was going on in the nature of the relationship between severely depressed mother and severely depressed daughter that made daughter behave like one of the problem pets Cesar is called upon to fix in *Dog Whisperer* episodes?

The answer is that the instincts, evolved through millions of years, that cause problem dogs to act out are the same instincts that have come by evolution to human children, causing them to act out. When there was an adult in my life who liked me enough and saw enough value in me to want to be my calm, assertive "pack leader"; who derived satisfaction from working with me and seeing me achieve what I wanted to achieve, I was generally cooperative. Mother was, with me, the opposite of everything Cesar tells his human clients they have to be if they want to elicit calm, submissive, agreeable behaviors from their charges.

After Mother's death, Coraya and I were discussing what a saint of a mother Leah and Mother's siblings were painting her to have been. Coraya and I agreed that if there were such a thing as a recognition for being the world's worst mother, Mother might have won it. Mother wasn't a disaster as a mother because she wanted to be. I feel sure she would have done her best to be a good mother if only she could have been divested by someone she trusted of the beliefs with which her roots and religion had crippled her. If only Mother could have had The Dog Whisperer come to our house and show her ... show her ... well, my daydreaming such things is crying over spilled milk.

Neither through my mother's years of depression nor mine, were we lucky enough to have husbands and children say to themselves and each other "Mother is suffering from depression. Mother needs some help here. We've got to all pitch in to wash a few dishes, sweep a floor, do this pile of laundry, keep things tidy, until Mother gets well and strong enough again to start doing these things for us as she did when she was feeling better."

Being severely depressed is being in more misery than I've ever been put into by any physical illness I've had in six plus decades of life. But, with our husbands, our children, extended family, friends, neighbors, and acquaintances, we don't communicate much about our depression. A kind of "don't-ask-don't-tell" cloud hangs over the subject. And what husbands do, if they involve themselves at all in their wives' depression, is call on some dominant woman from their own family to come and take charge of everything — the last thing a young depressed mother needs.

Take-charge mothers-in-law and in-law-aunts coming in and taking over a depressed mother's household make her look and feel even weaker and more useless than her depression makes her look and feel. Children stop seeing their mother as their pack leader when another woman takes charge in their home. Mothers have a deep instinctual need for their children to see them as their pack leaders. Knowing that there are living things depending upon them for everything has been a stimulus that has gotten many a depressed woman out of bed on many a morning. Children's allowing themselves to trust in their mother and be led by her gives her a spiritually uplifting feedback that is taken away from her when another female comes into her home and takes charge.

A dog is driven by instinct to find the leader of her pack, to follow that leader, and to attempt to ingratiate herself with the leader. Every human child is born with exactly the same instincts. If a mother cannot or will not step forward to take the position of pack leader to her child, the child is thrown into confusion; seized with a fear for her own survival born of instincts that override rational thinking. Any wild predator baby senses that without its mother's attention and care, it is in a desperate fight which it is hardly likely to survive. Human children don't feel differently just because they live in a society that will not let orphans perish. For the child to derive comfort from that, she would have to have sophisticated rational thinking capacity and little children who cannot get attention from their mothers have only instincts to guide their emotional states.

When a human mother ignores her child for long periods of time, the primordial fear of the abandoned infant wild animal comes to life in the child's insides. A depressed mother who doesn't want to see her child become her tormenter will recognize that the time she invests in giving her child calm, assertive attention will be well worth her time and energy in the long run, even if she has to drag herself from depression to focus.

A mother's recognition that she has an obligation to dominate her children — not insensitively and harshly, but calmly and assertively — will lessen the behaviors from them that contribute to her depression. A mother's establishing of a few important limitations and boundaries for all her children, and then never failing to back those up with bodily action when words aren't sufficient, will spare her so many horribly depressing events as the years go by, that it should be a psychotherapist's first focus in getting a young mother back on the road to feeling better.

Mother and I developed a highly dysfunctional relationship for various reasons, but the principal reason, I think, was that she unconsciously held an image of herself as being a family servant in her relationship to her husband and his older sister. Perhaps the fact that Mother's paternal grandmother really had been a domestic servant before her marriage to her husband (a manual laborer) had something to do with that. Daddy and his sister were products of wealthy families who had owned servants before the Civil War and retained them by wage after. That, too, probably contributed to Mother's sense of being an inferior underling whose place was not to assume responsibility, even for her children.

If Mother were today the depressed mother she was through the late 1940s and the 1950s, and receiving psychotherapy, how would her image of herself get changed from powerless to powerful? Feeling powerful is the opposite of feeling depressed. Would Mother get the "I can handle any child" attitude from going once or twice a week to talk to a psychotherapist who establishes his or her dominance in their therapeutic relationship with the logistics of the treatment paradigm alone? I think that's another one of those last things a depressed woman needs.

Imagine what it would be like if there were such a thing as a mental health professional who would come to your home if you were depressed enough to call upon a professional — would leave his or her turf and would come to see you on your turf where you would be the one sitting among familiar possessions in your own domain. Imagine the effect on your emotions and your self-image to be in a situation where the psychologist or psychiatrist realizes that he or she is a service provider (like Cesar Millan) and that you are a client, not a "patient" - a word that has more than a hint of association with the concept of recipient-of-charity.

Imagine having a mutual-respect and equal-control kind of relationship with a psychotherapist instead of having the kind that is almost all I've been allowed — a relationship where the therapist has all the control and the client none.

FORGET FREUD AND GIVE US CESAR MILLAN

Opposition

My depressed cousin provided me with a lead a few years ago in a letter that she wrote to me regarding my depression. She described a childhood episode with her mother in which her lack of obedience had been addressed at length. Her mother had brought out the Bible and used quotations to show my cousin that all people are sinners and that they need to be ever repenting and asking God for forgiveness and guidance toward a more sin-free life. I'm guessing that the message my cousin's mother conveyed to her was, "You were born bad, you'll always be bad, and you need to do something about that".

The situation might have been that my cousin suffered from oppositional disorder of childhood. (I believe that the name of this condition has been changed in recent years to Childhood Oppositional Defiant Disorder (or

ODD), but at the time I was receiving my formal education, it was ODC or OCD without inclusion of defiance.) I know that in my own childhood, from the earliest age in which I formed memories, I held a grudge against my mother and acted on it by belligerently doing what she asked me not to do. It seems to me that I had valid reasons for behaving in this way: Mother's refusal to protect me from my older sister's abuse, her refusal to pay any attention to me unless I was behaving in a manner so irritating to her that she couldn't ignore me, her ever present attitude that I was bad and that my badness was a burden that had been dumped upon her by hateful people (my father and his sister, my aunt) while she herself was good and an innocent dupe for their having forced her to bear me.

My resentments against Mother began with disbelief, agony, and utter despair, then moved on to become a mirror for her feelings toward me. I developed contempt for her, saw her as a person of no value, and made sure that I ignored whatever her stated wishes were about my behavior. After I had been through many years of study and therapy, I finally asked Mother, in a letter, why she had hated me so when I was a child. After a little delay, she responded by mail that she hadn't hated me. That was not the answer I wanted. I wanted her to confess that she had profoundly disliked me and that she had let me down and ignored my needs for that reason. That she could have cared about me and still supported my older sister in constantly abusing me made no sense to me.

Now I was left with a bigger puzzle. Had I been oppositional to my mother because I actually was bad? Had my arrogance caused me to want to believe she hated me?

Had I projected onto Mother my own demeaning attitudes toward her and deluded myself into believing that she had those feelings toward me? Probably the answer is that both situations existed. She opposed the notion that she held any responsibility for my welfare, and I was just as opposed to feeling warmth or respect for her.

By the age of three, it appears to me, I was already oppositional enough to be a menace to myself and a cause for hair pulling in my mother. By the time I was nine or ten, I had become a menace to my younger sister as well. Although I've seen, heard, and read accounts from various family sources that show me I haven't existed as an isolated case of ODC (oppositional disorder of childhood) or of ADD and ADHD (attention deficit without hyperactivity and attention deficit with it) or LD (learning disability) or intractable depression or obsessional thought disorder or addictive personality in my maternal family, I'm torn between attributing all that to nurture (lack of it, that is) and stultifying environment or to nature.

What I can see as I toss this issue around in my mind is that my surreptitiously sneaking off to the barn to draw water out of the cistern while my parents and Leah were occupied with garden weeds was not motivated by any chip on my shoulder toward anyone. I don't see ODC as being involved. What inspired that excursion of mine (one that, like my investigation of what it might feel like to fall down the stairs, could have resulted in my death) must have been my genes. Just as the rapper in a current Discovery Channel commercial chants, my genes propel me to undertake risky projects "since they wanna know, since they wanna know, since they wanna know".

On the other hand, I see my decision to purposely let

the front wheel of my Kiddie Kar ease over the top of the stairs to be reflective of a desire on my part to show Mother defiance in the strongest way I could devise. At that very young age, two to three, was I so pissed with my mother over her relinquishing me to Leah anytime Leah saw a way she could use me to her advantage that my heart was already burning with hatred for her? Since time and chronological order don't exist in the unconscious as they do in conscious awareness, it's impossible for me to determine how early in life my utter frustration and disappointment with Mother began. But I see in the episodes of the broken ceramic doggy and my near fatal fall a repressed hatred for Mother born of a panic over her refusal to give me what all humans think of as "mothering". I believe I unconsciously wanted to torture Mother, and the way I contrived to do that was to engage in self-destructive acts that would provoke in her great eruptions of anger and anxiety.

Of course, consciously, my instincts wouldn't let any such thought or feeling enter my awareness. Even as an adult, I wasn't aware that I was living and had lived all my life, on and on with few remissions, in a roiling base state of hurt, shame, guilt, resentment, puzzlement, fear, and unrequited longing — all over Mother. If ever there was anyone whose conscious self was completely out of touch with her unconscious self, it was I. At the time I entered psychoanalytically oriented therapy in my mid-twenties, I had a concept of my childhood relationship with my mother as being neither especially good nor especially bad. My conscious self-perceived it as a neutral sort of thing pretty lacking in emotional content and therefore irrelevant to my having developed severe depression that just would not go away.

Then — perhaps it was after I had cleared the decks of some little fear-of-father issue — I caught a glimpse of a fantasy that I had repressed as an eighteen-or nineteen-year-old home from college for Christmas holidays. It was pretty horrible stuff. The image I had conjured unconsciously but not allowed into my awareness was of shoving the handle of a broom up my mother's anus. This one image my unconscious allowed me to see in the late 1960s had the same sort of relationship to what lay yet unseen within me that a grain of sand has to the dune on the top of which it lies.

Being unable, as a child, to let such a thought as hitting my mother or even yelling at her enter my awareness (unthinkable in my world for a child to behave so to an adult), much less to fantasize murdering her, I acted on myself and on every most precious possession I had with the kind of frustration a person feels who picks up a priceless vase and hurls it against a wall. That self-destructiveness and that compulsion to destroy or throw away any priceless possession or indispensable relationship I come by has not only continued throughout my life, but has, it seems to me, escalated as decades have passed. For years, I have not dared to even attempt to have a relationship with anyone that calls for more closeness than is necessary for routine business activities.

I dare not buy a new car — within a few months, strangely, I would be in an accident in which the car would be totaled. When I shopped for a house here in the early nineties, if I had bought the one I picked out, I would now be living in a big wooden shack of such decrepitude fire departments might be asking me if I would let them burn it down for training purposes. My real estate agent all but forced me into buying this structurally sound and very attractive brick home. I imagine the only reason I've allowed myself to live on a property this nice as long as I have is that the real estate market here has been flat ever since I've owned this house, and its monetary value has not increased.

Beginning at about puberty, I began to throw away relationships with peers who loved and respected me — relationships that were so essential to my well-being that I was emotionally lost without them. When a boyfriend or girlfriend really demonstrated one-to-one love and loyalty to me, I, sooner or later, stabbed them in the back. I managed to let myself stay in a relationship with my husband and children about ten years, but from the day I caught a look of disgust on my psychiatrist's face over something I said, my negative transference to him of the identities of Mother and Leah changed my perception of my husband and children from asset to liability.

This understanding of my psychotherapeutic situation — this recognition of the negative transference, the identities of the caretakers from whence that transference came, and the extent and nature of the panic that negative transference had touched off in me — did not become clear in my mind until decades after my relationship with this psychiatrist was over. I knew that the image of his rather slight body, always seated somewhat slumped, head bowed over a book in his lap, never failed to bring to my mind the image of Mother, seated, reading, in a low chair beside my youngest sister as she sat crying on her potty while Mother waited on and on for her to come out with that which Mother knew was inside her little bottom.

I'm sure I related this association to the psychiatrist, but my memory of him is that he was like almost all male psychiatrists I've known — he thought he knew everything about me, I knew nothing about me, and there could be no possibility my therapeutically significant transference to him was anything other than from my father. Had I had my consciousness raised then to the level to which it has been raised since, I would have recognized that my decision to stay on and on in treatment with a psychiatrist who employed habits of behavior and who displayed attitudes toward me as identical to Mother's as his were was a decision that could come only from a mind in which unconscious desire to get Mother to relate to me, whatever the cost to my well-being, had told rational thinking "Fly away! Fly Away!"

When I caught on my psychiatrist's face that expression of disgust that was so like the facial expression perpetually turned to me throughout my childhood by Mother, by Leah, and by all those before whom Leah modeled the attitudes she wanted them to have toward me, my world went flat. To erase that feeling of disgust he had for me, I unconsciously surmised, I had to divest myself of those relationships that weren't doing anything to make me look good enough to arouse his respect; and, I had to win the love of some man so high in status my psychiatrist would be forced to feel respect for me through recognition that I had the feminine allure to land such a desirable champion.

What had transpired in my relationship with my mother by the time I was three that already had me seething with such hurt and resentment I was defiantly ignoring her warnings, leading me to plunge headlong down stairs, possibly inflicting permanent brain damage on myself?

My anger wasn't over any one event that had transpired between myself and Mother. My rage was over her refusal to own me - her refusal to get emotionally involved with me. You might be thinking to yourself, "Parents aren't supposed to think of their children as things they own. Why would you want your mother to think of you as something she owned?"

When I use the word "own", I'm thinking of it in the sense of, "own up to the part you played in this conception", or "own up to your responsibility to try to protect your child from harm" ... "own up to your responsibility to get your tubes tied if you hate children", or "own up to your responsibility to 'let your children come unto you' if you are going to represent yourself to the world as being a Christian" ... that's the connotation of "own" of which I'm thinking.

Because Mother refused to own me, I'm sure Leah found herself, over and over, in circumstances where she saw that I was a baby in dire need of attention, and no one was around to do anything about it but she. I'm sure Mother was often out of the house tending to farm animals or garden chores. If she was in the house, I don't think she felt any duty at all to oversee what I was doing. This left Leah (endowed to the max in genes for dominance) with a feeling that she had to fill the void in leadership Mother wouldn't fill and to do something about me even if all she could think of to do was to shame me and slap me.

I understood almost nothing of the stresses under which Leah operated during my infancy and minor years until I happened upon writings about gifted children by psychoanalyst Dr. Alice Miller. There, I found education in how inadequate and ineffectual parents, upon realizing they have a child so bright and innately competent she will readily assume and deal with tasks normally handled by adults, will often slough their responsibilities onto their child's shoulders. Such parents may mine their gifted child's precociousness to the greatest extent they possibly can, leaving her to handle, on her own, problems with which no child should have to be burdened. If Dr. Miller had known Leah and had been writing Leah's biography instead of presenting a compilation from the lives of her clients, she couldn't have portrayed Leah's situation any more precisely.

Leah was impressed into service where she didn't want to perform service. She didn't want the job of unpaid, no-training-invested babysitter dumped on her when she was six or seven or eight. No more did I want her there ruling over me coldly and harshly, taking out on me the resentment she felt at being left alone with a needy baby — a baby she hated because it was a competitor for adult attention.

Where there is a leadership vacuum, a child like Leah has an instinctual feeling that she must be the leader. Mother sidestepped the leader role assiduously in all family matters, leaving Leah to see herself as not only leader of me, but of Mother as well. Mother handed her crown to Leah, and Leah put it on and wore it grandly. For Mother to abdicate, allowing Leah to establish herself over me as my owner, judge, and correctional officer, was not fair to me; it was grossly unjust.

I wanted Mother to rescue me from being Leah's kicking post and scapegoat and to proclaim to Leah that I, too, was her child - a child of no lesser kinship to her than

Leah. Mother denied me that validation, always, and Leah reveled in the fact that she denied me — rubbed my nose in it. Like a wild animal caught in a trap, I was so desperate to be free of the jaws holding me that I did the emotional equivalent of spending my life trying to chew my leg off.

"You're not Mother's only child!" was the scream I wanted to scream at Leah from a time before I would even have had those words in my vocabulary — from a time when screaming incoherently was probably all I was capable of doing. It was humiliating and terrifying when I would cry in hopes Mother would come and advance my case before Leah — let Leah know what her place was, give Leah to understand that I was just as much her child as she, let Leah know that I wasn't a discard that Mother had left behind for her to pick up and do with as she pleased - and Mother would ignore me.

It may have been true that I was not uttering any of those words I've put in quotes in the preceding paragraph, that I was only screaming and begging Mother with my lungs and my eyes, but what baby animal, alone and facing a predator who's threatening it, isn't meowing or yelping or screeching out the message I thought I was screaming out to my mother? "Come and save me. Rise up between me and this horrible monster that wants to annihilate me. Please save my pride. Show her you do care something about me."

Unfortunately for me, I think Mother must have evolved from eagles instead of mammals. As you know if you've caught any eagle documentaries, Momma Eagle feeds the firstborn of her two and lets the other starve unless food is so plentiful Mom brings food to the nest at a time when her firstborn is so stuffed its gullet can't hold another morsel. In between Mom's visits to the nest with food, the firstborn is continually pecking its smaller sibling and pushing it toward the edge of the nest until finally the smaller fledgling is too weakened by starvation and wounds to protect itself any longer and falls out of the nest and a long way down to the ground, where it dies, unmourned by Momma. Mom never interferes with firstborn's dispatching of younger sibling; it's the scheme nature has evolved for the survival of the fittest eagles. Well, maybe this analogy is a little extreme to apply to Mother, but ...

Postscript 2020:

In the years since I wrote my first draft of this composition, I've further thought about the possible causes of oppositionality between mothers and daughters. Mothers (not just mine, but most) far overdo their surveillance of their daughters' behavior in respect to religious and social mores on what is acceptable in *females'* behavior. On the part of mothers, their admonishments against, and damning of, too many behaviors in their daughters results in resentment of many female children against their mothers and other female caregivers. (Not only on a mother—to—daughter basis, but in society as a whole, I think, females have a pathological need to see other females held back, kept down, required to be modest and self-effacing, made to excuse and forgive instead of being afforded justice — in short, seeing another female being "all that she can be" just seems to be an intolerable sight to far too many females. We'll make up any justification for hurting and humbling another who seems to be enjoying life too much and thinking too well of herself. As for blame rightly pinned to daughters, we don't often talk about the possibility that there could be such a thing as a genetic trait in the human species which might dispose offspring to compulsively bully their mothers in order to force their mothers to give more of themselves and of whatever goods and services their offspring think they should. I've spent many hours in these writings condemning my mother for not meeting my needs. I recognize that there may exist in me a gene which is constantly telling me I have been denied what I should have been given. Having such a gene would produce hatred between a mother and her child, but it definitely would promote the child's getting their needs met and thus surviving.

ROOTS, RELIGION AND DEPRESSION

OPPOSITION

The Stand-Up Routines

If a person has been given the mandate by the alphas of her family and culture, "You must make people admire you", it is essential that she have a store of entertainment ready with which to bewitch them. Being a naturally gifted musician like Leah provides one with that store. However, when one's instrument is a piano, as Leah's was as a child, even a gifted musician can be caught with no resources for using that gift to gain attention and admiration when there is no piano around. What was Leah to do then? Well, she usually had me and comedic talent.

An oft repeated bit of Leah's entertainment subject matter had to do with my birth. "I hated her", Leah would proclaim to visiting company (aunts and uncles, neighbors, whoever). "I told Mother to take her back where she got her." From the smile this statement of Leah's always brought to Mother's face, what could I think but that I was not a human child for whom they had feeling, but a thing — a toy to be used in communication play between the two of them and the audience for whom Leah was performing.

I think the stand-up deliveries of Leah's which brought her the greatest thrill were those in which her audience was male. I suspect that Leah knew she could ignite more shame in me and more loss of self-image when she uttered her lines and made faces for the ears and eyes of males than if she gave the same performances in front of females. Our Aunt E had indoctrinated both of us in how important it was for us to make boys like us (and, in the future, make men love us), thus our being irresistibly attractive to males was to be an attainment in our lives greater than any other. What would give Leah the greatest boost in the world to her self-image? Well, how about showing Emmy — "Daddy's little favorite" — that you, Leah, have total control over whether every male in her universe (other than Daddy) thinks well of her and treats her respectfully, or whether he spews scorn at her, laughs at her discomfiture, and runs her off.

When I began school, Leah and I had to wait a bit in the mornings in our community's country store for our bus to arrive. On our first morning there, several boys of about Leah's age were already seated around the stove inside the store when we walked in. One of the boys asked me in a very friendly way what my name was. Leah gave me no time to answer.

"We call her Prissy Britches", she broke in, "but she calls herself 'Pissy Bitches'". Of course, all the boys howled with laughter, and that was the last time any of them ever made any attempt to say anything to me that didn't consist of taunts and jeers. Until these boys graduated from high school and therefore were no longer in the same place at the same time as I, they shouted insulting names and comments at me whenever our paths happened to cross.

There were many stand-up routines of Leah's in which there was absolutely no comedy whatsoever, but they still seemed to be very satisfying to the children and adults in front of whom Leah performed them.

I have already recounted in another of these personal essays the alteration, by Leah, of my cousin Tommy's attitude toward me in no more time than it took for Leah to snarl a few words at me in his presence. At our first meeting, he had, in a very friendly manner, started to invite me to pet his cat. One sentence from Leah, "Oh, she wouldn't know how to pet a cat", accompanied by a face screwed up into one saying, "stupid, disgusting, ignorant", was all it took for a kind look on Tommy's face to change to one of complete rejection accompanied by the words, "No, you cannot touch my cat, and I better never catch you trying to!" That was the last word Tommy ever spoke to me.

The next time I saw Cousin Tommy he kept a good distance from me at a family reunion. Another male cousin was there too, one only a couple of years older than I and younger than my sister and Tommy. The three of them were in the yard playing, and I started to run toward them as any child would who was at a family reunion with children who were her closest relatives. This time it was Cousin Danny whom Leah had to influence to feel hatred for me, instantly, before I even got close enough to meet him. I could see Leah pointing at me, could see her mouth moving vigorously, her face enraged, as she made sure Tommy and Danny were looking at me and reacting to the alarm she was raising. I was barely within earshot of the three of them when they began yelling threats at me to keep away from them.

There were not only reunions but other get-togethers of maternal family members and friends where Leah felt she must create an image of me for them before they would have any chance to make the mistake of treating me as if I were "one of them" ... after all, does not a conscientious person have an obligation to warn her pack mates when she perceives a threat in their environs that they — being less wise and perceptive than she — do not see?

My mind often runs to the profoundly depressing fact that I endured being a stage prop and scapegoat for Leah all through the first decades of my life; then, when I thought I was well free of being used that way, ran into a scapegoater far more vicious than Leah when my ex's third wife put me in a position where I could not escape being the target of strategies so exactly like those used by Hitler to rob Jews I have had to wonder what on earth was being taught in all those psychology courses my children's stepmother had to take to get that degree in psychology that my children told me their stepmother had.

I've found myself wondering if quantum physicist Stephen Hawking's theories of Grand Design and predestination weren't right on, and there was a gigantic decider hovering over us all who wanted me to spend my whole life in slander hell. I've wondered if the Hindu concept of karma was right on and was the reason I could not escape having my relationships with all those in my life whose love I most needed destroyed by one image cannibal after another. However, being more realistic about why it has been so easy and so risk-free for my children's and my grandchildren's paternal family members and spouses to rob me of their respect and warmth, I have to look at what signals I give off that contribute to my being seen as someone safe to destroy with projection of themselves onto me.

Pondering what part I may have played in my having been set upon and stripped of my relationships with my children and grandchildren, what finally comes up in my radar is that old personal flaw that sent me tumbling down a long flight of stairs when I was three or so; I seem to be oblivious to what the consequences might be of my doing what I want to do.

The vulnerability of mine which I probably should have cited first — the one that all but assures that I can safely be accused of being, "that evil from which the weak and innocent must be protected" — is that I go everywhere alone. A bully does not attack if there appears to be a supporting body by their target's side who might be a force they don't want to provoke.

Always, when I went to visit my children after my ex-husband remarried, all the children observed was my being talked to and talked about and behaved toward with the most dehumanizing, humiliating words and prearranged games and actions their caretakers could get prepared for me. My children had no opportunity to witness my being shown the respect and humanity that non-self-deceiving civilized people, who think of themselves as Christian, usually show to each other.

Another significant vulnerability of mine is that I have

a greatly delayed response to environmental stimuli - the kind arising from humans – and that inability of mine to think on my feet, or to answer insult or accusation with an immediate, effective response, is the sign of weakness in me that makes me look like that clichéd sitting duck that projecting scapegoaters so love to have as their reflecting medium.

We humans don't form our opinions of other humans based on what we ourselves observe them to be in our interactions with them; we form our belief about them from how we see other humans talking to them and behaving toward them. Most of my life I have not been consciously aware of this at all. I have been thinking all these many decades that I formed my opinion of whether people were good or bad based on my interactions with them. That was surely self-deception.

In one moment, waiting at my local beauty shop for my hair to dry, my previously erroneous belief was set right. A woman came in and walked up to where the shop owner and I were. She was well-groomed and smartly dressed, and I took her to be a peer of the shop owner. Then, the shop owner began speaking to her as if she were intellectually impaired and less worthy of respect than others to whom I'd heard the shop owner speak. My own assessment of the lady went south on the spot. Prior to that, I had no idea that my modus operandi in judging my fellow human beings wasn't on any higher level than the MO of all those people I'd seen turn against me upon witnessing Leah, or my children's stepmother or grandmother, or some other slanderer talk to me or about me as if I were a proven deserver of their hatefulness and hurtfulness.

I really could hardly bear to acknowledge to myself

that I formed judgments of anyone from how I saw other people talk to them and behave toward them. How disheartening it was for me to face the evidence that we humans put a value on characterizations of others, talk and behavior directed at others, and falsehoods spoken about others above what we derive from our own personal, uncontaminated experience of them.

It seems to me that a tale I'll call the "Diaper Routine" was one of Leah's favorites for holding an audience's attention while shaming me to the greatest extent she possibly could. As was the case with the "Pissy Bitches" humiliation, Leah's dredging up of some incident or speech pattern that had occurred years before, while I was still not yet past two and still had been in diapers, when put out for the entertainment of teenage boys when I was now six years old, was as damaging to my image as any taunts with which a school-aged intelligent girl could be faced. At being shamed into the ground, that surely did it for me.

Although I have no conscious memory of a time the family spent in Florida when I was around two, events from the trip were a main topic of family conversation when I did begin to retain things Leah, Daddy, and Mother said; so I gather the Florida visit was a recent event when my long-term memory kicked in. Guava paste was under discussion quite a bit. Daddy vowed it was delicious. Leah made faces any time it was mentioned, implying that guava paste was putrid beyond belief. Daddy had made her eat it anyway. (He did that just because Daddy had a thing about insisting his daughters eat that which they did not want to eat even if it did make them sick.) I may have been oppositional with Mother, but with Daddy, I couldn't be compliant enough. I had to attest to how good guava paste was, although I doubt that I could even remember eating guava paste.

Mother related how wildly enthusiastic I had been about the beach and the water. In fact, I had been so excited about going, she said, I hadn't even stood still long enough for her to get a bathing suit on me but had dashed from the bedroom naked into a living room full of people. When telling this, Mother raised her eyes toward heaven and embellished her portrayal of shock and embarrassment with some body language effects that said my running out into the midst of company where more than immediate family members were present was an act on my part that ranked near the top of the scale in inappropriate behaviors. My thinking is; I was a toddler not even out of the diaper stage. Just how awful was it for me to run out naked in front of company?

What seemed to me to be the most memorable event in the Florida trip for Leah was probably most memorable for her because from it she got material for a stand-up routine she could bring forth for years to come that could get her center stage in a gathering and humiliate me so badly I'd immediately leave the room. After Leah had regaled a group with this tale in my presence, I was usually so overcome by self-consciousness around the people who'd heard it that I could hardly make eye contact with them thereafter, much less try to talk to them.

It seems that while on our stay in Florida, Daddy had wanted Mother to go fishing with him. Having two children, one of which was a baby in diapers, posed a problem but not enough of a problem to deter Daddy or Mother from making the trip. Daddy decided that Leah, who couldn't have been more than seven at the time, could babysit me. Mother, being one of those women who think that they must do whatever their husbands want them to do, went with Daddy and left me behind with Leah.

According to the account Leah liked to give, "Emmy messed her diapers, so I used her diapers to tie her to the table leg so she couldn't crawl around and drop her mess out of her diapers all over the floor. But Emmy crawled out of her diapers. They stayed tied to the table leg, and Emmy went crawling around naked. Oooooh."

I suspect I'm giving a shortened version of Leah's recitation, and I can't properly convey the entertainment value of the story as I can't show you the facial expressions and sounds of disgust Leah added, but there are the basics of it.

Intellectualizing tells me that this diaper episode when I was an infant being babysat by Leah might have been a significant precipitator in my lifelong bouts with thinking that something I had just done was so shameful I would never escape from people's disgust with me over it. The mental torture I went through before and during the birth of my first child was the most intense of these spells of shame I ever endured, though some other sieges lasted not for a day, but for months. This day was traumatic enough for me to repress memory of it for years.

As my contractions while in labor increased in strength and frequency, I experienced the physical sensations as being a more and more urgent need to evacuate. I had been given an enema and had already expelled the contents of my bowels privately in a bathroom before I had climbed onto the birthing table, but consciousness of the fact that my bowels were empty didn't stay with me as labor progressed. I was partially sedated with some drug that was supposed to mitigate the pain of giving birth. The drug was not mitigating my pain at all - I remember the pain quite clearly — but the drug was robbing me of my ability to rationally perceive my situation.

I had entered the hospital at about nine that morning, and my baby was not born until nine in the evening. From before noon, through all the hours in which I labored, I experienced every contraction as a powerful autonomic movement in my colon which was pushing a huge bowel movement down to my anus. In my drug-induced haze, I could see no image of a baby coming out my vagina. What I felt, what I visualized, what I believed, was that I had great feces in me that my internal muscles, against my will, were going to expel in spite of everything I could do to stop it from happening.

Long before my baby came, I was hysterical with the panic my belief brought me. All the doctors and nurses crowding around me were expecting me to give them a baby. I was going to eject poop. The specter of the revulsion they would feel for me, the disgust, when these feces I couldn't hold back would come piling out overwhelmed me with fear of my impending humiliation. How could I ever, ever, face the shame of what was about to happen?

I was far too much in the grips of drug and hysteria to explain to my birthing coaches that I couldn't stop screaming and I couldn't push as they were asking me to do because I was more terrified of the disgust and hostility I knew I would see on their faces when I passed my bowel movement than I had ever been terrified of anything in my life. I gripped and pulled on the rods in the head of the bed with all my strength. I squeezed my anal sphincter muscles and every muscle in my buttocks on and on in my desperation to keep this awful thing from happening.

I was getting anger and disgust from my birthing coaches, but it was my screaming and repeatedly begging to be allowed to get up and go to the bathroom that was exasperating them. When my daughter finally was born, I was so exhausted and depressed I couldn't feel one positive emotion toward myself or to my precious new daughter. My awful struggle to hold back what I thought was going to be a bowel movement had probably lengthened my labor by hours and accounted for how misshapen my poor baby's head was when she finally emerged.

My father had always been so disappointed that his children had been girls, not boys, and had expressed such contempt for femininity that I had no ability to adore a female infant. He had told me many times when I was a child that the reason that he liked me better than my sisters was because, of the three of us, I was most like a boy. When my birthing coaches held my daughter out for me to see her, my only thought was, "I've gone through all this work and pain, and this is all I have to show for it?"

As I write this, I am so overcome with grief, shame, guilt, and remorse at the attitude I had toward my daughter at the moment of her birth I can hardly type for sobbing. I realized far too late that this could have been the most significant, the most joyful moment of my life, but I had been robbed of all the love and elation I should have been able to feel by the thorough brainwashing I had received at the hands of my family members. Worst of all is the guilt I bear and will bear for the rest of my life. I now am fully aware that babies absorb moms' emotions through the skin. My poor, poor baby. No matter how sorry I am, I will never be able to go back and redo her birth with the joyful attitude I should have had. She and I never really had a bond with each other, just as I never had a secure, lasting bond with my mother or any other female caregiver during my childhood.

Resurrecting all the material in these essays out of my unconscious, reexperiencing it, and comprehending how it kept playing itself out throughout all the years I've been alive, has taken me decades to accomplish. According to the rationales of those who practice therapies aimed at resurrecting repressed memories and feelings, I ought to be feeling and functioning immeasurably better than I was while all this stuff was still repressed and unknown to me.

If I weren't taking a strong stimulant medication (luckily for me I'm also a recipient of a diagnosis of attention deficit disorder without hyperactivity), I'd be in even worse shape than I was when I was nineteen and went off to see my first psychiatrist. I wouldn't be writing this. I'd be doing anything I could to escape feeling — I'd be reading, watching TV, or dozing. If I were awake, I'd be eating or wondering what I possibly could eat that would quell my incessant desire to have something good in my mouth. Oh! I forgot crying. I'd be doing as much crying as I would be reading, watching TV, and dozing.

ROOTS, RELIGION AND DEPRESSION

THE STAND-UP ROUTINES

A Mind-Body-Spirit Perfect Storm

I see my lifetime of unrelenting depression as the manifestation of genetic, genealogical, physical, and sociological events, each one of which would probably produce a disabling melancholic condition in a female; and which, coming together in one woman, guarantee defeat of all treatment and medication inputs.

I've devoted some print already to the probability that I inherited genetic proclivities. Relatives and forebears have come up with many serious problems that suggest gene involvement. In my paternal ancestors there seems to have been an inordinately great number of stillborn infants or children who died in early childhood. My grandmother bore nine children. Only two survived to adulthood. A second cousin, whom I learned about only last year, told me Grandmother was diabetic. If that was true, I find it strange that neither she nor my father nor my aunt ever mentioned it. As no one ever spoke of Grandmother's being diabetic, I have no idea of the age of onset and cannot even be sure that diabetes was the cause of her losing so many babies.

My father, born nine years after my grandparents' first child, reached the age of four unscathed then fell prey to lethargic encephalitis. Miraculously he survived, but as is the case with severe encephalitis in young children, he sustained brain damage, one aspect of which was the lifelong affliction of narcolepsy. One other of my paternal grandparents' children, a boy, survived to the age of two or three. I never heard what caused his death.

Grandmother's first child, a female (the aunt for whom I was named) escaped serious childhood infectious diseases but had the misfortune of inheriting a nose of a size and contour that distressed her mother - and therefore her - unceasingly, as long as she lived. As I see it, the contribution my paternal side of the family made to my depression was the Duttweilor-McClelland attitude that only those who present themselves as enviable in all ways are worthy of respect; that to have defects, inadequacies, or mediocrities that the world can see makes one contemptible. That surely is the reason that my aunt's nose was a matter of such intense dissatisfaction to my grandmother. As you can see from my aunt's childhood portrait, she was a beautiful child, and there was nothing particularly off-putting about her nose.

If there were such a thing as a Duttweilor-McClelland coat of arms, I don't know what the graphics would look like, but the inscription might well be "Evocate Admiracionem", or, as my aunt put it to me once, "You must make people admire you".

According to one website I visited while doing genealogical work, all the McClellands in America are descended from that Scottish branch of the family that relocated to Ireland around the time of the English plantation projects; we Scots-Irish McClelland descendants are all related. I can readily believe that. While viewing a Civil War documentary that detailed General George McClellan's preoccupation with how admired he was after having whipped a bunch of rag-tag Union soldiers into such great shape that they wowed the audiences that came to watch them marching up and down on a parade ground, I could almost feel the man's genes in my own head.

As my aunt entered puberty, she developed a body shape that one would find illustrated in texts on Cushing's syndrome; large breasts, thick waist with an inordinate amount of belly fat, relatively thin extremities, and short neck over a vertebral hump. Ever conscious of being "homely" in comparison with peers, she concentrated all her energies on camouflaging with hair style and clothes what she considered to be her gross and disgusting physical defects and upon exuding such charm that those with whom she socialized would develop impressions of her as being pretty.

This was the way her mother had dealt with what she perceived as her daughter's ugliness from a very young age. My aunt related to me once that whenever her mother's sister, who lived in another state, announced intentions to visit with her, Grandmother Leitch, hating how the beauty of her sister's daughter would show up the homeliness of her own, would spend hours curling and styling my aunt's hair and would keep her dressed in her Sunday best for the duration of her sister's visit.

I include a picture of my aunt in order to show the mental pathology of my grandmother in the way she looked upon her offspring. Unfortunately for me, when I entered puberty with rapid weight gain, development of large breasts, and with hardly any increase in height, my aunt saw in me the ugly little girl her mother had seen in her.

Within the space of a year or so in my twelfth to fourteenth years, my aunt went from trying to correct my malnourished condition (nobody ever discussed with me that I had a tape worm, and when I passed it, in horror, in the middle of the night, I had no idea what it was) through buying me school lunches, to trying to badger me into letting her give me an enema in order to empty my gut of food in preparation for a three-day all-liquid diet to shrink my stomach. In the year of my gain in weight from eighty-five pounds to a hundred and fifteen pounds and the development of my ample bosom, my aunt developed the kind of fixation on me that a person might expect to see in a mother whose child has fallen into a life-destroying addiction to hard drugs.

As I look back on it now (especially as I look at pictures of me made at the time), for her to be all-consumed with how fat and homely I was and how gross and disgusting my big breasts were, was insanity. My aunt's pathological determination to control my eating and weight and to make me so conscious of how unattractive I was that I would never select an article of clothing or arrange hair or makeup without thinking about how I must use them to camouflage, destroyed the little emotional health that my older sister's abuse and my mother's hostility and neglect had left me. Any time my aunt and I communicated, even in her letters to me, there always had to be numerous references to my eating fattening things, to my weight, and how I should be dressing and grooming myself to hide all my ugly and gross features. By the time I was a sophomore in high school, she had so fully convinced me of my ugliness and of my sloth in not doing what I should be doing to hide it, that I just wanted to be dead. I remember standing in front of my mirror one day thinking to myself that I had no future; that I could not diet, and that being fat and ugly made me unfit, as a female, to have any reason to live.

I tried various ways of committing suicide, but I was just too faint-hearted about it. I tried to cut my wrists, but that hurt too badly to get past some superficial scratching. I ate wild mushrooms, but I guess the poisonous kind didn't grow on our farm. I consumed an entire bottle of aspirin. I probably gave myself some brain damage, but, disappointment notwithstanding, I was still alive and still feeling as hopelessly ugly the next day.

Being desired for marriage by men with prospects was just as important in my Southern environment as to those memorable characters that populate the pages of *Gone with the Wind* and *The Glass Menagerie*. In my aunt's case, her preoccupation with how a young girl could contrive to make a man fall "desperately in love" with her while she maintained a state of mind and emotion toward him that was absolutely free of such weakness, was an obsession that made Scarlet O'Hara's and Jenny's mothers' interests look unremarkable. In my aunt's eyes, a woman who didn't receive many marriage proposals and who couldn't afford to turn them all down until the most handsome, most knightly, most educated, and most financially secure man came along, was a flop as a female. And that is where I came in.

ROOTS, RELIGION AND DEPRESSION

A MIND-BODY-SPIRIT PERFECT STORM

The Longing for Listeners Who Want to Listen

Even in adulthood, after I had been without my sister Leah's daily presence in my life for years, following the most brief of encounters with her, I found myself in a state of dissatisfaction with myself, every relationship I had, and every personal possession I owned that surpassed any negative self-images that came to me following contacts with any other person I had ever known.

Sis Leah's analysis of why I felt so down was that I was jealous of her because she was so much more attractive than I. I did rate myself as less attractive than she, but what she had that I most wanted was the rapt attention she got from any third parties who were with us. At all times, all eyes were on her, and all ears were tuned to receive communication from her and to disregard audio waves from other voices. I had been intimidated into reducing myself to a mute observer in her presence, and what I observed was that everyone I had ever known was so eager to win her affection and good opinion that they were competing with each other to lay gifts at her feet that would be enticing enough to her to get them noticed. Who would not be jealous of a female having listeners like that?

What I didn't understand at that time was that she was so desperate to be the focus of everyone's attention that every cell of her being was going into getting that attention. She put an animation into her speech, her eyes, her mouth, and her movements that were all devoted to giving a performance that would go over with an audience. She spoke with excitement and at a pitch and volume of one who has a tale to tell that just cannot be held back from those waiting to hear it. Now I am able to understand that if I were as motivated to get everyone to pay attention to me and no one else but me as she, I would get at least a share of attention in gatherings. I don't have that much drive. Neither do I have that gene that tells me I can appear to look big by making someone else look very small.

That Leah had the think-on-your-feet readiness and the nanosecond wit to deliver an Emmy-destroying line to an audience before my brain had even got a whiff that she was about to do that to me, left me as stunned and confused as a deer must feel who has just been shot by a hunter. That stunned prey state seems to have stayed with me.

As tools go, language is one of the best (if not the very best) tool a human can have for getting his or her needs met in a competitive predator pack environment - the kind of environment in which all humans exist at all times except for the few who have become isolated; a living condition which is not natural or healthy for humans. Language, for humans, is the equivalent of fangs and snarls and howls in wolves or the astounding musculoskeletal structure of cheetahs.

Like wolves, humans must get favorable attention from fellow pack members or else die of want. If they should manage to survive as loners, they pass a miserable existence - too consumed with wanting and with fearing want to ever be able to stop their search for subsistence and to peacefully rest.

So, the biggest and most aggressive among wolf pups (and in most other species' litters) gets his needs met best because he can win the most attention from providers. The more attention he can demand from providers, the less the providers will have for litter mates with whom he is in competition for sustenance. Somewhat analogous is the situation in which I grew up; one in which language turned out to be the survival tool that won favorable attention for my older sister from providers of self-image sustenance. A human who instinctively, instantly, comes out with words that create an impression in third parties that paying attention to her is the good and the right thing to do, and that paying attention to her competition shows pitiable judgment, has a tool at her disposal that beats out all other tools where obtaining self-image sustenance is the survival necessity.

Being able to put the desired spin on things and being able to sniff out which voters will buy one's spin and which won't is what wins elections for candidates. Lacking the instinct to effectively spin favorable myths about oneself, and lacking the innate ability to sort out subconsciously, in real time, who'll run with the spin and who'll tear it apart, loses campaigns.

As a child, being so much younger than my sister, yet being under constant attack from her language as she used it as a tool to frighten me away from seeking attention and to influence providers to deny me favorable attention, I was abysmally outclassed. My efforts to defend myself against her language with my language were akin to a person's repeatedly trying to defend himself against switchblade attacks with a picnickers' plastic knife. My sister ridiculed me for being unable to defend myself verbally. Never, did I ever have a retort to any put-down from her that didn't leave me more vulnerable to more shaming and hurt than if I had just kept my mouth shut and departed immediately so that she could have the person whose attention she wanted all to herself.

In the presence of my older sister, I grew so accustomed to failing totally at using language for self-image survival purposes, for attention-getting purposes, for need-satisfying purposes, for intra-pack communication purposes, for bonding, that I largely quit trying. I developed language as a consolation tool, a substitution for human interaction, a solitary myth-making tool with which to entertain and delight myself. Alone, I would wander to some place on the farm where I knew my sister would never go, and there I would make up fairy tale stories in my head in which I was the important, loved, honored female in a group.

In these little sessions, where I might be seated high in a tree or crouched down in a gully deeper than I was tall - anywhere I could feel sure I couldn't be seen and that no human might ever catch me talking aloud to myself - I would speak freely and spontaneously to my imaginary little band of acolytes. I was Snow White, living in a cave, being cared for and loved by The Seven Dwarfs, and loving and caring for them in return. I was Bambi's mother, or father, or friend, depending upon my inclinations of the day. I was the mirror telling the wicked queen that she was fair indeed but that far, far away, in the deep, deep forest there lived one fairer by far than she.

I know now that I was instinctively using that most essential of all human survival tools, language, and its inseparable offspring, self-image mythmaking, to heal myself and to give to myself in fantasy what I could of the emotional and social necessities which I observed my older sister acquiring with language and with image mythmaking in real interactions with real people. Any use that I made of language to debate or refute my sister's linguistic representations of me as a disgusting embarrassment to her and a child of shameful, selfish, burdensomeness for our poor mother, took place only where I felt sure my words could never get back to her.

I haven't carried on imaginary subvocal conversations with my sister in many years. I can't recall exactly when they stopped, but when they did, I unconsciously transferred her identity to whoever happened to be in my life at the time whose communications to me were threatening my self-image. Although there have been many, the person to whom I most transferred her identity was a psychiatrist I began seeing in my late twenties who introduced me to what a little Freudian, psychoanalytically oriented free association-based therapy can do to irreplaceable mental and emotional assets that you are lucky enough to have when you undertake it.

What I wanted from him was what I had always seen

Leah getting that I couldn't seem to; the upper-class, cultured person who *WANTED* to communicate *WITH* me, who viewed me as being up to doing that. I did not get that longing satisfied in therapy with him.

By three or four weeks into that therapy, I was so consumed with my compulsive subvocal rehearsal of what I had said to the man, what I would say to the man next, how he had reacted to what I had said, how he would react in the future when I said thus and so, I ceased to even be able to take care of my children. Within a few months, as I recall, we had to call my husband's family to come take the children to their house until I could get my wits back about me sufficiently to be able to focus on what they were saying when the poor little things tried to talk to me.

I thought that my being in that pitiful a mental state was par for the course for a "patient" in psychoanalytically oriented therapy. I had no idea I had put myself in a situation where the perpetual terror I'd endured for years as a child would begin all over again, only this time, instead of that old familiar female face that was my sister's, here was a new male one to whom I'd unconsciously transferred my sister's identity. Now, I comprehend that what I did at that time, by undertaking that treatment, was to go with an old poorly healed wound to a medical person who thought himself capable of healing old poorly healed wounds, but who wasn't. I now understand the dynamics which caused his therapeutic approaches and his attitudes toward me to have the effect of introducing pathogens into my wound instead of healing it.

Well, I am certainly not the only person who has sought medical treatment for a condition which she has been led to believe is treatable, and who has discovered, too late, that she has been maimed by the treatment to such an extent that the damage is irreparable and that she will never be able to function as she did before the treatment or be pain free again. Thankfully, the awareness of the harm that "memory recovery" sorts of therapy can do to subjects is beginning to be known in the medical community.

Waking the Tiger, subtitled *Healing Trauma*, by Peter A. Levine, published in 1997 by North Atlantic Books, was recommended to me a couple of years ago by a very aware massage therapist who gave my bowstring-tight upper torso muscles a little yearned for peace with a few sessions of deep tissue message. Author Levine explains how therapy that guides a client to recovery of repressed traumatic childhood memories can put the client at risk of living the whole nightmare over again as an adult, with even worse damage resulting from the reexperiencing of it than occurred originally in childhood. In childhood we at least have that automatic defense of repression working for us, which is nature's very effective way of easing the pain fast; whereas, in adulthood, repression doesn't come to our aid very often. I hope the knowledge of the risk involved in therapists' trying to put clients through memory recovery is being disseminated widely among mental health professionals, because Levine speaks a truth that needs all the exposure it can get.

Why is all talk therapy - except for those cases where the client can generally feel, and the therapist generally feel, that they are members of the same pack and are pretty nearly equal in all things - such a failure?

For me, in most of my therapy situations, an ever-present problem has been that it reminds me just too much of a John paying for a liaison with a prostitute because he is so lacking in attractiveness to women with whom he would like to have sex that he can't find a partner who will be an inspiration to him (while also appearing to find him very inspiring) without paying big bucks.

This is a matter very hard for me to put on a page for people to read who not only know me but who might be providing me with medical treatment or psychotherapeutic help now or in the future. However, I feel it is best for me to stop trying to hide the fact that I have always felt this way about every therapist whom I have ever paid for treatment.

What a John wants from a prostitute is not just a sex act, but expressions and gestures and words from the prostitute that give him the impression she is enjoying the experience just as much as he. The prostitute doesn't, but pretends to.

When a woman goes to a therapist, the therapist is usually a substitute, for her, for the listener she wishes she had but doesn't have enough assets to draw.

In my own case, the listener I had always longed to find one day, would have been one like all those people that I, standing by mute and invisible, saw listening to Leah as if what she was saying satisfied their needs like no words they could have heard from anyone else in their world. Beginning with my mother listening to Leah's shaming of me, thoroughly entertained, and continuing on through the relatives and all the rest where Leah had gained status by making me look small, I wanted to be someone with whom the same people wanted to be, in the way all those people seemed to want to be, with Leah. I wanted Leah to want to be with me; to see something in me that lifted me up in her eyes to such an extent that she would want to play with me, share with me, and feel some kindred-spirit-ship with me instead of seeing me as nothing more than a thing to use in a performance for an onlooker. The listener I needed, if his or her listening were to, in any way, help me to complete my unfinished business from childhood, was one having a certain identity to my identity-transferring self

I don't know if other identity-transferring clients in psychoanalytically oriented therapy have the same problem as I, but my problem was, and always is, that I am so aware that my relationship with the practitioner is not a real relationship and never will be - that he or she is to me as a prostitute is to a john - that I simply cannot put my emotions and instinctual drives into the resolution of transference that I would into some relationship that had a small chance of satisfying some need of mine. I needed to be seen by the doctor as a colleague (just in my therapy - not in general) and the psychiatrist of mine with whom I wanted that sort of equals relationship found that need of mine to be "delusional".

Humans need someone, somewhere, in their lives to listen to them with the appearance of being interested recipients of what they are hearing. Women want to share about serious matters and get feedback that says their words had value to the listener. Women, even in areas of the country less misogynistic than here, just aren't listened to in the same way that men are - not only are they cut short and ignored by men; they're cut short and ignored by other females and children as well. That makes psychiatrists and psychologists women's last hope in their longing to have someone listen to them for a change, instead of their having to forever take on the role of being the interested, admiring, empathetic, agreeing, supportive listener. It is no wonder that when a woman gets to a psychotherapist – one who will sit quietly for a considerable number of minutes while she at last gets to say what she would really like to be saying to somebody who values what she is saying (and actually wants to listen to it) that she can feel almost like a John who is paying a prostitute to pretend interest in him. She knows the therapist is only allowing her to speak because she's paying for the time. The therapist's job is to role-play "listener". This is better than life without even so much as a therapist role playing "listener", but it is a long, long way from the way I saw my older female relatives being listened to in my childhood: I observed these women being listened to by men, even when they spoke about national and global matters - and even feelings - as if they were hearing words that mattered. No paid-for therapy could equal that in lifting up one's soul.

I believe that the best therapy for mental health clients is one where the authority figure the client sees is simply an arts-and-crafts-savvy person who maintains a site and materials where mental health therapy consumers can gather and talk with each other without having to take on the tasks of managing anything. I don't know why depression causes one to face alpha-type work and responsibilities as activity so loathsome we become unable to face it over time, but, I think, most of us do. Perhaps it is because deep depression makes us feel as if we were very, very sick - perhaps as one would feel dealing with a powerful virus or infection - and the ever-present sensation physically is of waiting for the illness to abate a bit before attempting to start back up again at the daily grind.

When I can see that, if I need to talk to someone, that someone who chooses to listen to me is doing so because they want to - not because they are being paid to - that difference makes all the difference in the world as to whether I derive any benefit from conversation or not. Still, not just any listener will do; a person with the capacity to give benefit to another by listening has to hold a certain identity in the mind of the talker.

The most depression-free months I have ever enjoyed have been the five months I spent in a state-run mental institution. Was my reason for feeling so much better there than I felt anywhere else that I was receiving great therapy? Heavens no! It is true that I was receiving a lot of different kinds of psychotherapy from the most well-prepared therapists money could buy, but the reason life was so good (in as far as how I felt every day) was that there were hundreds of other "patients" there. I was just as broken a human being inside the institution as I had been on the outside. The difference was that I was free from the awful burden of having to look and behave as if I were not broken.

I, as well as every patient I knew, was, mental-health-wise, in so much better shape inside the institution than out, that being released felt like being sent back to hell. There is so much talk now of the need of people bearing labels (color, LGBT, faith, etc,) to see others who look like them being included in groups that formerly contained no people of labels. We folks with closed-head injury and other differences that throw us into *Diagnostic and Statistical Manual* categories need some places we can be with each other too, but the stigma we acquire when we go anywhere to get together with others with that DSM label "mentally ill" is so off-putting it is not worth the effort to pursue such gatherings.

Groups can be found that are run by mental health professionals, but their presence in a group squashes the spontaneous socializing that gives attendees the benefit.

ROOTS, RELIGION AND DEPRESSION

THE LONGING FOR LISTENERS WHO WANT TO LISTEN

Revulsion and Redemption

If my writing goes today as it usually does, I will work all day without pausing even to eat and won't quit until I see that the sun is well on its way to going down and that I must get outside and do a few things in the yard, like refresh water in birdbaths to allay mosquito reproduction, while it's still light enough to see. My total output will be probably four pages or less. It's almost impossible for me to do anything fast, especially to express myself rapidly and spontaneously. I suspect there are reasons for that other than my genetic makeup.

One of the most painful aspects of my relationship with my older sister throughout the years when my body and brain were developing was that she thought me repulsive and disgusting and made sure that she let that feeling plainly show for her audience any time she and I were in the presence of third parties. She bragged about feeling those feelings toward me. She entertained our mother with the telling of little anecdotes about the revulsion she felt for me. When I talked in her presence where there was also another person to see or hear us, an expression was on her face all the while that said, "This is an idiot talking".

At the end of any utterance I made in her presence there was usually dead silence on her part while she stared at me as if offal or unintelligible gibberish had just fallen from my lips. The length of time in which she stared at me in this way made the communication about me in her facial expression very clear to observers. It may seem strange to you, the reader, that through fifteen or twenty years of experiencing this, despite being above average in a few kinds of intelligence, I had no conscious awareness of what was being communicated by my sister or what message was being picked up upon and digested by our mother, my younger sisters, other children, neighbors, extended family members, acquaintances, and first-time-met strangers. My obliviousness was due to that wonderful natural self-image defender, repression.

Finally, I did begin to realize consciously, only within the last couple of decades, how my sister was ingeniously using words, facial expression, and body language to influence feelings and opinions of anyone and everyone who might be witness when I attempted to interact with another human in her presence. Our Mother's death in the late nineties seemed to dislodge a clog in the cerebral pipes that connect my unconscious awareness with my conscious awareness where childhood repressed terror was involved. I began to be, not only unconsciously perceiving something frightening about what was taking place at times when I was in the same space at the same time as my sister and another human was audience, but I began consciously to be able to almost calmly analyze what that was even while I was feeling the fear.

Reflecting upon that, I can't help being stunned at how blind, deaf, and ignorant repression can render a person, and how astoundingly resistant my unconscious has been in giving me (the me that can make an adult, informed decision about how to deal with the contents) knowledge and feeling of its most misery-producing contents. I am a person who, in young adulthood, studied psychoanalysis, believed with all my conscious being that recovering repressed memories would free me from depression and dysfunction, went into psychoanalytically oriented therapy with a commitment I've never given to any other project in my life before or since ... and still, the security program in my brain that stands guard over and hides my repressed material would not give it up.

Early on in my work with my late-'60s-early-'70s psychiatrist - perhaps a year into my seven-year downhill slide under his care - he railed at me, "Mrs. Bowden, you are trying to control your treatment, and if you continue to do so, I'm going to stop seeing you".

Looking back I can only think to myself, "What stupidity for the man not to recognize that I did not have it within my power to stop trying to control my treatment; that if I had had a gun held to my head and been told by him that I must let him control my flow of free associations and emotions or he would blow my brains out, I wouldn't have been able to do it, and he should have known that".

When I entered therapy under him, he had given me a glowing validation of his competence to guide me in the psychoanalytic process. "I've had my own analysis," he had said to me in an early-on session when I expressed an inability to allow everything that entered my consciousness to come forth in speech because of fear that he would feel disgust for what I might say. "I would?", he questioned jocularly, "me, Dr. Searcy ... or are you thinking of someone I represent?".

I can't quote exactly the words he used as he continued in his reassurance to me that his disgust or hostility would not be aroused by any expression that spilled out of my mouth if I allowed myself to fall into un-self-censoring free association mode, but I'll try to paraphrase what he said with faithfulness to the sense and to the intent:

"I don't take personally anything my patients say to me in therapy sessions. I would react emotionally only if I myself had unresolved neuroses, but I've had my own analysis. I've worked through my unconscious emotional responses to people, and I'm able to listen to anything my patients say without emotional reaction. Now, there could possibly be a circumstance where a patient's conscious attitudes are so personally offensive to a therapist that he would find himself reacting negatively. A colleague of mine who was Jewish took on a patient who began to make a lot of strongly anti-Semitic remarks to him. My colleague did find his emotions aroused by that, so he terminated therapy with that client. But, that type of situation is extremely rare."

In the several months preceding my finding Dr. Searcy, I had devoured every book I could find that described psychoanalytic therapy, so I understood perfectly what he was talking about when he asked questions like, "Is it I, Dr. Searcy, who will be angry at you for what you say, or is it who I represent? You think that I am angry. Is that what I feel or is that what the person would feel whom I represent to you?"

In the books I read, clients talked to their doctors about all kinds of body products and sexual acts - their own, their closest relatives, and even what the therapist's might be. Feeling completely reassured, not only by what I had read about the complete appropriateness of freeing one's tongue from all taboos while speaking in sessions, but also by what Dr. Searcy was telling me, I did, in no time as therapies go, drop all conscious blocking of free association and of describing aloud to Dr. Searcy whatever that free association produced.

What turned out to cause the treatment to turn into a disaster for me - a years-long degenerative process - was that what Dr. Searcy said about his not taking personally or reacting emotionally to anything patients said to him in therapy was hogwash, and my own brain's unconsciously-operating, on-guard analyst suspected it was hogwash and just had to test that brag.

At the time, I existed in a conscious-awareness state of complete willingness and obedience to the psychoanalytic paradigm of which I'd read so much; where the patient has total trust in her doctor and the doctor is unconditionally accepting of her and of everything she says and feels. Further, I was so naïve I thought Dr. Searcy fully comprehended everything I said to him and could see who and what I was on the deepest level with a view undistorted by double-standard moral judgments and the belief commonly held among men that females were all just dumb little girls who desperately needed all the help they could get from males in any area of their lives where serious mentation was needed.

On a conscious level, I bought the hogwash psychiatrists and psychoanalysts put out about being able to see what's going on inside a client's unconscious mind just from listening for only a few minutes to what she (or he) says aloud while she can't see it or understand it herself - only a formally trained doctor can do that. I bought the propaganda that the patient who will eventually achieve success in therapy is the one who loves her doctor like a little child loves the best of godparents and who makes a verbal gift to him of every thought and feeling. Relying solely on what I'd read in books, what I'd heard famous people say, and what Dr. Searcy described as his type of therapy, my conscious self couldn't turn my life and my will over to Dr. Searcy fast enough.

On an unconscious level, Emmy was identifying bits of fantasy as fantasy right from the start. I'm using third person to tell about this phenomenon here, because I was not consciously aware at the time of the wholesomeness and the astuteness of this part of me that began to critically judge statements Dr. Searcy made and to sort out whether or not he was representing himself accurately. Or, whether like the biggest guns in my family always had done, he was presenting an image of himself to me that was more a product of his own mythmaking about himself than who he really was. I'm not saying that he was consciously wishing to deceive me into thinking that he was far more than he was. I believe he actually thought he was telling me the truth about himself, just as my sister believes that she is presenting things truthfully when she begins communicating to me and others what a vast disparity there is between her and me in every way that counts for something.

Add to this Leah transference the analogy of my relationship with the doctor to the relationship I had had with Aunt E, and this summed up to an unconscious attitude on my part of, "Oh, so you're going to play the role of God condescending to the lowly mortal, huh?". Aunt E had been out to fix things she saw as needing fixing in me for the sake of seeing herself in a certain way, and that appeared to me to be Dr. Searcy's motivation for behaving as he did toward me as well.

To give a summation that will dispatch that subject for now: the trouble with the therapy experience was that in addition to my imagining that Dr. Searcy had certain attitudes and feelings about me, he actually did develop attitudes and feelings toward me that were too much like those held for me by dismissive loved ones, and despite his deceiving himself that he didn't have those I'm-everything-and-you're-nothing attitudes, they showed. Emmy perceived them and was crushed.

Now, back to Sis: in our last interaction with each other, in the late nineties when Mother's estate had to be settled, in a phone conference shared by the four of us sisters with the estate executor, Older Sis was employing the same old communication strategies she always had to belittle me (and to a lesser extent our two younger sisters) and to make herself seem to the executor to be the only member of the family with thoughts about real and personal property that had value.

In probably the first contact with Leah that I had ever done so, I consciously could perceive her deploying her communication tactical weapons. Right out of the gate I heard, "When I was director of Habitat for Humanity

...". I recognized this as a phrase of the sort she uses and has always used around me for the same purpose that elk with bigger racks brandish them in the faces of elk with smaller racks - they want as much territory as they can get all to themselves, and displaying bigger weapons intimidates competitors into abandoning whatever aspirations they had when they came into the scene.

Sis's self-elevating phrases of the type, "When I was Director of Habitat for Humanity", always have been plentifully sufficient to intimidate me out of trying to participate in any conversation in which she, third parties, and I were thrown together, even if I needed to speak at least a little just to keep from appearing to be mentally handicapped or mute. In this telephone conference in 1998 of which I'm speaking, I was again intimidated by her presentation of evidences of vast superiority, but unlike the way I had shrunk back and closed up in probably hundreds of like episodes in times past, on this day, I felt my fear consciously while simultaneously recognizing the cause. I could express it to myself subvocally, linguistically, as the long phone conference progressed.

I had thought that I was afraid of the physical person of Leah, and I must still be to a certain extent, because my guts churn a little around women who are significantly taller than I. But it hasn't entirely been her six inch advantage over me in height, but rather her fantastically skillful use of communication as a weapon to run me out of my own territory and to influence my own pack members to help her to keep me out, that has kept me in terror of her all my life.

I forced myself to contribute verbally in Mom's estate settlement conference with the executor, and to keep on contributing, just because I could see that Sis was expecting me to shut up as soon as she presented her proof of being the only competent person, other than the executor, who was participating in the conference call. I always had been an instant pushover at being intimidated into shutting up. But Mother was dead and I knew that this executor was not Mother, standing by Sis's side, ready to glow approvingly over Sis's statements to me that were so humiliating and hurtful that I would just try to "disappear". Sis knew it too.

As the conference proceeded and I followed every block of discourse Sis offered to the executor with one of my own, I sensed that she was becoming more and more desperate to find some way to control the conference so that the executor and my two younger sisters would be paying attention only to her - never to me. Leah began speaking louder, faster, more excitedly, and tried to close up pauses that I might use as opportunities to seize the floor. I did the best I could to match her strategy for strategy although it is completely contrary to my nature to try to hold the floor when other people start speaking. It comes automatically to me to give up my effort to say whatever it was I wanted to say when another person interrupts me. Nonetheless, I didn't relinquish the floor on this occasion.

I noticed during the phone conference that despite the amount of expensive phone time she was expending in speaking, Sis wasn't providing any really useful information or suggestions that would help to get the stalled real property sales moving along. The same was true of other aspects of Mom's estate settlement that had to be completed before the four of us could get all our money. Comparing Sis's curriculum vita in estate settlements (which she presented to all of us involved) with what she actually accomplished in the tasks over which she managed to get control, I felt there was considerable disparity.

Up to the time of Mom's death, I'd always been a complete sucker for Sis's hype about herself. This was 1998, I was fifty-eight years old, and I'd been afraid all my life to display one sign of confidence around Sis because any sign of self-love or confidence I'd ever displayed around Sis had been punished by her - if not instantly, then as soon as we were away from whomever stood in the way - in ways that hurt me so badly I was ready to give up any good feeling I had if by so doing I could avoid having her show me how what I had imagined to be so admirable was really disgusting and pathetic.

Listening to Sis's non-stop efforts to communicate to Mom's executor that she was the only one of us four siblings who had anything to say to which it would be worth his while to listen, I wondered how I could have allowed myself to remain so intimidated by her name-dropping and bragging that I had spent a lifetime mute anytime I was in her presence. For the first time in my life, I was listening to her self-promotion objectively rather than through aural processes corrupted by emotional enmeshment.

Having discovered how snowed I had been for a lifetime by Sis's communication moves for showing herself to be unreachably above me, I soon after discovered that I had fallen for Dr. Searcy's self-promotive cons in exactly the same way. In fact, my gullibility for Leah's perpetual posture of superiority over me predisposed me to buy into the same approach from this psychiatrist by whom

I was so intimidated for so long but who was somewhat "heap big smoke but no fire".

I've wondered if my need to abase myself before Leah from my infancy onward in order to avert being painfully shamed by her - should I fail to maintain my mute facelessness - would account for the fact that anti-depressant medications make me feel more depressed, not less. Perhaps what is happening is that as soon as I begin to feel optimism and motivation, my unconscious recalls that whenever Leah caught me feeling "full of myself", she turned words and tales and facial expressions on me that made me loathe myself for having exposed my underbelly.

Serotonin is supposed to be the greatest feel-good substance known to man. Within only a few days of beginning any serotonin reuptake inhibiting drug such as Prozac, my sense that my life is a lost cause is exacerbated, and I lose the infinitesimal amount of motivation I had. Perhaps as soon as serotonin begins to alter my base autonomic pessimism/optimism ratio, an unconscious mental process kicks in of the sort that commenced in Pavlov's dogs when they heard the ringing of a bell and began to salivate because Pavlov had previously paired the ringing of a bell with delivery of their dinner.

Maybe my subconscious memory of experiences past is telling my neurons and brain chemicals that if I should slip up and allow myself to feel secure, confident, lovable, attractive, talented, successful - anything along those lines - that this will be to Leah what an out-in-the-open baby gazelle is to a cheetah. Baby gazelles that survive to adulthood instinctively lie for hours on end, low, silent, and motionless in tall grass where they won't attract the attention of predators like cheetahs. Perhaps depression in humans is instinctively lying low, silent, and motionless in tall grass when the predators happen to be fellow humans who feed on self-images.

ROOTS, RELIGION AND DEPRESSION

REVULSION AND REDEMPTION

LIONESSES OF THE PRIDE

Jane, my mitochondrial "cousin", and I introduced ourselves to each other by email in the fall of 2005 after I participated in National Geographic Society's *Genographic Project*, entered my test results at website www.mitosearch.org, and found her as one of my two Hypervariable Region 1 (HVR-1) mitochondrial mutation matches. Out of the thousands of people who have submitted their cheek swabs to various DNA testing facilities for HVR-1 mitochondrial analysis, and who have permitted their results to be displayed online, at the time that Jane and I found each other we knew of only one other tested person who had the same HVR-1 mutations as we.

We three knew this meant that somewhere in our female genealogical lines - probably many centuries ago, but possibly more recently - we had a common ancestor, a common mito-matriarch. We all plunged into investigating our own and each other's mitochondrial links, as far back in time as we had knowledge of names and places, to see if this mutual mito-mama was one we could identify. For a few weeks we sent emails flying back and forth to each other daily until we had exhausted our genealogical stores and had to face that our mito-matriarch probably lived at a time and place where births, deaths, and women and children's names weren't recorded except for those few who were in some way spectacularly high profile.

In Jane's first email to me, I found that both she and my other mito-match were librarians. This was the first piece of autobiographical exchange among us which left me a bit startled. Three mito-matches who also just happened to have made life choices which kept their noses stuck in books? Was that absorption with written word a result of mitochondrial inheritance, or was that absorption the thing that had led us to *The Genographic Project* and to sending off our cheek swabs?

My online correspondence with Jane's and my other match didn't continue past a few communications, but Jane and I seemed to have an ocean of ideas and feelings that began to spill out to each other as if we had each been waiting for a receptive inlet to receive the tide. Quickly, Jane and I found each other to seem so markedly like a sister we had always wished we had - but never had - that we went on to communicate volumes about our personal lives to each other.

Jane's first question to me was about my health, and although she made no mention of her own, I suspected that she asked because she, like me, had health conditions that were a constant vexation and for which she had found no relief in medical resources. It was many months before she finally revealed to me that she had suffered from recurring breast cancer. A sister of mine had surgery and treatment for breast cancer many years ago, and, as far as I know, the surgery and treatment were entirely successful. I was happy I could share that with Jane when she brought up the subject of her own battle.

My first question to Jane was about her relationship with her mother. To be exact, my query read:

"Up to my search for a mitochondria match a few days ago, I never had tried to find out anything about my mother's family members. My relationship with my mother and other women in my immediate maternal line had been so awful, I think I didn't care where Mother's ancestors came from or when they came. I hope to find, during my efforts to trace my mitochondria backward, that my mother's, my mito grandmother's, and my great-grandmother's (the only one ever mentioned by Mother) disliking of children had nothing to do with their mitochondria. I hope that you and Liz will tell me that you both had great relationships with your mothers and that love between mothers and daughters prevails in your pedigrees."

This was Jane's reply:

"Oh my gosh ... I had a terrible relationship with my mother, and no female in her family was very good at mothering. They just aren't good with small children, and none of us cousins got nurtured at all. Except the uncles were all warm and loving. My mother was an elementary teacher and great with people, but not a good mother. I was obsessed with my dislike of her until she died. I did what I could for her and to be a good daughter, but she drove me crazy. Loved my dad who obviously loved me too, but he had a horrible upbringing, so he didn't know how to parent. I got a little nurturance from him when he was around, which was seldom, but a lot of ridicule and yelling, too. Anyway, I liked men best all my life until now. After having lived in this red-necked bible belt community for the past 26 years where men still spit (and are supposed to show their masculinity that way ... and hunting), I don't much like men anymore at all. Thank goodness all the special ones in my past were good or at least treated me well and were civilized and gentle and kind, I would probably hate men because of the ones I'm surrounded by here."

"I felt very uncomfortable with person counseling!" (Working as a librarian was a sideline for Jane. Her primary profession had been counseling.) "I went through the counseling master's to become a career counselor which was a little more distant. Of course some personal issues came up, but I didn't have to deal with them for long ... they would be referred to someone who did personal counseling. What I loved was helping students find their interests, values, and personality types and match those up to majors and careers. I do love helping people one-on-one. I am a reclusive myself ... with pets. No one comes to my house, but mainly because it's a kennel. I was married once for a short while only. I fell in love many times and even spent 8 years with my first boyfriend but broke up right before we got married. No others lasted more than 9 months, but it was because I couldn't maintain a relationship. I have one son who is 34 and a deputy sheriff (lots of law enforcement in my father's line) and two granddaughters 14 and 4. I tried really hard to be a good mother and know I did better than my mother, but my son doesn't like me much. Great relationship with my oldest granddaughter."

"Wow, this is all pretty powerful. Jane"

As I read more of Jane's emails, which revealed layers of her personal profile just as this reply had, I marveled at how similar our attitudes were about so many of our fellow human beings' values and ubiquitous religious dogmas. I was stunned by how similar the outcomes had been in our struggles to safely navigate life's whitewater passages and emerge from them in as good shape as we'd entered, with all our possessions intact. At marriage, parenting, and careers, it looked to me as if we'd each slammed against every boulder in the stream. It seemed to me that neither of us had found the rewards we'd expected from our marriages, our investments in our children, or from the time, money, and effort we'd poured into reaching levels of knowledge and competency in our chosen professions that should have earned us at least a little recognition and respect from our superiors and co-workers.

Sadly, the career experience of each of us had been that no one over us or around us looked for anything in us other than whether or not we were sucking up and conforming to those we were expected to suck up to and conform with. I think of all the disappointments and disillusionments of our lives, this purposefully-acquired blindness, in our superiors and fellow-workers, to our professional credentials, intelligence, and to the job descriptions of our positions, was the diminishment by our fellow humans that brought an end, for each of us, to our last great dreams.

I know that the last great dream for my future that I had entertained had been of multiplying through education the talents that were inherently mine, then of contributing from the proceeds of what I had made of my talents to my family members and to those with whom I would work. I was so sure that once I had degrees and a professional title, my family members and society in general would feel the respect for me that, so far, I hadn't seemed to be able to win. I imagine Jane had dreamed similar dreams. I don't think either of us had so much as a glimpse, during all the years when we were struggling so conscientiously to make of ourselves better parents and the best we could be professionally, that the reward waiting for us at the end of all that effort would be devaluation and ill treatment.

One of Jane's communications touched me especially deeply. Why? How many humans are there among us who, knowing that a woman has been diagnosed and treated for depression, feel any compassion or empathy for her in her discomfort? My reply to Jane's query about my health follows:

From: Emmy
eclb@rootsdiggers.net
19 January 2006
To: My Mito "Cousin"
Dear Jane,
So great to hear from you again.

It touches me deeply that you expressed concern about my depression. I can't remember any of my more immediate mitochondrial mates or my children doing that in many years. I do have one cousin, younger than I, who has been in a nursing home for several years due to severe depression who remembers me each Christmas with a card and a sentence of sympathy in recognition that I, too, am not having the time of my life.

There was a somewhat encouraging article in the local paper today about research that is showing why antidepressants just don't work for some people and, chemically, why those people are depressed in the first place. The article referred to a protein, which the writer identified as p11 - posited by some researchers to determine if a person can metabolize serotonin for mood benefit regardless of whether that serotonin is endogenous or comes from drugs. I doubt they'll have medications on the market that will work on p11 within my lifetime, but it is of some comfort to me to visualize women of future generations not having to live as many of us now do and have in the past.

There was a long article in yesterday's *Wall Street Journal* about a prominent figure in the financial world, a sufferer from recurrent severe depressions, who had just ended his own life despite having been through years of the best treatments and medications money could buy. In all the ways (to outward appearance, at least) by which the world measures a person to be a complete success at living, he had qualified. He had close friends, the esteem of the financial community, a loving wife, well-established grown children, and plenty of money. None of that had the positive effect on his sense of well-being that the poverty-stricken and faceless beings among us would imagine worldly success would bestow.

I think you may put your mind at rest that I might end my life before my time. This suicide victim was an older man. In my experience, women who commit suicide do so when they're young. After they get to be my age and older they're so used to feeling awful and they're so exhausted by decades of feeling awful they haven't got the energy or enthusiasm to do anything as pro-active as offing themselves. On top of that, it's been so many years since they've felt good or happy they forget what feeling good or happy was all about - at least I have. Once the memory of feeling good and happy is long gone, so is the torture of longing to feel that way again.

I think it's somewhat like having arthritis in your hands. When arthritis first hits, you have your former dexterity fresh in your mind, so your stiffness and pain is "in your face" with every familiar activity you attempt. After a few years of frustrating yourself by continuing to expect of your hands that they will operate efficiently, these expectations gradually reach some kind of expiration date and this lets you forget how satisfying it felt to be able to move your fingers freely and nimbly. Whenever you move your hands, you always have pain and stiffness, so over time, you get so used to that pain and stiffness it almost stops registering in your awareness. Depression is like that. You just gradually give up trying to make your personality work properly because you've long ago forgotten what a personality's working properly feels like.

As to whether or not my depression and numerous other physical and psychological problems are a result of mitochondrial disease, I can't make up my mind on that issue. I'm sure you must be very apprehensive about that as you and I share at least the same Hypervariable Region One mutations and might share others as well. You are younger than I, so you might be thinking that the complaints I'm now having might be in store for you in the future. Although I'm still at the most primitive level of understanding with regard to how mitochondria expresses itself physically, emotionally, and mentally in humans, I believe I do comprehend enough to be able to say, with some credibility, that the probability that you and I will deteriorate with age in similar ways and acquire the same diseases is next to nil. We already know that our most recent common ancestor had to have lived more distantly than five generations from us - most probably fifteen to fifty before that.

    In all the investigation I've completed so far, I've found no evidence that either of my HVR1 mutations is associated with any physical, neurological, or psychological complaint that I have. At this point, I'm leaning toward thinking my problems are due to some genetic material other than mitochondria (even though I've read that all cell energy comes from mito, and my cells seem to think they're producing energy for a hibernating bear instead of a human). It seems to me that one study associated mutation at position 519 of HVR1 with deafness in some geographically distant tiny population somewhere; however, my hearing is exceptionally good so I concluded that a person needn't worry about mitochondria-produced deafness unless she is in that population's haplogroup and subclade.

    I need to go back to www.familytreedna.com and www.mitosearch.org and look again at my genetic matches. Did I really write to you that my new perfect match has the same given name as our only other match, Liz? I must have really been in a confused state when I wrote that. I've been so under the weather for the past couple of weeks between being one-eyed and having my all-consuming rash, I can't even remember the name of the person I did see as our newly found additional match, but the name definitely wasn't Liz. I could well have been in a cognitive fog while I was trying to work online last week. There have been many times since mid-December when I have felt more like a ninety-five-year-old than a sixty-five.

The additional test that I paid familytree for was just the "mtDna Refine". I haven't had the HVR 2 test because the HVR 2 test, I reasoned, would not give me any additional matches besides you and Liz. Just to verify that, I wrote to the familytreedna site folks and got an answer back confirming. I chose the H haplogroup refine test instead of the HVR 2 test because the H haplogroup refine test was touted by familytreedna as being able to narrow down, geographically, my origins so that I wouldn't be looking at 40% of the population of Europe to see who my genealogical geographic mito-mama's mates might have been preceding g-g-g-g-grandmother Phoebe's appearance in America.

I had high hopes the H haplogroup refine test would tell me from which British Isle my mito line had come. When I got the test results and found out the computer had put me in Hl* (which I see as the equivalent of an H haplogroup recycle bin) I was profoundly disappointed. The long and the short of being identified as haplogroup H1* says to me, "Emmy, you don't exactly fit any of the H subclades, so we're putting you in the H misfits' haplogroup".

Your question about what career I would have chosen, given my druthers, was quite thought inspiring. What work do I wish I'd chosen? Although I never got paid a cent for the work to which I've given most of my time and energy over a lifetime (self-directed research and investigation) I'd have to say that I have done the work I most wanted to do - I think. Maybe I should call it obsessive/compulsive activity instead of work; because I'm not sure I spent my life in endless searches out of choice.

When I was a toddler, I can remember an elderly aunt sermonizing to me about my curiosity; giving me to understand that curiosity was anything but a good character trait for me to have, and that "curiosity killed the cat". I have paid for my unquenchable drive to know and experience the novel so many times and so dearly one would think I would put a strait-jacket on my doubting-Thomas self and take up being an in-the-box thinker and believer with all my being. My need to go where none of my fellow pack members has had any interest in going has resulted in my becoming more and more, in their eyes, just a loser.

That's not how I see my insatiable desire to get at knowledge though. In spite of all the lack of interest and low opinion my life explorations have inspired in family members and others who have comprised packs in which I've wanted to have good standing, I admire myself for insisting upon being led by my own brain instead of somebody else's even when thinking and behaving like a "good little girl" would undoubtedly have spared me a lot of suffering.

I've known few who have had innate analytical and evaluative skills sufficient to enable them to appreciate the courage and intellectual power of humans who aspire to a higher level of cognitive operation than to automatically assimilate beliefs and values fed to them by their packs. And, by the way, may I tell you how profoundly impressed I was when you mentioned that you had discarded the religious ideas of "the pack" when you were only a teenager? That strikes me as so courageous and so out-of-the-box for such a young person, I'm awed that you could do it.

Back to my treatise on non-conformity ... I trust my brain to give me those analytical and evaluative skills that few have - the skill to see great worth in people and their ideas when others can't recognize any value. I see the steadfast confidence I have in my own brain as the one thing about me that makes me extraordinary, admirable, wholesome, good, and a valuable creation. The reason behind my great self-estimate on this account, I imagine, had its nascence in the heart of my first-grade teacher and the sense I always got, when reading for her, that she experienced joy and admiration for me when she saw me "getting it".

Probably, work doesn't qualify as a career if you don't get paid for it and if it doesn't seem to benefit anyone other than yourself, so perhaps I'm not answering your question in keeping with the meaning you intended it to have.

I didn't foresee when I was transitioning into adulthood that I would be spending my life in work for which I'd receive no tangible reward - studying psychology and psychoanalysis and pursuing every possible strategy to gain awareness of the material in my unconscious. As I was working diligently on whatever I was working on, I was always imagining that someday those whose good opinion I most wanted would look at the great results my work would surely bring in the end and think me somebody really special. In every case, I thought I was engaged in work that would eventually bring me great admiration and worldly success.

Even when I realized I was getting nothing for my efforts but scorn and ostracism, without exception, from all sides, I kept gravitating to doing the work that something inside me compelled me to do. I dedicated myself obsessively to one research project for decades - the project to bring out of hiding memory of some childhood traumatic event that had surely occurred - all the while eking out my subsistence with hourly wage clerical work. Is that way of working evidence of pitiable mental illness (as most who have known me seem to think); or is that the way geniuses have pursued demystifying the mysterious since the world began?

Whatever job I ever had, including my recent brief profession as a speech-language pathologist, nothing ever captured my attention and mind-body involvement like immersing myself in some novel life experience and concurrently reading literature that would enlighten me as to what the unfamiliar life experience was all about.

One of my grandchildren's other grandmothers made a remark to me upon one of the few occasions when our paths crossed, as we sat in her spotlessly clean and carefully furnished house, about how she had never done much reading as she had always considered reading to be a frivolous waste of time. I perceived in the remark a desire on her part to deliver a put-down to me. I don't know whether it was there or not. Unfortunately, as you have said in one of your emails to me, most of society judges women by how spiffy and spotless and fashionable they and all their belongings look - not for the wisdom they've got inside their heads. That's far more likely to inspire hostility and put-downs than admiration.

So, when it comes to pats on my back for years of work to enlighten and educate myself, I have to give me my own pats because I'm not getting them from any relatives, neighbors, or old schooldays friends. A woman with a lot of money who practices "conspicuous consumption" is what impresses my family members, not a bookworm who doesn't keep her dishes washed and for whom almost every day is a bad hair day.

Nonetheless, I suppose I'm just as happy that I didn't try to make a career in research or investigation even if that is my spontaneous passion. If I felt obligated to do research because I had to do it to make money, I'd probably lose all enthusiasm for it. When you work with no hope of ever receiving worldly reward, just because you have a passion for that work, doesn't that lift your psychological core into a bit of a spiritual realm? ... or, have I spent too much time thinking about what I've read in the *Bhagavad-Gita*?

ROOTS, RELIGION AND DEPRESSION

LIONESS OF THE PRIDE

Mitochondria Multiplied

My compulsive verbosity is going to make it difficult for me to keep my written summation of my life as short and concise as Jane's, but I'm going to try. Here it is:

My relationship with my mother was so hurtful and disappointing that during my childhood and through most of my adulthood I entirely repressed conscious awareness that it was hurtful and disappointing. Consciously, until rather late in life, I had no idea that my childhood relationship with my mother was remarkably bad. The only woman in my family who had any interest in me (my father's older sister) asked me on one occasion when I was eight or so if my mother didn't prefer my older sister to me. I answered with full belief (consciously) that I was telling the truth when I responded that I didn't think my mother showed any favoritism where we (her children) were concerned. I had no idea at the time that I unconsciously harbored such rage against my mother that had I been a wild animal instead of a socialized human child I would probably have tried to kill her.

None of my three sisters, with some exceptions from my next younger, have seemed to entertain hatred for my mother at all ... quite the contrary. That seems to be one argument disproving a theory I might hatch that the mother-daughter hostility that arose between Mother and me was a result of mitochondrial inheritance. On the other hand, only I, of the four of us, ever undertook psychoanalytic therapy and self-examination. Had I not purposely gone looking for my repressed feelings, perhaps I too would have lived on forever seeing my mother as a sweet, caring, good, mother who unselfishly and unwaveringly put others' welfare ahead of her own. I would have retained her myth as my myth, I guess.

Continuing back in my mitochondrial line, as to my mother's mother, I don't remember the woman's ever speaking to me but twice, and each of those breaches in her shunning of me was brought on by something I did that aroused her ire so much that she interrupted her silent treatment of me for the length of time it took to give me a good dressing down. The year that I turned five Mother was seriously ill for several months, and my year-old sister and I stayed with Mother's parents during that time. Surely Grandmother must have spoken to me on more than these two occasions that I have mentioned, but I don't remember any other communication from her to me - definitely no positive communication.

I suspect Grandmother's own children got the same kind of treatment growing up. I remember my mother's voicing the belief that if adults paid any attention to a child it would spoil the child. I never knew my mother to express an original thought in all the years I was around her, so I feel confident this belief about the immorality of paying attention to a child came straight from her mother.

Pulling tiny bits and pieces out of various family members' accounts of what a wonderful woman Grandmother was, I don't see the warm and loving woman they're attempting to portray, I see a parent who was just as cold and inaccessible to her children as she was to me during the miserable months I was in her care. An uncle wrote about my grandmother's gathering her children together after suppers and reading to them from the Bible. This sounds all warm and fuzzy on the surface of it, but I feel sure the time Grandmother spent reading Scripture to her children and praying for them was not done with any eye to increasing their enjoyment of life. The only interest any members of Mother's family seem to have in anybody is whether or not they can get out of that person the words they want to hear about Salvation. What I've observed is that they live only to see themselves as having saved somebody; having led somebody to fall to their knees and beg Jesus to please forgive them for their terrible sins and enter into their heart so they won't have to spend eternity in Hell. In having eight children, Grandmother just produced her own captive audience to which she could play Apostle Paul evenings.

I feel that I see everywhere in Mother's family repetition of this refusal of parents to relate to their children and parents' redirecting of their children's bids upon them for love and attention to a mythical provider of nurturance, Jesus. A cousin wrote in a religious publication about leaving the house for school each morning while her mother sat at the kitchen table reading her beloved Bible.

If I write a letter to any cousin, I usually get no response at all; but if the cousin does write back, regardless of what I've written about, her response will be limited to a few words that focus on Salvation or something closely related. Members of Mother's clan don't seem to want to communicate with me at all, because I have no interest in endlessly repeating something that paraphrases "I found Christ. I've been saved. I was born again" on such-and-such a day in such-and-such a year.

I made the mistake of blurting out to an aunt something one of my children had done to me that had hurt me unbearably. She wrote to me about being hurt by something Grandmother did or didn't do to her, and how a therapist had opened her eyes to forgiving Grandmother in order to heal her pain. Along with the note came a book of two or three hundred pages which stated on every page the same thing, "Forgiving people who hurt you will erase your pain". That wasn't the end of it though. I'd given this aunt a foot in the door by breaking down and sobbing in her hearing, then telling her why. In Mother's line, if you should let it slip that you are hurting because another human is doing something hurtful to you, then you are the sinner; you are the one who needs correction, preaching, and teaching. That is because Jesus said things like, "… whosoever shall smite thee on thy right cheek, turn to him the other also", so that's the sort of thing you should be doing if someone is abusing you – not ratting your abuser out to someone from whom you hope to get support.

I had the misfortune to spend a day alone (most of the day, at least) with this aunt - whom I'll name Evangeline -

when I was in the fourth or fifth grade. Aunt Evangeline and my older sister decided that Evangeline would give my mother the great gift of relieving her of my burdensome presence for a day, and Aunt Evangeline took me by bus to Grandmother's. If the visit was unrewarding in some way for Aunt Evangeline, I didn't pick up on it. Evangeline was a student in a Bible college somewhere in the North at the time, with the end in mind of becoming a missionary, and perhaps she thought this would surely put a light for her in Grandmother's eyes. Maybe that didn't happen on this visit, and Evangeline felt let down that she hadn't been fussed over. Maybe that notion is all in my imagination. I have no idea what caused the depression into which Aunt Evangeline fell as we left Grandmother's to return to my house, but her depressed state of mind turned into a trauma for me.

We had to sit side by side on the bus, of course, but Aunt Evangeline seemed to be almost unable to bear having to be that close to me. She sat in the aisle seat and turned her body somewhat in that direction, keeping her eyes focused away from me. I suppose I was thinking that as I was by the window, and a person would normally look out the window while riding a bus, she was keeping her face turned away from me because she wanted to be free of awareness that I was there. Frequently she sighed deeply, and I took that too to be a sign that she felt mentally and physically almost overcome by having to sit beside someone as repulsive and disgusting as I.

As we had been preparing to leave my house that morning, Evangeline had appraised me head to toe with discernable disgust because I was making the trip to Grandmother's wearing a dirty dress and dirty socks. I didn't have any clothes to wear that were clean, and I got the message that it was I, not Mother, who was responsible for that. If I had been a wholesome, good child, I could see, I would have washed and ironed my own clothes; not expected my poor mother to do what I should have done for myself.

Now, whether Evangeline really did find me so disgustingly dirty she couldn't stand me, or whether that was all in my imagination and Evangeline was really depressed and preoccupied with some issue that had nothing to do with me; to me her depressed state was all about me. We rode mile after mile with me trying to will myself to merge into the bus wall beside me. I was rigid with shame that my presence beside her was causing Aunt Evangeline to suffer such disgust; disgust she wouldn't have had to endure on and on through this long ride had I been the clean child I should have been, I thought.

The trip back home was only a distance of fifty miles or so, but it felt to me as if we were not even moving and that we would go on not even moving forever. After what seemed like hours, Evangeline roused herself as if she suddenly had thought of a way to find escape from the terrible effect I was having upon her. She opened her briefcase of missionary preaching/teaching objects and publications and began to teach Salvation to me.

As I said, I was a fourth- or fifth-grader and had been in Sunday school and church every Sunday since before I could walk or talk. Almost every summer I went through two weeks of Bible school. I must have heard about who Jesus was and why God sent him and what I had to do to keep from going to Hell a few hundred times and had comprehended what a person was supposed to think and do to get saved from the time I was about four. After all, does a person really have to have John 3:16 repeated to her hundreds of times and explained to her hundreds of times before she is able to grasp what "For God so loved the world ..." (etc., etc., etc.) all means? Aunt Evangeline and all the other of Mother's relatives to whom I've had exposure seem to think so. So, Aunt Evangeline shook off her black despair of the moment by donning her servant-of-Christ hat and proceeding to follow the charge of "our Lord and Savior" to preach Salvation to the ignorant and lost - me.

Of course, high IQ or not, I didn't think I had the right to correct Aunt Evangeline's assumption that I was ignorant of what she was teaching me ... the right to say, "Aunt Evangeline, I learned all that in Sunday school and summer Bible school by the time I was four. And, besides that, every morning at school the teacher reads to us from the New Testament, and she always reads from Matthew, Mark, Luke, or John, so if I hadn't learned about God and Jesus and Salvation in church, I would have learned about that in school."

Here was a person so blindly averse to having any "soul" connection to me, so needful of seeing me as one of the ignorant "lost sheep" whom God in Jesus had appointed her to try to save, that she couldn't allow any particle of the contents of my mind to get through to her mind. My experience of other members of Mother's family have been the same - each wants to see herself or himself as a Paul-like figure in a First Century world where everybody on earth (except them) is ignorant of who Jesus was or is unless they teach them.

Aunt Evangeline once told me that Mother had shared

with her how she had met Christ and been saved as a teenager. If that communication weren't enough to put a little dampener on Evangeline's clung-to fantasy that Mother wouldn't have adequate knowledge of Salvation unless she, Evangeline, fed it to her, I would think Mother's frequent letters to this sister would have made some impression. Mother was a member of a Christian church, was there every Sunday, and got herself to almost any kind of church service that came up between Sundays. I'm sure she wrote something about her church activities in every letter she ever sent to anyone.

Still, Evangeline bombarded Mother by mail with literature from her own evangelical sources throughout my Mother's lifetime as if Mother wouldn't know anything she needed to know about getting herself saved right unless she, Evangeline, sent her some kind of publication from her own denomination explaining it to her. Did Mother find Evangeline's flood of religious literature insulting? You bet she did. Did Mother ever even hint to Evangeline that she didn't feel she needed to be taught and preached to? She didn't.

In my mother's family, the only way in which I've ever seen or heard members relate to one another is through the speaking or writing or passing back and forth of evangelical-style religious utterances and stories. Telling one of my mother's relatives that you really are not as completely ignorant about Jesus and God as they assume you are, and that you don't think you need for them to lead you to God or Christ - that you think you might be able to get there without their guidance - will put an end to your relationship with them almost immediately. As I said, they need to see themselves as playing pivotal roles in the preparation of the world for the final judgment, and if you aren't going to play the role they want you to play in their play, you cease to be of interest to them.

When I set myself the task of giving a short summation of my life in keeping with the concise summation of her life that Jane sent in email to me - the email contents I quoted earlier - I doubted that I could stay on task, and here I am many pages later having found, once again, that my cognitive processes work in only one way - freely associating and nomadic. I blame the sessions I spent many years ago in Freudian-paradigm, psychoanalytically oriented psychotherapy for my inability to think or act in the sort of focused, straight-line manner that I see in Jane's abstract of the highlights of her life.

Upon further reflection though, I have to realize that I was already spacey as a four- or five-year-old child. What the free association verbalizing in therapy did for me was to erase all spontaneous repair of that spaciness that had occurred in intervening years (I think).

MITOCHONDRIA MULTIPLIED

Stop Attacking - I'm Dead Already

Throughout the years in which I have envisioned writing this book, I have seen myself producing a work with organization, cohesiveness, and coherence. I have imagined that each chapter would have a novel topic which would be launched at chapter's beginning with an adequate explanation to readers as to where I intended to go; a topic fleshed out with all pertinent details but pursued without deviation into extraneous matter and summed up neatly at chapter's end. I intended for the book to have a central theme and for all chapters to contribute to that theme.

Now I have a hodge-podge of floppies and CDs dating from the mid 1990s as well as many folders of paper copies of chapters I began but was never able to complete. As soon as I began the attempt to make my fingers translate the focal points of my thoughts to corresponding printed words, the focal points seemed to flee my mind or vanish much like dreams do when one awakens. Instead of sticking with the idea to which I had intended to devote myself when I sat down and opened a new document, I would find myself, over and over, in a mental free association state where I was wandering away from my original idea in the same way that one wanders away from a home page at an internet site by clicking on a link.

Seeing this go on month after month, year after year, as I have clung to my dream of writing and readying a book for publication, has plunged me into such despair on so many occasions that I have often wondered why I don't forget all about my dream that I can do this, and fall, instead, into doing the only kind of work upon which I do seem to be able to keep focused and to sustain effort - that work is digging out or pulling up weeds ... anywhere, anytime. That is not the work to which the executive functions of my brain want to be confined, but my muscles, tendons, and bones seem to be violently opposed to doing anything to cooperate with the desires of my conscious mind. My physical body seems to be as inaccessible to my conscious will as the security programs on my computer are to me after they've been corrupted by viruses, worms, or hackers. I assume that what has put my ability to perform beyond the reach of my desire to perform is analogous.

That this "paralysis" has genetic roots seems clear to me. Recently we all have had the sorrow of seeing on TV scenes from the areas around the Indian Ocean which were over-washed by the tsunami waves. In one brief interview, a man stood in a sea of rubble with a look on his face and a slump to his body that bespoke shock. The few gestures he made seemed aimless and automatic. Behind him were many other people who were working with items of rubble in what appeared to me to be a purposeful way. They seemed to be engaged in the task of salvaging whatever items they might be able to use and cleaning away what they perceived to be useless rubbish. The man being interviewed was almost sobbing as he said, "I'm not able to make myself do anything. Before this happened I had so much energy. I was always working. Now I can't make myself do anything." How I felt for this man who wanted so desperately to be working alongside the others of his community as they pursued the common goal of getting something of their former lives back.

What, in the active, performing survivors enabled them to put their bodies in motion to accomplish the good goal that their minds envisioned while the man being interviewed was just as desirous as they of getting the mess cleaned up and some kind of normalcy restored but couldn't get himself in gear? To state his dilemma in the vernacular, he was standing around with his thumb up his ass while everyone else in camera range was doing something productive and beneficial for the community as a whole. The man's frustration with his inability to make himself perform at the task which his fellowmen were performing with purpose and focus was obvious. If he wasn't feeling self-loathing already, he soon would be if he couldn't "snap out of" his immobilized state. If those around him who were working with vigor hadn't begun expressing their scorn for his lack of contribution to the common effort at the time of the interview, they soon would be, and the chorus would only grow as his lethargic state dragged on, intensifying his paralysis and his mental torment with every disgusted look or reproachful comment.

    This man had probably lost no more in the disaster than all those around him who could get their bodies to do what their conscious thoughts wanted their bodies to do. Why couldn't he make himself work when they could? What other answer could there be than that his brain chemistry and function differed from theirs? If I could have any influence over researchers' endeavors as they attempt to discover the underlying etiology of the most incapacitating forms of depression, I would tell them to examine the brains of animals who "play dead" when frightened. This phenomenon seems related to the interviewed tsunami survivor's hated inertia as well as to my own. There are other animal instinctual behaviors, such as hibernation, that I suspect of being related to human manifestations of depression, but "playing dead" seems to me to be the instinctual state most applicable. I'm placing "play dead" terms in quotation marks because the words imply that the animal consciously wills his frozen state. The animal isn't willfully "playing" anything and neither are human beings overcome by debilitating depression.

    On the occasion when I saw, at close range, a possum that was being attacked by my dogs, I had an opportunity to see just what might be going on with this awful symptom of human depression referred to as "leaden paralysis". When my dogs began to bark and screech so vociferously that I knew something other than the ordinary was happening in my yard, I ran out of my house and saw that they were jumping at something that was just at the front edge of my work shed. Rushing up, I saw that they were attempting to get at a possum that had his back to a hole under the shed that was too shallow for him to retreat into completely, and that the possum couldn't go forward to escape because my two dogs were in his face. The possum had his mouth, which was amazingly huge, spread open as widely as that of an aroused alligator. His mouth was lined with pointed teeth which, together with his strident hissing, were intimidating enough to keep the dogs from going in for a kill.

Analyzing the situation, I quickly concluded that the only way to save the possum's life was to get the dog carrier, put the carrier with the door open between the dogs and the possum, then push the open door of the carrier toward the possum until he would have no choice but to go in, whereupon I would haul the carrier up, close the door, and transport the possum to an area where the dogs couldn't reach him. Unfortunately, I was thinking of myself as a big strong savior of the weak and the helpless, but the possum was not tuned in to my myth. The perception that I was saving the possum was all in my mind, not in the possum's. When I pushed the opening of the cage toward him thinking that he would be forced in, he jumped sideways, evading the cage completely and dashed away across the lawn.

My rat terrier, who is hardly bigger than this poor creature was, had his jaws clamped onto a mouthful of the possum's flesh in an instant. Before I could make a move to intervene, my terrier had the possum's whole body off the ground and was shaking him with such force and such amplitude of oscillation that I knew, had the possum been human, he would have sustained irreparable brain damage. With screaming and shouting and clutching I managed to jerk my terrier back, forcing him to drop the possum which fell to the ground like a corpse. Grasping my dogs by whatever body part I could hold on to I got them into the shed (where I would have put them in the beginning if I had any capacity for quick-thinking) and locked them inside. The possum continued to lie in the same spot, unmoving, all the while I was containing the dogs. He certainly looked dead. However, most of us know that possums "play dead" to save themselves from predators, and having seen the teeth in this creature's mouth, I wasn't about to take the risk of picking him up with my bare hands only to have him possibly come to life and slash me wickedly.

   I found a shovel and after some huffing and puffing got him situated on it centrally enough to be able to cart him out of the dogs' fenced enclosure and into the woods. Dropping him on the leaves, I looked down at his cadaverous body. His mouth was agape, his lips slack, his teeth showing; not purposefully now, but rather as if there were no muscle action going on that would automatically hold his mouth shut. His body was drawn up in a fetal position with his little fingers and toes in the retracted position which we are accustomed to seeing in dead chickens. I pushed at him a little with the shovel, still trying to ascertain as to whether he was alive or dead, and seeing that his extremities sprang back to their drawn-up position when I forcibly extended them, realized he had muscle tone. Recognizing that rigor mortis might bring about such muscular rigidity, but that rigor mortis hadn't had time to set in, even if my terrier had killed him, I concluded that he was very much alive, and that his survivalist's instincts, which were imitating in his best interests the appearance of death, were working very, very well. My findings were confirmed an hour or so later when I looked out at the spot where I had laid him and saw that he was no longer there.

Did that possum consciously recognize a need to feign death, develop an intention to do so, and then purposely affect the physical signs of death? I find it absurd to imagine that any conscious recognition of need or conscious plan to deal with need came to this possum's awareness when my dog sprang on him. It all took place so fast I couldn't even keep up with what was happening as it happened. Had I been able to, I would have grabbed my terrier before the terrier grabbed the possum. The possum's intention (if he had such a thing as a conscious intention) was to escape my cage and my dogs by running as fast as his little legs could cover the ground between us and the fence under which he had crawled to get into the yard in the first place. That he went "dead" in the fraction of a second that it took for my dog to grab him out of mid-run had to have been a state into which he was plunged instantly by automatic brain function.

That possum's brain was hardwired before his birth, maybe before his ancestors' births thousands of years ago, to proprioceptively pick up the feel of a predator's teeth puncturing his skin and to relay that perception to a cerebral motor control strip where "move" signals being disseminated to all parts of the possum's body from that site get switched to "freeze" signals in nanosecond time. The "freeze" signals - electrical, chemical, or both - are automatically sent to still-moving muscles, tendons, bone, skin, and eyes where they bring an instant shutdown to the "flee" program and open a more efficacious one; that program being "You can stop attacking now, predator.

You've finished the job. I'm dead already". It is my belief that something completely analogous to this is happening in my brain when I attempt to carry through to completion work of the quality and complexity that my administrative/executive prefrontal consciousness tells me is entirely within reason to expect of myself ... and can't.

What has happened within my brain's structure and function, I suspect, is that very early on in my life my brain ascertained automatically, instinctually, that I was in a situation that I couldn't flee, that I hadn't the resources to fight, but that I had to deal with in some way. My observations and experience tell me that when one is in pain or terribly frightened, one's unconscious store of animal instincts, a store of survival programs accumulated through perhaps millions of years of evolution, begins to compulsively try different subroutines beginning with the preferred first. When we've gone through "fight", we've gone through "flee", and we've hit "feign death", I don't think our brains can ever go back to using "fight" or "flee" as our primary strategies again.

Getting down to the subroutine "feign death" is an admission by the whole system - brain, muscle, the works - that we lack what it takes to mount an effective defense. It seems to me to be an admission by the whole body of weakness and inadequacy. I think that as long as we can survive through the use of strategies that leave us free to move our muscles, bones, tendons, vocal cords, and all other classes of body parts to the greatest extent they can move and with the greatest power they are capable of exerting, we grow in self-image and self-assurance. I think that when these active measures fail and we are dropped into "feign death", something psychologically the opposite happens to us.

If we can protect ourselves by meeting a threat and fighting it with all stops out until we've intimidated that threat into turning tail and leaving, we gain some kind of great spiritual inner fill-up; a stomach, grit, the security to go about our business without having to keep scanning our environs for danger. In other words, we don't have to attend to every sight and sound; we can keep our focus on that which is providing us with enjoyment. Or, alternatively, if we discover that we needn't fear threats because we have the ability to flee faster than our attacker can pursue, that too is empowering.

Now, true to form, I guess I have wandered pretty far afield from the topic I began some pages ago which was to be an apology to you and an enumeration of reasons why I can't do right by you, the reader, and give you material to read that doesn't evoke for you the image of being caught in an endless loop in a computer program which has been constructed by a person too technologically incompetent to be attempting programming. As I keep trying to bring some order to the disorder, I'm rather of the opinion that I'm a little uncertain what the point of the chapter is, myself, even while I'm attempting to lay it out for you with clarity. The chaos in my writing, I'm afraid, is not something I now am able to fix, nor will I be able to in the future. Perhaps it is the umbrella subject, depression, which brings on the chaos in the writing.

Out of all the books I've read by authors who absolutely had the answers, and all the therapists I've consulted who were of the highest professional caliber, and all the authoritative advice I've received from those who knew just what I ought to do to cure myself, I don't believe I've seen much reality checking in any of it. What I believe I've seen, rather, is a global and persistent denial of befuddlement over the components of clinical depression and why one person emerges from it and another can't. All the people from whom I've heard, who have come across as the most confident that they were at the pinnacle of understanding, look to me now as if they were nowhere nearer comprehension of the condition in which they pictured themselves experts than my ancestor physicians were when they applied leeches to the bodies of sick people who needed more blood, not less.

My writings probably seem like wanderings without any clear goal because they probably are wanderings in which I have no clear idea of where I'm going. Through writing down my thoughts with the visual image before me of a few other human beings possibly wanting to sift through my thoughts along with me, I hope to discover ideas, beliefs, processes, methods - whatever - that will make the voyage or trek or safari profitable for you, the reader, and for me.

Having attention deficit disorder might be one reason that I find it almost impossible to keep any work that I begin from undergoing a sea change from a well-formed plan into chaos. What was the origin, in me, of attention deficit disorder? Nature or nurture? In my inability to stay on track I see the behaviors of an animal who knows that it doesn't have the resources to effectively defend itself and who therefore keeps looking in every direction at all times to make sure she is not being stalked. Who, pray tell, is stalking me? Not a soul at the present time. I don't mean to imply that there is a real person who is dedicated to jumping me. However, once upon a time, in my earliest years of life, there was someone who was always watching for any opportunity to jump me when I was going about my business in a happy manner and to deliver such a shaming to me that death would have been a welcome escape for me.

I have to consider that I possibly am unable to maintain focus on a goal long enough to reach it because I incorporated, very early in life, into my brain's modus operandi, the process of turning such a scornful eye on my performance at any job that I lose the heart to stick with it. I can't relax and accept that the work I'm producing is good and worthwhile, because during its years of greatest growth my brain was consumed with developing neurons and synapses for coping with being shamed, slapped, and having my actions described to me as contemptible by a much older, much larger sibling, who, most of the time, found no reason to hold back in expressing her hatred of me. Perhaps the instinct of all animals to mimic those behaviors which they observe in their caretakers and pack mates came automatically into my repertoire of instincts, and my unconscious, sixty years later, is telling me to feel disgust with myself and everything I do, just as my sister did when my brain was developing.

I've given a great deal of thought to how fear of my sister's psychological control over how I and others perceived me has stayed with me throughout life as unalterably as the color of my eyes or the pattern of my finger prints. The terror that took over my soul as I witnessed repeatedly how she could own any relationship I wanted to have with anyone, if she chose to do that, is a terror from which I have never escaped even though I have avoided actual contact with this sibling since my twenties. Thanks to that great process of transference, however, my fear of her contempt and my greater fear upon seeing her get anyone whose aid she wanted to enlist to regard me as scornfully as she, has been a fear I've revisited in almost every work or love relationship I've ever attempted. She demonstrated, to my horror, that my own mother wouldn't want to have anything to do with me if she didn't want her to. That was the coup de grâce for me.

My sibling's physical abuse of me along with her ridiculing, sneering remarks to me and dehumanizing stories about me told in my presence were largely delivered because the abuse and shaming were so satisfying to my mother, other members of her family, and to my sibling's friends. The extent to which she diminished me as a human being was the extent to which she grew in stature in their eyes. Had it not been for this, had my sister's abuse and shaming of me been met by my mother and her family members with disapproval and condemnation instead of with admiration, I believe my self-image and self-esteem would have had a chance to survive.

As it was, I suspect that the personality having traits of joyousness and exuberance that might have been mine, had been so attacked and mortally wounded by the time I reached the age of five or six, that thereafter it never had a chance to emerge, for long, from its "feign death" state. Between my third and fourth year, I seem to remember, there arose in me for awhile, when my sister was deprived for a few months of my mother's encouragement of her abuse of me, a beautiful, happy, lovable child, but that child was one that my sibling and my mother would have none of. A child who thought that she was beautiful and lovable just as her older sister was, was one the older sister was not going to allow to exist if she could help it. Fortunately for my older sister's development, with a mother who believed that a smaller, weaker person should give bigger, more aggressive people anything they wanted, she didn't have to allow my good self-image to continue to live.

It's tempting to detail here all the reasons why my mother and older sister could not tolerate my having self-esteem or a good self-image. Farther along or in other chapters I'll attempt to explore some of that. In short, they hadn't received the self-image nourishment they themselves needed. They were starving in that regard, and in such circumstances, self-image cannibalism is the means of self-image self-feeding to which humans invariably turn. Women have a hard time finding nourishment for self-esteems, I think, unless it is at the expense of other women.

It was terribly unfortunate for me that my mother, most of her family members, and the playmates that my sister wanted to impress were very impressed when she talked to me in front of them as if I were so disgusting, bad, and ignorant that I wasn't fit to be in their company. She saw herself as a dedicated defender of the common good, performing a great service for those who didn't know me, when she educated them about my rotten character and deceitful self-representations. Her audiences generally believed the myth she created for them. My sister and those who bought what she was selling weren't any better or worse than most humans. This "we have an enemy in our midst" maneuver goes on around us all the time and always has. Most of the time it's projection operating (self-deception), but that doesn't keep it from working well.

My sister perceived herself as helping our asleep-at-the-wheel family members and acquaintances by disabusing them of their misguided predisposition to regard me with a positive attitude. The message she got across to her audiences was, "If you were as clever an analyst of underlying human character as I, or if you were as infallible in your recognition of quality as I, you would be able to see that Emmy isn't quality. And, you would see right away as I do, that badness, dirtiness, ignorance, inferiority, and repulsiveness underlie that first good impression she's made on you."

Those of us humans who buy into myths of this sort, and we do it all the time, are hooked into doing so and into acting in concert with a myth-creator's designs because we all have a fear that a person pointing out a great threat has access to some higher source of knowledge and insight than we do. We are prone to dismiss our own judgment when a myth-fabricator confidently presents herself or himself to us as possessing a higher level of knowledge than we about our fellow human that they are describing as such a lowlife and such a deceiver of good, trusting people and to jump on the myth-creator's bandwagon so he or she won't look down with scorn and hostility on us, too. This, I think, is how movements that have resulted in the torture of innocents have gotten started. A myth-creator begins telling anyone who will listen that there is a person (or persons) who is masquerading as good who is really bad and who constitutes a threat to unsuspecting people because ... And, the myth grows from there until the innocent is attacked en masse.

In my case, being incessantly informed of my badness by my sister, mother, grandmother, older cousins, and anyone else my sister could influence (and there were many) was, to me, what my dog's puncturing the skin of the possum with his teeth was to the possum. Animals may have real coverings such as dense hair, thick hide, shells, and the like to protect them, but I think that human beings are dependent for all their protection on virtual coverings - their images and self-images. My awareness, throughout my childhood, that my image and self-image were owned and controlled by a sibling who hated me about 99 percent of the time was an ever-present awareness, I think, that altered the course of my brain's development. It is possible that my genetic inheritance is such that I would have developed attention deficit disorder, body dismorphic disorder, visual-spatial deficits, musical notation dyslexia, social phobia, chronic "leaden paralysis" and depression, allergies, and assorted other problems with or without the highly successful campaign to destroy my image and self-image that my sister undertook while I was still in infancy - but, I don't think so.

I believe that my brain, in the first few years of my life, began to funnel all resources into preparing for the recurring experience of seeing those humans whose good opinion I so desperately wanted, look at me with expressions that changed from smiles and acceptance to distaste and rejection as my sister regaled them with accounts of disgusting things I'd done that had put her capacities for dealing with revulsion to the ultimate test. Throughout my childhood, I saw so much of the expression she put on her face to show me that I was pathetic and disgusting, and I saw that sneering, scornful expression turned on me by so many who seemed to think that mimicking my sister's attitudes toward me made them cool, that the horror of it influences almost all my thoughts and actions even when I'm not consciously aware of it at all, up to this day. In fact, until recently, I haven't even seen clearly how chronically feeling, on an unconscious level, that I am bad and repulsive and others clean, or else that I am clean and it is others who are bad and repulsive, has prevented my ever being able to sustain any close relationships.

I didn't realize how overwhelmed my whole system is with this sense of being offensive and repulsive, even after living with this horror governing my life for almost all of it, until I began to have, last year, some deep tissue massages to relieve the pain of hard upper-torso muscle contractions that wouldn't release even with ice, vibration, or medication. As the massage therapist rotated my limbs, I became aware that my limbs were resisting even while, consciously, I could think of no reason why they were doing that. Consciously, I thought I was cooperating with the therapist fully. I could think of no reason for not doing so. When my limbs didn't want to go where he obviously wanted them to go, I had to recognize that some part of my brain, with which I wasn't in touch, was trying to accomplish something I didn't know anything about. After two or three sessions I realized what my body was trying to do. It was trying to hold my repulsiveness in so that my repulsiveness wouldn't get out of my body and disgust the massage therapist.

Finally, I got the courage up to tell him what was happening with my muscles. I could hardly bring myself to do it because I was sure that even talking about the reason my muscles were resisting his control would make him aware of my repulsiveness if he hadn't seen it already. I wavered between bringing the subject to the light of day and keeping it hidden. The motor control area of my brain was obviously instructing my muscles to hold in all my repulsiveness that might spill out and alienate the therapist. I figured that now that I was consciously aware of what my cerebral motor strip had been unconsciously doing, I could consciously make a decision that I wasn't any more repulsive than a lot of other women and didn't have to go on shrinking when someone touched me.

However, I never was able to arrive at the conclusion that I really am not repulsive and offensive to people. When the message therapist assured me that I was not repulsive, I still could not shake the fear that I really was repulsive and that he was just trying to be kind by assuring me I wasn't. I can see that I either don't believe people when they tell me I'm attractive or else I think that they really do find me attractive because they have the discernment of Neanderthals. I had hoped that talking about my problem with my massage therapist might dislodge that overpowering sense of being distasteful to clean people of high standards and make it go away. It didn't. Now that I'm consciously aware that I'm terrified of seeming repulsive to people, my muscles have loosened up well and I'm no longer in constant pain because of their automatic contractions. That's good, but now the problem is that having brought my unconscious sense of being disgusting and repulsive into my full awareness, I'm really afraid of people and don't want to be around them at all if I can avoid it.

Getting back to what I believe to be the originating source of this state of affairs, I'll elucidate a bit farther on my sister's mythmaking about me that I bought into so completely as a child, although I might have already explored this subject ad finitum. Perhaps the insight that I have into how my self-image became so bad so early in life could be of help to others in understanding more about the dynamics of the development and maintenance of bad self-images. Perhaps I don't understand the subject myself as fully as I want to believe I do and am being automatically propelled into pursuing the topic to some closure or peace of mind because it's unfinished business that keeps calling for a finish. For whatever reason, I don't seem to be able to, as yet, let the explaining of my sister's and my relationship rest.

My sister saw herself, throughout our childhoods and into adulthood, as having been endowed with a moral duty to expose me to unaware humanity for the substandard person that I was. Each time she was successful in influencing another human being to see me as pathetic and flawed where before they had been thinking of me as pretty neat (and it looked to me as if she always has been unfailingly successful at this), she came away with the conviction that she had carried out the great moral duty that was hers to carry out. Under her influence, people jumped on the idea that I wasn't fit to be "one of them" with the zest demonstrated by Hitler's followers as they joined him in demonizing the Jews. When my mother, my cousins, and my sister's friends supported her in diminishing me, their self-images swelled. They felt themselves to be bigger, stronger, to be allied with the leader of an important and righteous cause. Like Hitler and his followers, they imagined themselves to be working together to defend the good, the clean, the wholesome, the more civilized against a contaminant which would bring them down if not fought and banished. When my sister pointed out my shortcomings to me in my mother's presence, she perceived her enlightening of me as to my unsavoriness as being helpful to a wonderful, taken-advantage-of person, my mother, who was being preyed upon by a big ugly parasite, me.

Most of us human beings do entertain this sort of myth at our core. We like to think that we are the threatened ones, valiantly gathering together good people to fight those who are bad. However, in most cases, when we launch these campaigns, we are victims of our own predatory instinct to deceive others and ourselves. On a level of our being at which most of us never look, we enjoy seeing a weaker, smaller creature being mauled by a large aggressive one. Of course, in our minds, it is always other, bad human beings who admire and support bullies, never us. We believe that we are on the side of the gentle, giving, healing providers of our society, if that's not what we are ourselves. It's other human beings who are the bullies and the bully-supporters, and it's our job, the job of us good individuals, to lend a hand in getting them set straight. I, of course, also see myself as being one of the good sorts of humans whose duty it is to straighten out the bad. The message that I too am a pack predator that sides by instinct with the most aggressive of other predators came clear to me recently as I watched a cheetah documentary on TV.

The mother cheetah was teaching her juvenile cubs to hunt, and as is the case with human parents when demonstrating their competencies to their offspring, Momma Cheetah must have entertained an image of herself that vastly exceeded her real size and strength. She outran and attacked a full-grown springbok which appeared to me to be in the prime of life; optimally nourished and blessed with huge horns. The springbok was far larger than she and she could not pull him to the ground. Her cubs were clueless as to how they might assist her and milled around her and the springbok throughout the cheetah mother's long struggle to bring the springbok down. The cheetah's effort to overpower the animal that she thought would be her prey lasted many minutes. As time wore on, it looked as if she were prevailing in stamina, exhausting his strength, and that she would drop him. Then, in a stunning reversal of fortune, the springbok surged forward, dragging the cheetah off her center of gravity and rendering her helpless. Her grip being broken, the springbok's head was free to move again, and with his horns he stabbed her through the side, wounding her mortally.

As the narrator explained what was transpiring, and as I saw the springbok repeatedly stab the helpless mother cheetah with his horns, I was horrified. I think I even was saying aloud, "No, no, this can't be happening, no!" After the springbok backed off, the mother cheetah arose and limped slowly into the thicket adjacent to the site of the battle as the narrator told us, the viewers, that with the mother cheetah dead, all her cubs would also die as they lacked the experience as hunters to be able to provide for themselves. The last scene of the documentary segment showed the mother's carcass lying on the ground with the great wound in her side exposed.

I took stock of how emotionally distraught I had become over the mother cheetah's inability to kill the springbok and over the turn of events that I had taken for granted would never happen. As I had watched the drama unfold, I had been assuming all the while that no cameraman or nature documentarian would ever show us, the viewers, a predator mother being killed by her intended prey as her offspring looked on. As I realized how emotionally involved I had been in the cheetah's efforts to kill the springbok, a grazer that eats only plant material, I had to recognize that I had, at no time, had any rush of compassion for the springbok. All the while that I had been anticipating the springbok's impending demise, my guts hadn't churned, and I had not once had the "Oh, no, no, no" response of brain and breath that had overtaken me when it became clear to me that the springbok was mortally wounding the cheetah.

Then my thoughts turned from how shaken I was over the mother cheetah's death to how blah my emotions were toward the springbok who had miraculously saved himself from becoming the carcass on the ground that the cheetah now was. I had to realize that I hadn't cared a whit about the intended victim; no empathy, no sympathy, no compassion, no thrill when he suddenly came to life and effected a rout and a defeat of his attacker that was truly stunning.

My own lack of concern for the springbok's pain answered some questions in my mind as to why my mother, my cousins, my sister's friends and acquaintances, my aunts and uncles, and others have felt no urge to support and defend me at those times when my sister has set about to demonstrate to them that I am a pathetic and valueless person whose inadequacies should be highlighted. I believe I can comprehend why humans fall right in line when a Hitler or an Osama Bin Laden or a politician or a local housewife creates a myth about themselves in which their crusade is righteous and the target of their aggression is someone who really needs to be stamped out.

I had to also question, in myself, why I had thought no documentary would show intended prey turning on his predator attacker and killing her. The answer has to be that although this must happen rather often in the wild, nature hosts must not want to film it and we viewers must not want to see it. If we humans didn't want to see powerful predators overtaking terrified, fleeing grazers, there wouldn't be so much programming on TV showing that. I guess in spirit we are right there with those predators, getting a surge of adrenalin from watching them because some ancient part of our brain knows what hunting down and killing prey feels like and identifies. I suspect we have a gut, rather cold, compassionless feeling for passive, timid people and animals and a great instinctual rush that smacks of worship for those who attack them.

What doubt can I have but that my mother and members of her family who witnessed my sister's crushing of my self-image and who joined the cause were of this ilk. Deny it or confess it, face it or hide from it, we enjoy seeing weaker things hurt. Those of the relatives about whom I am writing, who wanted to be a part of my older sister's ongoing attack on my self-esteem, were like the members of a predator pack who never make the first attacking move themselves, but who, seeing that an aggressive pack member has identified a victim and is after it, throw everything they have within themselves into helping the leader accomplish his kill. When a human becomes the focus of this kind of enjoined campaign there is seldom an out. Every use of brain or muscle to escape will only expose another part of one's being to attack. Perhaps, as in the case of organisms like possums, it serves a survival purpose to close down functions: metabolism, muscle enervation, pre-frontal cortex executive function-whatever would cause one to move. Perhaps that is "leaden paralysis".

The "feign death" survival strategy of animals like the possum and the "leaden paralysis" condition of us depressed humans in whom this damned shutdown gets involuntarily invoked in the presence of every little stress, could have, I think, common denominators. When I discovered that my possum, which appeared to be dead, had muscle tone and was obviously using muscle to draw limbs back toward his body when I stretched them out, I saw that "playing dead" was not an inaction. Probably my despised "leaden paralysis" isn't either. The possum wasn't doing nothing. He was at every second doing something. He was restraining his muscles from doing what one would expect of a terrified living thing which had just been through the kind of experience he had. How did he keep himself from trembling uncontrollably? How did he keep his sides from heaving in response to his body's great need for oxygen to replace that he had expended in running? The answer has to be: with great, sustained effort consuming considerable energy.

Considering his physical response to his brush with death helps me see my accursed, everlasting, no-reprieve "leaden paralysis" as not an absence of energy but rather as an ongoing effort, by some ancient-brain instinct of mine over which I seem to have no influence, to prevent my body - all the moving parts of my body, at least - from doing what my conscious mind would like for it to do. In fact, at times when I've tried to force myself to do little jobs around my home or related to my personal appearance that I knew would result in my having a much improved attitude toward myself and my life, I've encountered self-opposition that has grown to such extremes that when I persisted in my efforts to accomplish the task, I've ended up damaging and destroying materials and tools with which I was working and one time injured my hand quite seriously.

There seems to be something about the "play dead" instinct, the instinct that comes up automatically as in the case of my possum or possibly in humans who get socked with the "leaden paralysis", that I think is the human equivalent of "play dead", that puts the user on a downhill course, even when the "play dead" instinct works and the accosted victim-user survives the fray. As I said, my possum, who had been bitten severely and shaken like a rag doll by my dog, came out of his "I'm in rigor mortis" state when he sensed that he was no longer in danger. The possum's senses must have continued to work well all the time he was "playing dead" and his brain must have continued to process all the information his senses were sending to it, else he wouldn't have known when it was safe to go into motion again and scurry away from the spot where I had laid him. I wonder if the possum felt as awful while he was in his posture of muscle rigidity and non-movement as we humans are who are in the grips of "leaden paralysis"? I believe it was a day or two later that I saw the body of a roadkilled possum on the highway near my house. Was that the possum whose rescue from the dogs I bungled so badly? I'll never know for sure, but I imagine it was.

If one could voluntarily choose the strategy of feigning death to survive, I don't think permanent harm to one's psyche would result. I've heard people tell of their intentionally pretending to be dead after being wounded by an attacker. This act has apparently served them well, and I don't recall hearing of any adverse psychological effects. Involuntary, automatic, instinct launched freezing is, I think, an entirely different matter. I see these shutdowns as having a disastrous effect on brain function. Assuming that the dead possum I saw on the road was the same one I had earlier hoped I'd saved, was my possum's being struck and killed by a car just something that would have happened to him anyway, even if he hadn't gone through his traumatic encounter with my dogs and my misguided rescue? Or, had his alertness to his environment been compromised by a disruption in his brain's natural operations - a disruption caused by the instinct which came upon him automatically at his moment of no escape, causing his brain to reverse a natural mode of energy expenditure and to utilize energy in holding muscles back instead of sending muscles into motion? Had "playing dead" had a lasting effect on his alertness to information coming in from his surroundings? Perhaps it was being shaken by my terrier that impaired him in a lasting way and led to his poor judgment in trying to cross a highway. There really isn't any way to sort these things out any more than there is any way for me to sort out whether my cognitive and physical deficits are due to genetics or to early childhood abuse and neglect which, in turn, prevented my brain from developing in the way that it would have if given a better environment.

❖ ❖ ❖

What I started out, day before yesterday, intending to do with this segment of writing was to apologize to you, the reader, for not giving you a better book. I intended to very briefly explain to you that, due to circumstances that seem to be beyond my control, I can begin a story but I can't ever seem to get to the denouement and end. The first time I noticed that I couldn't devise a plot, then resolve the business that I'd created, was when I was presented sometime around 1968 with the Thematic Apperception Test (TAT) which was one in a battery of tests I was being given by a clinical psychologist to whom my psychiatrist of the time had send me. In this test, when shown a picture by the psychologist, the client is supposed to make up a story from which the clinician is then supposed to be able to interpret details, thereby deriving information which can then be used, supposedly, to help the client who made up the story. I was able to begin stories with no problem. I could develop characters, explain their inner turmoil and fully detail reasons for that inner turmoil. What I couldn't do, with one single picture out of the lot, was spring the trap. For the life of me, I couldn't get my characters out of the untenable life situations into which I'd gotten them. I could think of no way for them to achieve the getting of that which they wished to get, and I could think of no way for them to escape from wanting to get that which they couldn't get.

That was the dilemma, for me, into which all my life experiences up to that point in time had gotten me. It's little wonder that I couldn't create resolutions to any unfinished business in those little stories I created for the psychologist. In my life I'd never, myself, been able to bring about any successful resolutions in my own accumulating mountain of unfinished business. I didn't have any experience with completing a life cycle in a wrapped-up, finished manner. Just considering things, as far as lifecycles are concerned from a Freudian point of view, I'd never made it through a psychosexual stage of development with any success.

My potty training, I'm sure, was taken control of by my older sister, whose greatest desire, where I'm concerned, seems to be to this day that no living human being should ever see anything admirable in anything that I am or that I do. Why do I think my mother just handed me over to my older sister as if I were just a doll that she really didn't care enough about to keep for herself? There are some things you just know, aren't there? My Electra stage went along probably more successfully than any other stage because my father liked me and enjoyed having me around. However, I wasn't able to enjoy that very much, because the conflict between my father and my sister was terrible and unceasing. My father had sustained significant brain damage at the age of four as a result of a nearly fatal case of encephalitis. He was handicapped cognitively and had narcolepsy to boot. My sister was precocious, gifted, as quick-thinking as a fox and as perceptive at picking up on power and vulnerabilities in humans as an alpha wolf is in sensing which elk in a herd is weak and unable to defend itself. My sister could easily outwit my father. She knew it and he knew it.

Our father wasn't the kind of man who could feel generosity of spirit toward a daughter who was more intellectually competent than he. He couldn't establish his dominance over my sister by earning her respect with intellectual displays of skill and competency so he resorted to brute force to intimidate her. He made her eat food items that were sickening to her and provoked incidents that would create in his mind a justification for paddling her. He was, in short, often hateful to her. He was determined to do away with her being "sassy" to him. My father was like that with all four of his children, but the sister of whom I'm speaking seemed to me to be much less willing than I to yield to tyranny. Given a choice between arousing the contempt of my father and the contempt of my sister and mother, I didn't really see myself as having a choice. No matter how much my sister slapped me around, I didn't think she would kill me. I wasn't sure my father wouldn't if I made him really mad. The upshot was that I was toadying to my father when he was around, then hung my head in shame over my perfidious nature when I was with my sister and mother and my father wasn't with us.

Once out of sight of our father or his supporters, who were few, my sister could influence almost anyone with whom she had a chance to speak that she was an abused child and our father was an ogre. I know that I certainly was convinced. So were my mother and every member of her family with whom I ever witnessed my sister speaking. There were a few relatives who didn't look at my sister when she talked as if they were groupies privileged to catch a rock star, but she could always point out their shortcomings to me so convincingly that I figured they must be bad, stupid people if they didn't see everything exactly the way she explained it to them.

What could I think, when my father was kind to me, but that I was part and parcel of the devil? All the while I was escaping my sister's needling and my mother's purposeful neglect by going to wherever my father was and hanging out there, I had to endure my conscience's telling me that to actively seek the companionship of my father amounted to traitorous action against my sister of such magnitude that, just like she said, I wasn't of high enough character to deserve any goodwill from any good person. This sort of situation doesn't lead to neat resolution of a Freudian psychosexual phase of development; a neat resolution in which the little girl realizes, on an unconscious level of course, that she can never marry her dad and will settle for becoming like her mother - that woman that her dad loves in a romantic manner which will never be the manner in which he loves her, but which she will enjoy someday in adulthood with a man who will be her husband.

With many more Freudian psychosexual stages of development to go, I believe I'll cut the account short and state simply that the rest of the stages didn't open, bloom, and close for me with any more sense of fulfillment and willing relinquishment than the two did that I've just mentioned. I guess my goal has always been to find my lost self-image, wherever it is and whatever it is, and get it back inside me where it belongs. It probably would help if I could recognize it when I saw it.

My life story seems to be that I got on the road at the beginning with a destination clearly in mind that I had no doubt I'd reach in due time. I guess the destination at which I thought I'd arrive was the state of being so satisfied with myself that I could forget me and just be free to enjoy life. I'd been given the map, had the destination pointed out to me, and the route designated that would get me there. However, every evening when I got in my motel room and pulled the map out to see what kind of progress I'd made that day, I discovered that the road I'd just come off was not leading to the destination at all, and that instead of decreasing the distance between myself and the place I'd wanted to reach, I'd put myself farther away.

Thereupon, the next day, I had a more complex task. I couldn't just get in the car and drive as I had on the first day. I had to figure out what road I was now on so I could figure out whether this new road would get me there or whether I had to find the original route, pinpoint where I'd switched from it to this new road, and try to backtrack until I could get myself straightened out. After driving all day in an effort to do this, I entered my motel room, pulled out the map and discovered that not only had I not gotten back to the original route, I hadn't even stayed on the new route as I tried to get back to the original route. I'd gotten sidetracked and ended up farther away from my intended destination than ever and farther away than ever from the route that would take me there. Eventually, I found myself driving on and on and on without any idea where I was or where I was going. I'd even forgotten why I'd thought my self-satisfaction was going to be at the destination I was heading for when I began the trip. Nonetheless, I had to keep driving; because, although I'd forgotten what my destination was and the reason I was trying to go there, I also couldn't find my way back home.

This book was supposed to be a really good book, but I'm going to settle for a book - any kind, good or not-so-good. What I have are many chapters that got sidetracked and ended up in the wilderness. So far I haven't been able to get them back on a road that led to anywhere. I have many letters that I never sent to those to whom I was writing, because those people wouldn't have appreciated what I was saying one bit. If I wait to submit my writings for publication until I can fix all that's wrong with my writings and whip them into shape so that they comprise a good book, my writings will never get published.

    As was the case with my inability to give conclusions to stories I created from pictures in the TAT I took in '68; and, similar to that, my aging out of each psychosexual stage of childhood without concluding the developmental business of that stage; just so, seems to be where my dream of publishing a book may be headed. It seems to me that I have wanted to be an author forever. If I allow my inability to make order out of chaos stand in the way, I'll never see a book with my name on the cover.

STOP ATTACKING - I'M DEAD ALREADY

Help! I Need Somebody's Help!

When recently I had to face that I had been writing for years and still didn't have a manuscript that would meet even the lenient criteria set by the Library of Congress for awarding authors copyrights on their material, much less one that would meet the requirements of a publisher - even a subsidy publisher - I decided I'd try to find a local freelance editor who could and would review what I'd written and help me organize it into something resembling a cohesive whole.

I'd tried finding an editor by advertising at the closest university and had had only one applicant - a lady whose resume said she'd graduated summa cum laude from the university where she'd earned her bachelor's in English and who said she was currently employed on several editing projects, both by individuals and by a business. As I read this editor's emails to me and her resume, I saw so many errors in her writing mechanics, I couldn't imagine her catching the errors in mine.

Next I told the editor of my church's bulletin of my need. His editing work for the church is gratis, and I had no knowledge that he had serious literary resources, but he was able to provide me the name and email address of a professional editor almost overnight. Quickly, I emailed her an informal proposal to contract for her services.

She was a woman of few words (and I subsequently found that she apparently wanted a lot fewer from me than I had the compulsion to give her). The initial inquiry that I emailed to her - an inquiry I hoped would launch a long and mutually satisfying editor-author relationship between us - stated my objection succinctly enough, I think. My inquiry included this short summarization of my greatest yearning; "I want this collection of mental meanderings I've churned out over the years to get whipped into something that I can leave behind of which I needn't be too ashamed." What prompted me to explain my need in that way was my awareness of my neurological state - a state deficient enough in many ways to disable me from doing with my writing the things I most want to do - make order out of chaos, recognize and eliminate repetitions of identical material, and fix errors in mechanics and facts.

I assumed that a person who had hung out her "Editor" shingle would have the same vision of "editing" that I had. The presumption I had was that I was a prospective client to her, and that she was prepared to perform the editing services for me that I requested of her should she agree to accept payments from me.

If I were God and had set myself the task of creating the universe, I would get the Big Bang accomplished well enough, and I would get the soup created out of which I envisioned making spectacular cosmic systems, but when I then moved on to coalesce out of the soup galaxies, and from the galaxies stars, and so on, I would find myself overwhelmed by the very soup I had created, drowning, unable to get my head high enough above the surface of it even to see what I might grab onto and use to pull myself up and out.

I have commenced many a big project with great expectations of myself, then have begun to see, as I worked, that the project was expanding entirely beyond my capabilities; that instead of my speeding to completion of my project, fruition was speeding away from me at a furious rate. I would feel desperation to find a higher level god than me to rescue me from the morass into which I felt I'd inadvertently worked myself. Most times wherein I've thought I've found that human higher-level-than-me god who could accomplish for me what I could not accomplish for myself, I have found myself in a relationship that has left me obsessing on questions like, "What in the world is going on here?".

"This person obviously has some vision in mind of what my work (or I) would have to be in order for it (or I) to look to them as if it's (or I'm) worth anything. Credentials or licenses or public opinion has put them on a far higher level than I in this work, but I would have to lower my standards so far to be what they want me to be or to give them the work they want me to give them, it would be for my spirit like having to go back and earn a GED to please them when here I sit with a BA and an MS from two of the scholastically highest ranked universities in the country. Where is this person coming from? What is going on in that head that is telling that person - that higher-than-me person whose help I'm trying to get them to give me - that everything I am and all the work I'm trying to show them (the work into which I've put the best of which I'm capable) is worthless as is?"

And so it developed with this editor - the one I was hoping to hire to pull me up and out of my metaphorical soup. Her response (of about seventy or so words) began with: "I'll be glad to look at a few pages of your meanderings, if you'd like for me to, with the idea of seeing if they're something I can improve for you".

"My editing fee is $40 per hour".

Her concept of editing as improving an author's work struck me as bizarre. Nonetheless, I figured if she could command $40 an hour for professional editing in our remote-from-civilization, out-of-touch, economically-depressed rural area, she must be pretty darned good. Having lived here as long as I have, I should know better than to make such an assumption, but...

As usually happens when I ignore those negative realities to which my own cerebral cortex tries to alert me and go heedlessly onward in the pursuit of a dream, trusting all the while that the flashes of insight coming at me from my own brain can't be valid since they're not the flashes other people are getting, I paid a little for failing to recognize that my self-discounting and elevation-of-others processes were doing their thing again. The cost was $70 and several days of painful constipation.

This particular anecdote happened this way:

Being unable to comprehend how seeing only a few pages of an author's writing could tell an editor anything about the overall nature of an author's project when that author's project is the publishing of a book, and being unable to comprehend what an editor could possibly be thinking who intends to make a decision about whether or not she will accept a contract to edit a book based on her reading of only a few pages of it, I decided that she had to read at least one chapter if she were to be anything other than clueless about whether or not she should accept my job offer.

I inquired of her how long it would take her to read forty pages and tell me whether or not the complaining, bitter tone in my writing would turn readers off. "Three hours", she responded.

"And I thought I read slowly", I said to myself. I mailed her twenty-eight pages and a check for seventy dollars. I chose to send her a chapter describing how devastating long term depression can be on one's visual-spatial cognition and ability to cope with activities of daily living.

When she had already communicated to me what was, for her, the job description of "editor" (to improve an author's writing), and I had concluded, "Weird!", when I had already remarked to myself that needing three hours to read twenty-eight pages and tell the author whether or not her "voice" was a turn-off was weird, why I went right on trying to get out of this editor what it should have been plain to me she would not be able or willing to give, was a question I didn't think to ask myself at the time. I just blindly plugged in and used the same compulsive, instinctual routine for dealing with frustrating and disappointing interactions between myself and other people that I always have.

When interactions between myself and another person reveal to me that we just aren't on the same page (and often when we haven't been, this has made itself evident in our very first contacts with each other), I suspect that a person free of crippling neuroses would cease trying to force the co-actor to get on the same page and would move on. I almost never have done that. I've transitioned immediately to bombarding that person, who doesn't want a part in my play, with words, as if giving enough devotion to the task, eventually I will get a communication to them that will excite their interest. This encounter proceeded no differently.

Some time elapsed, after I sent my twenty-eight pages off to the editor that I thought was going to whip my reams of writing into shape and make of them something of which I could be proud, before she remitted to me her assessment. I had thought I had prepared myself for a negative opinion on my "voice". What I got was not a negative opinion on my "voice" - she didn't address that - but a negative opinion on my writing as a whole that was so all-encompassing I would have had to go back to my conception and be reborn as a different woman to be able to fulfill her demands.

My writing didn't have any point, she opined, and if I wanted readers to keep reading, I was going to have to decide what the point of my book was. I needed a "well defined theme". Next, she posed to me eight or ten questions that instructors of English 101 almost always address to students in their classes; students whose exposure to the work of writers has been limited to whatever they had to read to graduate from high school. "If you answer these questions", she wrote, "I think you can start creating a sense of destination for your book".

"Your work is overwritten and would be better if you

would cut at least a third of it", she continued. "Of course you could pay an editor to do that for you, but I really think you are a good enough writer to handle this step for yourself." When I hit this advisory and considered the autobiographical material contained in the chapter I had sent her that stated clearly that this was precisely the step in writing a book which I could not perform due to my neurological impairments, I wondered to myself where her head could have been when she read my material.

Here, I could go on for another page quoting the directions she gave me in how to write if I expected any reader to want to read what I had written. "She wants to teach me how to write crap for the literarily challenged", I huffed, then quickly had to acknowledge to myself that people pay her good money for doing what she thinks of as editing. If she were totally off track in her concept of what services a freelance editor owes her clients, would they? Self-doubt set in. Surely she must be right about the sorriness of my writing rather than I being right about her sorriness as an editor. The obsessive thinking which takes over my every waking moment any time my self-image gets a jar was off and running.

"She wants the simple-minded, answer-to-all-your-problems non-fiction that regularly makes it onto best-sellers lists", I thought, feeling contempt for any editor who would hold the opinion that was good writing. I reviewed the long list of shortcomings she had said I needed to do something about in the little bit of my work I had sent her. I took stock of the fact that she was telling me to select a third of everything I had written and to cut it on the basis that at least a third was useless or redundant wordage.

I realized that meeting her expectations for my work, if I wanted to make of it something she would consider editing, would require me to rewrite my entire body of work - more than a decade's worth of the greatest effort I was capable of investing, not only in creating the work in the first place, but in editing and rewriting it insofar as I had done that.

She was far too polite to sum up her two pages of criticism with a paragraph stating, "Your writing is so verbose and dull, the story you're trying to tell in your writing is so obscure and uninteresting, and you've given me so little reason to feel sympathy for the protagonist and author (you), I don't want to have to look at any more of this even if you pay me $40 an hour to do so. No reader would want to either." That's the message she communicated to me even though she didn't say it quite that crudely.

Did I read what she had to say and immediately and instinctively save the good feeling I'd had about my writing before her critique by discounting her ability as a judge - something that would have been a very healthy thing for me to do both mentally and emotionally? A little, but not enough to rescue my self-image. Did I think, "Anything I write and give to her to edit will be casting pearls...?" No. It would have been healthily self-image-preserving to think that, but I didn't think that.

My whole system went into as defensive a mode as if this editor were the older sister of my childhood years; the older sister whom I was always afraid to disbelieve no matter what grievous flaw or shortcoming she attributed to me. If she was right in her analysis of me, I believed her, felt unbearable shame, and tried to fantasize something about her or myself that would make me feel better;

but I kept those fantasies to myself. If she was wrong in her analysis of me, I believed her just the same. I was sure all her scathing opinions on me were infallibly correct and that any opinion I had of myself was a hoot if it was good. Whether her criticism against me or against something I'd done was justified or not, I never sprang forward to debate her verdict after a few attempts in my early childhood where those who were audience to my sister's pronouncements against me couldn't move fast enough to support her.

No, I didn't dare open my mouth, in the presence of my sister and third parties functioning as my sister's audience, when she cut me down with word and sneer to nothing. What I did do, by the time I was in the second or third grade, was to begin to develop adversarial relationships with females I didn't think would have the cognitive and linguistic capabilities to humiliate me in front of people as my sister was invariably able to do. What I constantly sought, without having any conscious idea I was doing so, were opportunities where I could safely do to others what was being done by my sister unto me, or where I could at least be free to fight others instead of having to play dead because I knew my adversary had weapons in her arsenal that could make mine look like sticks and stones opposing guns and smart bombs.

After a few days, sanity began to return to me. My subvocal voice was once again saying to me that, poorly written or not, the goal of publishing a book was just as rationally sound as a goal of keeping one's house structurally maintained or of having beautiful flowers every year around one's house, and no more grandiose. My subvocal voice was again saying that my years of writing hadn't been a foolish use of time that I should have more profitably spent fertilizing my lawn. The reams of paper on which I'd printed out much of my writing weren't just stacks of waste paper that I should shove to the back of a cabinet and forget.

Calming down and believing that all is not lost is a process that always takes a remarkably long time for nature to get me through any time I've had another encounter with the negative transference from my sister in which I've unconsciously clothed somebody in my environment. Even when some days had passed after I'd received the editor's castigation of my writing, I was still, in my head, at the joust - still consumed with the obsessive subvocal linguistic battling with Sis-stand-ins that my brain practices incessantly any time I think I've let my image down. I was, however, thinking in a little more clear-headed way than I had been.

But I wasn't out of the woods yet. My church's bulletin editor, the one who had provided me with the name of the freelance editor who found my writing so un-editor-worthy, emailed me a follow-up inquiry, setting off for me a new round of unrecognized negative transference. Unbeknownst to me, this time I unconsciously began to equate him with one of those many attendees to Sis to whom she was able to convey the impression that I was so pitifully deficient in knowledge and intelligence that if they were as astute as she, they wouldn't waste their time listening to anything I had to say.

This brought on a new round of obsessing, constipation, and - this time - skeletal muscle contractions so severe they sent me to bed for a day before they began to relent. Excerpts from our correspondence show how besieged I felt my image to be:

From: Emmy
To: John
Date: March 3, 2007

You asked in your email of today if Sue, the editor whose name you had found for me, had proven to be the pro who would do for me the work I wanted done to get my writings on their way to becoming a published book. Sadly, no.

Sue's concept of "editor" and mine don't seem to be elements of the same job description. Her response to my first emailed job offer to her was, "If you want to send me a few pages of your work, I'll see if they're (sic) something I can improve for you".

I don't think I'm ignorant of what "editing" entails - I took a very good online course in it a couple of years ago. Also, I worked in the editorial department of a newspaper in my youth, and I have a BA in English from Wm & Mary (besides my MS in speech-language-hearing from Chapel Hill). I think my vision of "editor" couldn't be too far off track. Nonetheless, I never could seem to get a handle on what "editing" meant as Sue envisioned it.

John, I should have dropped my correspondence with Sue as soon as I read her response, as I *know* my writing is vastly in need of improvement. But if all the writing and editing courses I've had to date haven't made an acceptable writer of me by now, I think I've got to go with what I have - not what I wish I had - and look for an editor who will focus upon spotting my errors in writing mechanics and factual information. I have neurological deficits (always have had but have only begun to let this sink into my psyche fully in recent years) that include some types of visual processing. I'm guessing that is one reason I cannot organize and competently prune what I write. Too, I often forget linguistically what I've written previously and write the same thing all over again.

I'd hoped I'd find an editor who might comprehend how hard it is for even a well-educated intelligent person to organize many parts into an orderly whole and to recognize when she's writing again what she's already written. when her brain has limited activity in a number of skill areas. I'd hoped I would find an editor willing to point out to me passages in which I'd repeated myself and in which I'd put the cart before the horse leaving a reader clueless as to what I was talking about.

Anyway, wondering what on earth an editor could find out about a ream body of work from only a few pages, I must have decided that I knew better than she what she needed. I asked her to quote me her fee to read a chapter and tell me whether or not the author's "voice" elicited some sympathetic interest in the content or was a turnoff. She replied that it would take her about three hours to perform that task on forty pages (single-side print, double-spaced) - the amount I had proposed to send her. I was stunned that such a small task would take her three hours (at $40 per), so I sent her twenty-eight pages and $70.

Reading her critique of the work I'd sent her evoked in me memories of instruction on the subject of writing-in-general that all my fellow students and I had been given by English teachers when I was a high-schooler. At first, I was so incensed at what I perceived to be grossly insulting to my intelligence, I went into the defensive mode that disables all my capacity for rational thought anytime anyone finds fault with me or anything I do.

I compulsively composed a long explanation to Sue of why I could not - and did not want to - rewrite ten to fifteen years' worth of work to make it all conform to rules that would bring it down to middle-school reading level. She responded to that with the utmost in professional, courteous verbiage, which said basically, "Your writing is so over-verbose, so dull, and so lacking in anything that would arouse in a reader a feeling of sympathy for the protagonist (you), I wouldn't read another page of it even for $40 per hour. Good luck with your book".

❖ ❖ ❖

John, what I want my books (I've written enough already to make several) to show, is why psychotherapeutic treatments for those suffering severe depressions (treatments almost always based in Freud's client-destructive notions of what the therapist's relationship to his "patient" should be) make murderers and suicides out of people who are sick but harmless before they undergo treatment. Society's beliefs about why severely depressed people are that way (i.e. depressed people fail to get off their sorry butts and get themselves undepressed as they could perfectly well could do if they wanted to) are so simplistic and kindergarten-level-ignorant it makes my stomach churn every time I read or hear medical people's commentary about depression.

Is there a magazine, newspaper, or TV day that doesn't have somewhere in it some nationally recognized expert in mental health stating, "Depression is caused by thinking negative thoughts, so if you're depressed, find a psychotherapist who'll give you cognitive therapy" (i.e. teach you how to think right)? Or, maybe your brain chemicals are out of balance. "You've suffered all these years because you didn't know that depression was a curable illness! You felt lousy but you didn't take the first step and make an appointment with your doctor to find out if you might be depressed: You didn't know that your doctor can tell what brain chemical you've been shortchanged on (serotonin, to be sure). He'll prescribe the medication for you that will fix you right up, and you will live happily ever after."

John, the mental health professionals and pharmaceutical companies which are propagating this bull are misleading the public far more than tobacco companies ever did when they told us their low tar cigarettes could make smoking safe for us again - in my opinion.

You asked me what my proposed book deals with. What I write goes back and forth between how my own personality got formed to be what it is, and how evolution has formed, over millions of years, the various personality types found among members of predatory packs. The depressed individual in a predatory pack may survive because he or she, due to evidencing depression, may be seen by other members as no competition - no threat.

Language did not precede cognition in human evolution and language does not arise (ordering discrete events sequentially) in our modern brains preceding cognition and feeling. Language is the servant of cognition and feeling - not the other way around. Therefore, to imagine that thinking negative thoughts is what causes a person to be depressed is ludicrous. Both animals and humans can experience horrible depression without attaching any linguistic thought to the feeling at all.

How can experts with doctorates and years of experience in treating depressed people fail to see that depression is the cause of negative thinking - not the result? No wonder their clients so frequently get much worse off almost immediately after entering therapy. What a terrible letdown it is when you find your therapy demeans you rather than validates you and doesn't alleviate your depression one iota.

Well, John, I can look at the volume of what I've written to you and recognize that Editor Sue was right about my being verbose.

John's next email to me read thusly:
From: John
To: Emmy
Date: March 5, 2007

I know you and my good friend what's-her-name didn't hit it off. Let me say a couple of things.

I can't really speak about Sue or whatever her name is, but I know my friend Mary (who was just getting back to teaching when I contacted her) and how she would edit, and maybe I can speak to her style - it may apply more broadly or not, I don't know.

Mary (and I suspect the rest) are going to edit for style as well as content, grammar, and spelling ... she knows what kind of writing sells and what doesn't ... Americans today want stuff quick, short, easy. So, if you want to sell it in America today, it has to be able to meet the reading requirements (no matter how much we all lament it) of today's reader.

Of course, some markets are different, and you can write somewhat above a 3rd grade level, but it still needs punch to sell.

❖ ❖ ❖

"Why", I wondered, "is John teaching me on the subjects of editing and writing, when I have just told him that I hold a BA in English from Wm & Mary, have taken an online course in editing, and once worked on a newspaper's editorial staff? What have I said in my communication to John that has left him thinking I am ignorant of what editors do. Why is he assuming I would be clueless as to what the masses are preferring to read these days? Why is he assuming that it is my desire to produce writing that will be, in style and content, what the masses want?"

Never being one to realize what I'm doing when I'm hitting my head against a brick wall in which I'm unlikely to create an opening regardless of how long I persevere, I persevered in trying to make John see what John wasn't interested in seeing.

From: Emmy
To: John
Date: March 7, 2007

Just had the idea to look on amazon.com to see if Sue had written anything that was there. See that she primarily writes promotional literature. I did find one fairly lengthy example of her writing. I see now exactly what the problem was in my expectations of her. I don't see anything in her professional profile that would suggest she has knowledge, interest, or life experience in the subject matter I write about. My writing is very psychoanalytic and also very much rooted in the views of the zoologist Dawkins. John, I make a big production of my neurological deficits, but I hardly ever bother to also mention that my verbal abilities have consistently tested out in the top one percent of the population. I could see in reading Sue's material that I am more qualified to edit her work than she is to edit mine. That's not being arrogant - Wm & Mary is just a top-rated school for majoring in English, and I did very well there. On my GRE for admittance to UNC-CH graduate school, I scored at 99th percentile on verbal and 24th percentile on quantitative.

Unfortunately, I think people size me up by looking at my "quantitative" abilities instead of my "verbal". Having looked at what Sue writes, I can now see that had I done some research on her work before I asked her to edit mine, I would have recognized that she and I are not on the same page and apparently don't have any common denominator. Now, I will know that before I submit any work to another editor, I must try to find out how she herself writes and what works she has read that have made the most lasting impression upon her ... I'm learning.

Have you ever read *Zen and the Art of Motorcycle Maintenance* by Robert Pirsig? If you haven't and thought it was about motorcycle maintenance, it's not. For many pages of that book, I wondered where on earth the author was going; he seemed to be rambling all over the place aimlessly, pointlessly. But, soon I grasped that the aimless wandering effect was absolutely essential to the author's showing his readers who he was - what his soul was like, bared. From that point on, I was spellbound. I read very slowly for someone of my verbal ability, and it took me all night to finish the book, but I couldn't put it down once I got on the same track with the author.

When I realized that even after all he'd been through (his life makes mine look like a cake walk), Pirsig still had the heart to try to put together a book that would tell the world his story and that he kept faith with his work through many rejections from publishers, I knew I must not let self-disparagement keep me from trying to do the same.

❖ ❖ ❖

Back from John came a response:
From: John
To: Emmy
Date: March 7, 2007
Yes, I read Pirsig's book years ago...
On the subject of editors, I'm not sure that your editor necessarily needs to have a higher verbal score to be a good editor, just enough smarts to know how to move your work toward your goal. So, try the new name I've given you, and if she doesn't work out, maybe by then Mary will be finishing with teaching her course in New Bern and will be available.

On and on I went in my campaign to show John how misguided he was to think that I did not know what editors do and needed him to tell me. The silliness of my devoting all the time and effort to this project that I was devoting eluded me. Blindly I plunged onward, probably insuring that John would move my name to his blocked senders' list as soon as he opened the following message from me:
To: John
From: Emmy
Date: March 7, 2007
What I also haven't happened to mention is that I took a very good online course in editing in 2003 (and I worked in the editorial department of the Roanoke, VA, *Times*, before I married an editor and journalist whose writings on Gary Powers and his U2 were then being carried all over the world by AP). I've always had a problem with present-

ing myself to people as a glass half empty instead of half full. I suspect I've done it again with you. Let me see if I can portray my knowledge base in a little more accurate light than I have done so far. This is what my job on an editorial staff, my notice of my ex-husband's work, and my online editing course have taught me about editing:

It is in the job description of an instructor or professor of writing to critique students' work and teach them how to write. Unless this instructor is asked by someone who is not a student of hers for an assessment of his writing, she's being presumptuous to lay her criticisms one-to-one upon him. It is not professionally acceptable for an editor who has been offered a job by an author to presume to do anything other than what the author asks her to do. There are many kinds of editor. Unless an editor (working freelance) is asked by an author to edit for content or style, she has no business addressing those issues. To do so, unasked, is not professionally appropriate. If I had asked Sue to tell me whether or not my work was suitable for marketing to the masses, then the criticisms of my work she sent me would have been professionally appropriate.

I have no interest whatsoever in making of my work something mass marketable - I'm writing for the very few who will have a knowledge base broad enough to understand what I'm getting at. But Sue assumed if my work didn't fit the formulaic fast-food mold she equated with "good writing" (and I'm well acquainted with what kind of writing that formulaic fast-food mold chums out) it was no good. My idols as authors are James Joyce, William Faulkner, Joseph Conrad, and Frederick Perls. The last thing I want to do is write like Danielle Steel or the Kellermans. Yes, I read bestselling fast-food writing; I use two or three pages of it to put me to sleep every night.

If Sue had been an editor on the staff of a publishing house which I was hoping to interest in my work, then her sending me two pages of excoriating commentary on my writing would have been rightly within her duties. In that case, she would have appropriately assumed the position of judge, and I would have been the supplicant in her court. That was not our situation. When a person, functioning in the capacity of freelance editor, accepts a job offer from a writer, it is outrageously out-of-line for her to take it upon herself to teach her client how to write.

I can't tell you how clearly my online course in editing stressed this point; a freelance editor's job is to do with the author's work what the author asks the editor to do. In freelance work, the author is the client, the editor is the service provider. To make an analogy of it, if you went to an architect and asked him or her to draw up plans for your dream home, what would you think if the architect presented you a few days later with plans that didn't include the features you had requested and were full, instead, of features you had not asked for and didn't want in your home at all?

Which is not to say that Sue didn't give me some feedback that roused in me a desire to try to do for myself what I have been telling myself I cannot do - organize, order, and find my repetitions of material.

❖   ❖   ❖

It was at this juncture that I became aware I had passed the point of being tiresome in my communications to John three browbeating emails back - that I was compulsively fighting on and on in defense of my self-esteem when it made no practical sense at all to do that; when all I was accomplishing with John was turning him off so thoroughly he would cease having anything to do with me.

HELP! I NEED SOMEBODY'S HELP!

Lead-Up to a Meltdown

The day after Halloween, 1944, Leah and I began the trip back home after five months at Aunt E's. As we made our way southwest to the mountains, I was feeling exactly what I had been accustomed to feeling throughout the preceding summer and fall: I was happy and full of energy, and I felt as wholesome, feminine, smart, and good as any well-cared-for little four-and-a-half-year-old girl would feel.

As would have been the case with any normal preschooler, I had elicited my caretakers' disapproval on occasion and had even received some tear-drawing discipline from time to time. However, in this period of my cerebral development, I don't believe I had the hypersensitivity to pain of all kinds that I remember so well from later events. Neither can I recall being hypervigilant constantly for signs coming from another child or adult that they had negative feelings for me. During this stay at Aunt

E's, her disapproval or Leah's, a spanking or two, or being confined to my room and deprived of play time, had done nothing to disturb my sense of being secure in Aunt E's love or Leah's good will (to the best of my recollection).

I don't remember hating myself or being overwhelmed with shame when I did things that made Aunt E angry and for which she had to correct me, nor did I have the perception, when Leah had been witness to my provoking of Aunt E's ire, that she was joyously gloating and sneering at me; conveying to me as pointedly as facial expression can (without being noticed by onlookers) that I had slipped up in my phony act of being a good child and had allowed my sorry real self to be seen by this adult I had so wanted to think well of me.

There may have been undercurrents of some less than ideal feelings existing between Aunt E and Leah as we rode along on our trip back home, and those rivalrous or resentful suppressed feelings might have been there during all the previous months. But, if they were, I was oblivious to all of it. Perhaps I hadn't noticed any negative undercurrents because I hadn't been in a state of perpetual fear and therefore hadn't been living every minute of every waking hour like a mouse who knows that there might, or might not be, a cat just outside the opening to his hideaway; a cat waiting patiently to grab him as he emerges (something that the mouse sooner or later will have to do) and who will surely get him if he fails to attend with all his being to the feedback from his hearing, sight, and smell that he is depending upon to warn him of the cat's presence.

A few might have looked at all the seemingly unconditional love coming to me from Aunt E and voiced some suspicion about the sincerity of it all. Retrospection leads me to the possibility that Aunt E had been treating me like a little royal, and Leah like a nanny (a commoner) hired to take care of the little royal. Was there an agenda going on there; a use being made of me by Aunt E to achieve some personal objective? I didn't see anything like that going on during my preschool years, but somewhere along the way I grasped that my bearing Aunt Emmelia's name caused her to project onto me every failure she had ever incurred in being that more-attractive-than-peers girl that her mother and she had so wanted her to be. An astute onlooker might have spotted a streak of sadism going on in my "blue-blood" aunt; an instinct to diminish the young Leah, who at nine was already displaying social acumen with adults and children that rivaled hers and threatened to eclipse her center stage spot on many occasions. Was Aunt E seeing me as her preschool self, put into competition by her mother with a cousin?

I don't know how my relationship with Leah got turned into one that Leah saw as a vicious rivalry in which she (the good girl) had to be constantly defeating me (the bad girl), but I know that it was not I who created that nightmare of my every waking hour. I did always sense that something about Leah's personality made both Daddy and Aunt E want to see me develop into an adult whose successes would leave Leah's in the dust. There I was, a child five years younger than the sister who was seeing me as her competitor - a child with many neurological and physical deficits being made to believe I was under obligation to meet or exceed, every step of the way, all the accomplishments of Leah; this girl with precocity, drive, talent, and physique ideal in femininity and symmetry. Looking back,

I wonder how any family members could have subjected me to comparisons with Leah if they even liked me at all.

Decades after my 1944 stay at Aunt Leah's and others of shorter duration, I have an understanding of what I was to Aunt E that is very different from the way her narratives always portrayed it to me. That mismatch between reality and what Aunt E and others led me to believe was reality (beginning with this extended visit to Aunt E's and our day of return home) led me into so much misery, not just in my preschool years but continuing through my life afterward, that I would rank socially-induced delusion right up there with genetic disease or brain damage as a probable precipitating factor in my spending years in psychotherapy. Even decades after my intelligence and higher education had rejected the "blue-blood" stuff that had been put in my mind as a child, it hung on in my system the way pursuing a diet of insects would live on in the brains of birds that, as fledglings, watched their parents catch and eat insects.

In my alliance with Aunt E, I was always committing myself to the relationship between us as if she was committing herself to the relationship in the same way I was. She wasn't. I don't know, conclusively, how she was viewing the "love" for me that she so effusively would go on about during my visits with her. I do think that her love for me was one hundred percent conditional - "I'll love you when to do so adds in a positive way to how I feel about myself or how I look to people who really matter to me". Aunt E's interest in me was merely in making of me something she could use to enhance her image. I think that when showing love to me didn't get her the image improvement she wanted, the underlying contempt for me that was always there because of my father's and mother's poverty and disabilities came through loud and clear. I don't know if the word *LOVE* even should be applied to what she felt for me. I do know that I desperately needed for her to love me because of the negative narratives that stood in the way of my being able to bond with either Leah or Mother. The mythology created by Leah about what I was to Mother and what she was to me filled all the space that would have been occupied by reality had Leah not existed.

Perhaps the over-the-top expressions of love with which Aunt E so liked to shower me gave her a sense of satisfaction such as I feel when I've surprised my dog with a piece of my roast chicken after she's had a dry-kibble dinner and has gone back to her bed thinking that was all she was to have. More than that, Aunt E's professions of love for me were probably a tool she realized she could use to entangle me in her agenda; maneuver me into trying to make of myself an enhancement to her image. Perhaps she also feared that Leah and my mother might undermine her behind her back, and that the love attestations she was making to me would cause me to feel guilty if I should listen with openness to anything negative I might hear said about her.

Those many sessions of "I spoil you, don't I? You are my favorite. I don't like Leah because..., Coraya because..., Do any of your other Aunts spoil you as I do?" ... the uncomfortable sessions in which I found myself trapped by Aunt E, may have been set up by her with the subconscious forethought of isolating me from other family members and making me dependent upon her. Although in my childhood I failed to recognize (at least consciously) the extent of the deception and self-deception that was behind so much of Aunt E's "spoiling" of me, I was able to see, early on, that her professions of love were verbal cues she was using to elicit from me effusions of love and loyalty with which she could assure herself that she was god to me, the only human who was god to me, and that I would have no other gods before her.

These episodes of being a captive audience to Aunt E's (and Daddy's) negative remarks about Leah and Coraya hadn't yet begun on this happy, sunny day, homeward bound, in '44. Those began when I was several years older and would visit Aunt E while Leah stayed at home. In the months preceding this day's interactions, narratives about people and feelings had focused most of the time upon people in Lexington and were mostly glowing. I'd seen and been introduced to many of Aunt E's and our father's family members and lifelong friends. While all these people had looked like strangers to me, Leah seemed to already know them all and to be perfectly at ease with them, whether adult or youngster.

The people (especially men) whom Aunt E, Leah, and other females of our circle talked to and talked about - those subjects falling into the category of "our class" - took on mythological proportions in my heart and mind. If we were talking about men, the context was usually, "Will I marry a man like him someday?" Aunt E's husband, who had died a year or so earlier, had been a divinity among mortals (from all I heard) - absolute perfection in the way he had honored Aunt E and rewarded her for her faith in him at a time when he had been in debt (at the depths of the depression). He had been such a gentlemen, so immaculate and well-tailored at all times, always enjoying nothing in life more that doing things to please her or selecting the most exquisite gifts with which to surprise her. I suppose the same process was going on in my brain that had taken place in the minds of ancient Greeks when oral-tradition poets like Homer spoke about everyday people with language that evoked visualizations far more colorful and powerful than the people, places, and things from which these story-tellers were drawing their myths' skeletons.

A verbal account of an event, along with a description of the person central to the event, may begin life very closely associated with reality. Ask anyone who observed to tell you about it, and the account they give is likely to be within the bounds of reality. However, any person who stands in higher status in observers' eyes than themselves and the person central to the event can take hold of the observers' factual account, spin a whole 180 degrees different narrative, and those same observers will abandon what they had previously said they saw, heard, and felt and will adopt the narrative coming from the higher status human as what they themselves witnessed.

Watching chimp documentaries on TV, I can see that we primates have been preferring fictionalized versions of beings and happenings to what's really going on all the way back to our origins in the jungle. At age four I apparently announced to Leah that I was going to marry Daddy. After she let me know that she certainly would not go that low class and unworthy in choosing a husband, I believe I did a complete about face in my evaluation of Daddy and decided that I found him just as distasteful as Leah did. In allowing the belittling things Leah and Aunt E said about my father to influence me against him, I scorned the only real supporter I had among my family elders.

This preference of humans for narratives spun by deceiving self-deceivers to narratives adhering to reality must promote survival, else the majority of humans would not believe that fabrications by deceivers are where the truth is to be found, and that what can be seen, heard, and felt by oneself is best not believed. I can see examples of this principle (this principle of winning by supporting alphas' lies and denouncing truths when truths are told by those that look powerless) from my extended family and my ex's all the way up to global powers. In my own case, from my earliest years, I couldn't get enough of the tales Aunt E, Daddy, and Leah would spin about their (and by extension, my) genetic superiority and all the other superiorities that being inherently superior to other people gave us. That has been anecdotal evidence, in my mind at least, of the validity of the theory I've just advanced stating: given the choice between believing that reality is reality and believing that delusion is reality, humans want to believe that a delusion is reality.

When passing judgment on the mental health of any individual, the first thing psychiatrists probably ask themselves is, "Does this person seem to be in touch with reality?" A few mental health experts have alerted us to the fact that this is a question that cannot be objectively answered, since what reality is (as with beauty) lies in the eye of the beholder. How many of us can look at our own view of factuality and spot the many ways in which our convictions about ourselves and others come not from a factual rendering of what we ourselves see, hear, and feel, but from what we have been told by parents, older siblings, and others in our childhoods?

This society in which I'm now living (America, 2020), doesn't have any marker, government designated and enforced, that uses a particular religious belief or lack of it as the criterion by which an inhabitant's sanity is determined. There have been many periods of time in human history when one's acceptance or rejection of the religious delusion ruling the brains of the powerful of the country have become the yardstick by which a citizen's worthiness to live has been the measure. Religious myths embraced as *Truth* by alphas of families, communities, and groups of all sizes have always been a tool used by the most powerful to sort out which individuals were "one of us" (one who, like us, sees what the truth is) from those they could disempower by calling them deluded.

Mental health professionals' use of religious belief as one factor in their list of factors that influence their decision when diagnosing a client as either delusional (insane) or sane is probably a use they try to avoid talking about these days. In the society in which I grew up, The Apostles Creed was taken as truth, and a belief in the superiority of rich WASP privileged humans over those humans who were not, was taken as just as much reality as The Apostles Creed.

There have always existed among humans trust in falsehoods presented as truths by competent orators, faith in pantomime by fellow humans that imply there are beings with us that only the mimers are privileged to see, and belief that words recorded in writing in a certain book or on a certain surface came not from the mind of the human who put them there, but from an all-powerful being no one could see but the authors holding the writings. In each case, these products of deceptions created by deceiving self-deceivers have been accepted as reality in the groups within which they appeared and rejected as delusion by those in other groups.

If the delusion about themselves and others in which an individuatl is living is also the delusion of the powerful of their family, community, country, or other type cluster, then the delusion is not a delusion but is reality. It is reality when the sharers in the delusion think and act as if their delusion is not a delusion. In so doing, they change themselves and those they act upon. There is no doubt whatsoever, in my mind, that I and my close relatives, my ex and all of his relatives that I knew well, our children, and my granddaughters are very different people from what we would have been had we not grown up within our elders' falsehoods about religion and social matters.

Few of us who are alive in Europe or America today realize that in the years in which our great-grandparents, grandparents, and parents were alive, most of those of their generation believed just what Hitler did - that certain humans were superior genetically but that a far greater number were just like those individual horses in a herd of thoroughbreds that stood no chance of winning races and therefore needed to be culled. A majority of the citizens of America and northern European countries subscribed to the idea (ostensibly derived from scientific findings but surely derived more from unacknowledged prejudice) that animal husbandry was just as good and necessary a practice to apply to the human species as to farm animals. The South has always been an agrarian society, so I deduce from that fact that a belief in Hitler-like theories about genetics and therefore about oneself and one's fellow human beings has been particularly dear to Southerners for several generations. This is a belief system most Southerners would claim doesn't exist here.

The reason I bring all this up is that in the family in which I was born and in the family of my ex-husband in which I became embedded, I can see that in the years in which I was in touch with my relatives and in-laws, there was hardly one of us who was not held hostage mentally, at all times, by narratives that had been spun in the past or that were being spun in the present by those family members who were belief creators. Those beliefs centered around convictions of the superiority of themselves over others, but each of our families had criteria directly the opposite of the criteria of the other.

Most of us who were not the creators of the exalted belief of the moment were nothing more than pawns in the service of it. The overarching myths had been fed to us early enough in life for us to be unable to see that these were delusions created by one or another myth-making alpha of us all, for his or her own benefit mostly, although they were presented to us by our alpha-status mentors as if they were gifts to us of information lifting us out of darkness.

The alternate realities that were often being spun and presented as truth frequently arose from those personality defenses of humans that spring automatically to the fore when we are about to face our own judgment of ourselves if we don't, in a nanosecond, escape reality. Most characterizations of this or that fellow family member were presented to us because the presenter needed a scapegoat upon whom they could project; that is, the presenter had unconsciously analyzed themselves, then unaware of what they were doing, claimed their own flaws were in the person they were unknowingly using as a mirror. Most of these narratives related as truths were concocted by only a few family members but were listened to, embraced, and acted upon by the majority as if the fiction was indeed fact. As I see it, these narratives had effects on family members that have resulted in tragedy for some, if not most.

I don't know of anyone, other than myself, out of all the family members with whose convictions I'm become acquainted, who sees any delusions at all going on with their evaluations of themselves and others. I suppose that indicates that they are comfortable living within whatever delusions they've been gifted by family alphas. I never have been comfortable with the delusions in which these families have entangled me.

When I write, fifty years after my Aunt E's death and sixty years after my father's, that all the while that my sisters and I were growing up we were in a delusion Aunt E and our father had fed us that was poisoning us, most who ever knew my aunt at any time would probably say that was a ridiculous idea - no support of that in reality. If focus shifted to my father, whose delusion was the same as Aunt E's (that we were of blue blood; had superior genes), opinion would probably be that he was deluded. That is because he was neurologically impaired and poverty stricken whereas Aunt E had money, property, and had been married to a man with prestige in the region where she lived. Also, she held a position of some power in her church, where forebears had been members and influencers.

If I had been in a position to win friends and influence people unchallenged by competitors, been adept at performing social routines by which I could make myself look good and others inferior, and think on my feet when caught out (all those things Leah was able to do), I probably would believe to this day that all the garbage Aunt E taught me about how to show myself to be "upper class" and draw the "right people" as friends and suitors was good stuff. I had to face a different reality because I could not fail over and over again to exhibit superiority and go on believing there was something better about my genes. Cognitive dissonance made me face the fact that I couldn't come up with the right stuff to make people admire me as I'd been led to believe in my childhood I would have to do all my life if I wanted to have any value in the eyes of fellow humans in my world.

I have recently had a change of opinion about where Aunt E's and Daddy's belief in their genetic superiority originated. I had always thought it was handed down to them generation after generation from ancestors who were of the English royal family. Information I've come upon far too late for it to make a difference in my life says that my father's and aunt's declaration of their superior blood came out of the eugenics movement; an amalgam of survival of the fittest science with the idea that the human race would be improved if the best specimens of humanity were encouraged to marry and have offspring while those less fit should be prevented from reproducing, even if that took state ordered sterilization.

Popularity of the notions related to modern eugenics was greatest in England, Germany, and America from the late 1800s to 1940. These would have included the decades when Aunt E and our father would have been in their teen and young adult years and therefore the most open to sociological movements.

Eugenics was the base upon which Hitler built his rationale for genocide, envisioning that and portraying that as being an altruistic campaign to rid the world of the "least fit" who, if not weeded out, would drag down the whole human race. Once the Second World War came to an end, and the world saw what had transpired in the extermination camps as a result of Hitler's great plan for bettering the human race, I don't imagine there were many Americans who had been ardent supporters of the myths advanced in the eugenics movement who wanted to admit they had been full-throated advocates for all the beliefs about superiority of some humans over others that they had previously felt so free to speak about. When Daddy or Aunt E spoke about their "heritable" superiority, the usually tied it to ancestors' coats of arms and such.

I have to wonder if their obsession with being among the superior was not more shaped by eugenics principles, against which they feared they themselves might be judged as among the inferior, than by what their past connection to European royalty might have been. All the claims among the eugenics adherents that evidences of the fittest could be found in wealth, in physical perfection, in the intelligence to maneuver others into doing one's manual labor, etc., seem silly to me when it looks obvious that the fittest-for-survival among humans are those who have the most children who survive to have the most children who survive to have the most children, and so on, generation after generation. Those who do that are not the alphas of humanity – they are the followers of the alphas. Christ said that the meek shall inherit the earth. Undoubtedly they will because there will be so many of them.

Nonetheless, something about the beliefs of the eugenics movements must have made a powerful impression on Aunt E, Daddy, and their more senior family members regardless of irrational deductions and inferences.

My aunt's appearance was quite Mediterranean. She, as well as her mother and those sisters and brothers of her mother that I had a chance to meet, were all short, thick in the middle, a bit swarthy of complexion, and brown-eyed. Given these physical characteristics along with the size and length of my aunt's nose, the conviction held by so many Americans and Europeans of my Aunt E's parents' generation and her own, that Anglo-Saxon features were evidence of racial superiority while darker skin and short stature spelled inferiority, must have weighed on the minds of my aunt and those of her line who most resembled her. Imagining that it was others who were the inferiors of the society in which she lived might have been projection; an unconsciously activated personality defense that is synonymous with self-deception in those who happen to have well-functioning self-deception genes. For whatever reason, I seemed to have ended up being the human upon whom all her dissatisfactions with self fell.

The beliefs of the eugenics movement were probably embraced with joy and affirmations of validity by Southerners who had been wealthy land owners and slave owners before the South's defeat in the Civil War. Aunt E's and Daddy's grandparents would have been among those former plantation dwellers with lives centered around daily socializing and enjoyment of recreational and cultural activities. I know that there were some women who were daughters or granddaughters of former slaveholders who were so deluded about their superiority over working women they would perform acts as silly as refusing to speak to waitresses who served their tables in restaurants or maids who cleaned rooms in hotels where they stayed when they traveled. I know about this because one of those women so deluded was very close to Aunt E. The eugenics theory most dear to the descendants of former slaveholders would surely have been that being rich, successful, and in command of lesser beings (whom you could get to perform all the tasks necessary to free you from ever having to lower yourself to engage in manual labor) was proof in itself of genetic superiority.

Upon reading William Faulkner's 1929 masterpiece *The Sound and the Fury* when I was in college in the late '50s, I saw myself in Faulkner's tragic character, Quentin Compson. I felt total empathy with Quentin as he stood on a bridge near Harvard Law School preparing to commit suicide. He was there finishing up the only year of a Harvard education that his family could afford. This waste of a valuable year of his young life and of his family's last bit of assets was a result of his mother's refusal to let go of the delusions about class and inherited superiority that had hold of her thinking and emotions. Her persistence in trying to live on in her delusion through her children - in this case, her son Quentin - had robbed them of their ability to adapt to their real circumstances. Faulkner gives the mother character dialog that is so like what I remember as Aunt E's way of speaking, that it evokes memories of all those childhood years of mine lost to Aunt E's presentations to me of a fairy-tale life as if it were one attainable by me.

In *Sound and Fury*, Quentin is introduced to us with words his father is saying to him about an heirloom watch he is about to give him - (people like Aunt E thought the gift of a family heirloom was a really big deal even if changing times had rendered the item useless) - "You will use it to gain the reducto absurdum of all human experience which can fit your individual needs no better than it fitted [your father's or] your grandfather's". That seemed to describe how I felt about the trip to Europe Aunt E had treated me to the summer before I gave up my relationship with her. I had not been able to escape for a moment my perception that she was visualizing our tour as a field of play in which I was to meet men of higher class than I would be able to meet on my own back home on the farm.

I would have been thrilled with my travel together with Aunt E through Europe, I think, if she had had at least a little interest in the history of the places we visited or in the art, music, and literature our guides were talking about as we visited homes, museums, libraries and such. By that time in my life (1959), I had been socially isolated from others of my age for so long I'd tried to escape from my obligation to be social, and my shame over my inability to do that, by switching my focus to learning. Aunt E wasn't interested in my new concentration. I didn't see a glimmer of delight in edification coming from Aunt E.

The only things on which Aunt E had her mind as we toured through Europe were social alliances within our tour group and which individuals within the group were the "best people" like her. What I couldn't escape, long enough to enjoy much of any part of our trip, was my feeling that the whole thing had been conceived by Aunt E as a project in which she was going to put her little loser niece, Emmy, in opportunities where she would be with more of those "upper class" people she didn't ingratiate herself with back in the states. Of course, a real coup for her would be if she got me a perspective husband who would be more wealthy and more desirable than that very desirable man Leah had landed only a few years before.

Aunt E's unending plans for turning me into something that would look attractive to some "right" people somewhere had been going on for years - for decades - and I was sick of the lack of respect she so frequently showed toward me in my incapacity to wow people who looked like important people to her. Having no girlfriends and no beau at twenty is awful enough without having the family matriarch you've practically worshipped all your life feel contempt for you over that lack. It was clear to me that without my showing myself to be the "upper class society girl" she was constantly telling me (and everyone else) she had been when she was young, there was nothing about me of interest to her.

With Aunt E, I had come to feel, every minute, her disgust that I wasn't enticing "society" girlfriends and some wealthy or titled bachelor to "fall head over heels in love with me". I knew that had I been Leah, I probably would have attracted all the "best" girls as my friends and the most impressive male around into swooning over me; but I wasn't Leah. I knew that no matter how much "making a silk purse out of a sow's ear" effort Aunt E had poured into the project of turning me into a completely different person than I was or ever could be, the reliving of all her own younger years' hopes and dreams about herself was not going to take place for her in me.

ROOTS, RELIGION AND DEPRESSION

LEAD UP TO A MELTDOWN

From Basket Weaving to Shots in the Dark

Behind almost every venture of mine into a new effort to find help in psychotherapy, there has existed the same problem - a gnawing feeling in my gut that surely amounts to simple loneliness.

Here in northeastern North Carolina, a few years ago, scientists tried to reintroduce red wolves into habitat where hunting had previously wiped them out. In the first pack with which scientists had some success, there was a female who had the terrible misfortune to become an omega; the member of a wolf pack whom the others attack and run off.

On the evening I made the trip up from my home to the location where (newspaper articles said) there would be a "wolf howling" to which the public was invited and where spokespersons would talk about these animals, I went alone except for my dog. A drive at night to a place hours from my home, anticipating I might hear wolves howl who had once populated my home states, would have been really pleasurable for me had I been able to share it with another person with whom I felt comfortable. "With whom I felt comfortable" is the operative phrase here, because it is not for lack of humans with whom I could spend time that I am alone.

I am alone all the time because I'm more miserable with human company than I am without it ... in fact, unbearably miserable. There have been people in my life whose company I have wanted so badly (I thought) that my longing for it has blotted out every other thought in my awareness. In the end though, there is no doubt in my mind that if any of these people - my "love objects" - had done an about face, had felt themselves to be so in need of my company that they couldn't live without it, I believe I would have lost my fixation on them overnight.

Up until my late seventies, I not only felt lonely all the time I was alone, but I felt crushing shame, too, because a person's being by themselves everywhere they go makes them look socially abnormal. To this instinctual reaction of pack predators to one of their own species who appears to belong to no pack, add the contempt that existed in my family for me because the few friends I was able to make weren't the "right people", and you can see how it was that I was almost squirming in discomfort over my social status twenty-four/seven.

When I got to the wildlife refuge, it was well into dusk, and I found myself in a group of couples and families. The only other loner there was our instructor/guide. Actually, even she wasn't a loner in the same way I was, because she was in touch by radio with another guide who was communicating to her in real time the location of the pack as it moved about over the terrain. Our presenter began to fill us in on how the pack as a whole, and some of its individual members, had fared since their release a few years previously.

Then our guide came to the little female red wolf they'd lost. From the first, the other wolves had tried to run her out of their midst. There was sufficient food for all members of the pack, but that hadn't stopped pack members from trying to prevent her from getting any of it. Handlers had to step in to keep her from starving. Any and every member of the pack would attack her if she didn't keep herself far out on the periphery of the area where they were hunting. Whenever handlers checked on the pack's whereabouts, they could see her wandering up and down, anxious and depressed, outside her line of exclusion; her instinct telling her to join her fellow pack members and experience telling her how far away from them she needed to keep herself to avoid getting attacked.

Then a brief respite came for this unlucky female. The alpha female of the pack had pups, and after a certain time, these pups were put into an enclosure where they could not be reached by the pack. The handlers saw this as an opportunity to get the little adult female who was being mistreated so by her pack mates into a safe place by putting her in with the pups. Her whole personality came to life with the pups as her companions. The pups were too small and inexperienced to bully her. With them, she could behave as an alpha sort of wolf; an elder or caretaker.

She began to romp with a freedom and joy they had

never seen in her before. With the non-threatening pups as her companions, the appearance of anxiety and depression they'd always seen in her disappeared. But, pups grow up, and when these did, the separate enclosure was no longer needed. Once again, the omega was back where she had been; always drawn by instinct toward the pack and always pulling herself back from it out of fear. "This is truly a sad, sad story", I thought to myself as our guide was relating this wolf's history. But the story did have a conclusion. Apparently, the little omega wolf could not resist the instinct to be with her pack with enough will to stay far enough away to save her own life. Handlers had found her carcass not far from where the pack had last been seen.

Leaving the refuge that night, I felt as if I'd never heard a human's story before that I could relate to in the way I could relate to that little omega wolf's.

By the second semester of my second year of college the first time around, I'd seen myself fail in all the opportunities I'd had to succeed socially or musically that might have elicited a little interest or admiration in my female family members. Scholastically, in anything language based, I was doing quite well. For whatever reason, this did not seem to be worth a moment's notice in my family. What I could accomplish had no value to the females in my family.

Most importantly for me, it had been Aunt E whose aspirations for my adult life I had always fantasized myself fulfilling, and I now couldn't see one chance of my satisfying any of her ambitions for me, ever. I couldn't bear to see her disappointment in me - her boredom with my lack of social conquests to introduce to her - on her face anymore. It looked to me as if the only things that would put a light in any of the eyes of the females of my family for me were things at which I'd tried to succeed my whole life so far and absolutely could not.

After Christmas of 1960, I returned to school and began to find empty rooms here and there on the campus where I isolated myself during the day when I wasn't in class. Somehow I ended up in the dean's office, where I remember being unwilling or unable to even talk to her. She told me she was sending me to a psychiatrist; one in a town about forty miles away, as the town in which my college was located wasn't big enough to have a psychiatrist. I would have to go by Greyhound to the bus station in that town, then walk about a mile or so to the psychiatrist's office. This would take up a whole afternoon, so I would be going to these once-a-month sessions on Fridays.

I began to travel to my appointments, very hopeful at first because I thought the doctor was going to do something to help me feel better. Once at his office, I talked and talked, crying all the time I was talking, I'm sure. Not long before this, I had essentially told Aunt E goodbye forever, though not in so many words, and that had felt like the end of everything to me. Alienating her was going to cost me dearly, I knew, in a family where I already felt I was only there because I'd been born there. At the end of the appointment, nothing was different than it had been before the appointment.

I started my walk back to the bus station - a walk which took me through a part of town in which it was really scary for me, a nineteen-year-old female, to be walking alone - and took my seat on the bus that would take me back to my school's town. For a teenage girl, being alone on a bus when the male who has taken a seat beside you seems to have gotten himself a whole lot closer to you than has been necessary, is not too pleasant a thing either. Nonetheless, I went through the whole deal over again for the next session and for the last one in the last month of the school year. Not one thing in my life or how I felt about my life had changed in the three months I had received treatment from this psychiatrist. In my last week at school, I got the bill.

Getting a bill following three sessions of psychotherapy should not be a surprise to any client who gets one. However, it came as quite a shock to me. I suppose I must have thought this was some health service my college would cover. I had no income. There was no adult in my family that I would have dared tell I had run up a bill at a psychiatrist's. I decided I had better kill myself. However, as in several other attempts I'd made at fourteen or so, I must have lacked real commitment to going from alive to dead because I didn't come close to making the gate.

Once home, I gradually got myself into facing life again and moved into town after I had found a job there. Working every day was therapeutic, and living away from home helped too. By fall, I had met my husband-to-be, and for the next five years the births of our children, my husband's promotions, and our geographical resettlements kept me thinking that my change from depressed to happy lay just ahead when whatever circumstances we were in at the time would be better.

The concepts of mindfulness and of maintaining in the foreground of one's attention the "here and now" were not ideas I had ever come across in any way that promoted them as concepts I could use to make my life less miserable. Life had always been presented to me as something that had been glorious for my ancestors and would be glorious for me in the future when I accomplished all those things I wasn't accomplishing in the "here and now".

By 1965, I was in that future I'd pinned my hopes on. I had the husband and children that were supposed to lift me out of depression and drop me into happiness, and depression was with me as overwhelmingly as it ever had been. My children's pediatrician recognized it on my face as I talked with him in his office about my daughter whom I'd brought because of some common childhood symptoms of illness she was exhibiting. My daughter's doctor advised me to seek help at the outpatient clinic in the city.

At this time we were living in Tulsa, Oklahoma, and I could see, as soon as I met the psychiatrist/administrator at the large clinic to which I'd been sent, that in Tulsa, immediate relief of misery for those suffering from depression was the priority for professionals there. My time with the psychiatrist was brief, as I recall, and consisted more of the doctor's telling me what my schedule for my coming weeks of treatment would be than in eliciting from me an account of how I felt or why. Two or three mornings a week, I would be coming to an arts and crafts workshop along with other people in treatment for depression, where I'd choose a project, and an arts-and-crafts-trained person would provide me with the materials I needed and with help in developing my idea, if I wanted help.

Along with these sessions in the workshop, appointments would be set up for me with a psychologist who would act as a counselor, providing me with strategies for getting more enjoyment out of my relationships with my children and my husband and less stress; more effective handling of unwanted behaviors in my children and a re-constitution of the couple-type relationship with my husband I'd had before the birth of our first child.

With every one of my arts-and-crafts sessions, from the first onward, I felt better. The fulfillment there came, not only from creating something in which I could take a little pride, but in the satisfaction of social need that I derived from being able to talk freely about those terrible effects on mental and physical functioning that depression brings at the times when a person most desperately wants to have energy and to be quick thinking, clear headed, motivated, and performing efficiently. To not be able to force oneself to do work or physical activities from which a person would receive reward - if only one would take up the task and keep at it - is one of the most frustrating features of being depressed that I've ever experienced. I've heard other women express the same feeling of despair over that type of functional paralysis.

My husband and I began to again do things as a couple. He had virtually no interest in doing anything that a preschooler wouldn't have wanted to do, so our date nights had to be limited to his interests: food (steak and potatoes) and sports. I took the meager options he gave me and felt lucky I could get some alone time with him. Things seemed to be going much better for me, then my husband got a promotion which meant a transfer to the state of New York. In New York, I fell into depression as soon as the cold weather set in that kept me from taking the children to amusement parks.

When I had left Tulsa, I had thought that my improved

state would stay with me. That improved state I had gotten to in Tulsa had been a result of socializing, brought into my life by the treatment program. In New York, all of that was gone again, and the only therapy available that I could find was the fifty-minute-hour kind with a male psychiatrist.

My husband was an editor with an international news organization. I had thought that should give me at least a little status with the "shrink" I began seeing in Schenectady in 1966. When this doctor told me, "You should get a job", and holding up the classified section of the newspaper said, "I see here there's an opening for a counter girl in a doughnut shop", my face surely must have visibly turned red. I felt so "shrunk" tears came to my eyes.

When I mentioned to my doctor Schenectady that almost every person I talked with in New York, upon noticing my Southern accent, would begin some question having to do with "How are Blacks treated down there?" and in the course of chatter would comment on how slowly I spoke, this doctor responded with, "You're in the North now - time to pedal your bicycle".

I would leave sessions baffled as to what it was all about. I guessed there was supposed to be something therapeutic about whatever it was the psychiatrist was doing, but I couldn't for the life of me see in what the man was saying to me anything that constituted help for depression.

When one day I came to my session feeling a little better than I usually did, Doctor Schenectady had to know the reason and finally pried out of me that I'd had intimacy with my husband the night before for the first time in awhile. But", he said, "you really didn't enjoy it very much, did you?" That question had surprised and puzzled me profoundly. The lovemaking episode had been very, very satisfying, I had thought. We had orgasmed together and had fallen asleep embracing each other, still connected. "What was there not to enjoy about that?" I set to thinking after my session with the psychiatrist.

Still having bought propaganda from somewhere that had presented psychologists, psychiatrists, and psychoanalysts as being able to read minds by way of different sorts of evidences their patients (or even people who weren't their patients) were unconsciously putting out, I thought that surely was how Dr. Schenectady had gotten this information from me that I had not enjoyed sex with my husband the night before.

Due to my naïveté and my having no confidence in my own beliefs when confronted with a psychiatrist's, I was completely intimidated by this man's show of omniscience, deciding that he could see straight through me because of very personal information that I was somehow letting slip out to him while I thought I was safely chatting.

Following this session, I dreamed I was in a stone multi-storied building under siege by soldiers. (Maybe I had been watching too much of Vic Morrow in *Combat*.) I knew I had to find some way out of that building. I saw there was a garbage chute going out one side. In my dream I jumped onto the chute along with piles of trash and food waste and was carried out of my besieged refuge unseen and safe from those who were trying to capture me.

I'd never come close to having sex with anyone but my husband. I had nothing with which to compare the experience that would have shown me that having foreplay and intercourse with a partner to whom I was physically attracted would have had an element to it that just wasn't there in my relations with Bobby. If you've never had truffles, you're perfectly satisfied with mushrooms.

When Doctor Schenectady said to me., "You really didn't enjoy it very much", I assumed he meant that there was something wrong with me that kept me from responding in marital intercourse with my husband as a wife who was sexually mature and healthy would. It didn't enter my mind to think, "At no time in our six years of lovemaking has any bodily contact with Bobby ever made me feel high. Yes, what we do sexually works because the right buttons get pushed and the right levers get pulled. Intercourse with Bobby is fine, enjoyable, and orgasms are satisfying, but, as far as kissing and other things that would probably be called foreplay - caressing my breasts, lingual things? - Oh, yuk! And looking at his naked body and feeling lust? Never, ever has happened."

If at any time Doctor Schenectady had asked questions or introduced topics that would have differentiated sexual functioning from erotic feelings, perhaps therapy under his guidance might have at least made me admit to myself what I'd denied throughout Bobby's and my relationship - that I'd settled for him because he'd been in a place at a time when I was so desperate for the recognition society (and especially the women in my family) afforded to women who had fiancés and husbands, I'd have choked down any reservations about any man who was educated and had some professional status.

Bobby was college educated, was top drawer as a news writer and editor, and further, was every bit as desperate as

I to replace the humiliation of past love life failures with a here-and-now relationship that might allow him to forget. I had met Bobby when I had landed a job as an editorial assistant on a newspaper where he was a state editor. The best thing of all about him had been, for me, that he was in a lost-cause marriage to a woman who had been unfaithful and who had moved out on him and back to her family's home in a distant state. Bobby had seemed *landable* to me. I couldn't see him as being confident enough in himself to play the field, find someone more suitable for him than I, and dump me. I saw my risk of being rejected as very low.

I was so terrified of being found uninteresting by someone who was appealing to me that I practically had panic attacks in the presence of men holding a lot of cards. I had settled for what I thought I was capable of getting and keeping. Bobby probably wasn't all that excited about me either. I had just been someone at the right place at the right time and available. As the years had passed in our marriage, and the children grew to an age when they could communicate well, Bobby had seemed to lose interest in doing anything with me. He seemed to have interest only in his job and in watching TV with the children. His idea of having a couples-level social life was spending hours drinking beer and talking with the husband while leaving behind awareness that I and the other wife were even there.

Still, when I finally did admit to myself a couple of years after I'd left Doctor Schenectady that I really just didn't love my husband, my recognition of that had anything but a positive effect on my depression. I can't see how the outcome of facing how I really felt about Bobby could have ended up any worse for me than if I'd gone on conning myself into believing that Bobby and I had a hot romance for the rest of my life.

In Schenectady with every session with my psychiatrist, I'd grown more and more depressed. When I got fired from my job as a sales clerk because I couldn't tolerate supervision and couldn't get along peacefully with co-workers competing for commissions, I was at the end of a six-month slide straight down. Dirty dishes were piled high (Bobby was not about to do housework), and my three-year-old daughter was making her own peanut butter and jelly sandwiches to take to the babysitters. I took the medicine that Doctor Schenectady had prescribed, which knocked me out so effectively I could hardly remain standing after taking it. I fantasized about just running away from home and trying to stay disappeared forever.

The last time I saw the Schenectady psychiatrist, I shrank from him as if from evil itself, and when he addressed me by my nickname, Emmy, as he usually did, I snapped back without thinking, "Call me Mrs. Bowden". He had some information to pass on to me to the effect that my feelings were all mixed up, that I felt anger when I was supposed to feel love, and some other enlightenments of that nature, but my defenses were up to such an extent I couldn't bring myself to utter a word, right though he might be.

Doctor Schenectady directed Bobby to take me to a hospital where he should tell the staff to begin shock treatments on me. Bobby never displayed much of a caretaker sort of personality in his relationship with me, but in this case he did. He found the cold detachment with which Doctor Schenectady had told him to ask a hospital staff to give me shock treatments to be just a little more uncaring than he could support. Instead of relying on me to make all family decisions as he usually did, in this instance he made the decision to ignore Doctor Schenectady's directions and to bring me and our children south to his family's home where we would stay while he waited for his transfer request that would move him to a bureau in Miami.

Before Dr. Schenectady, I'd already had a couple of people - my nurse aunt and my college-grad sister - in my life who had intimated to me they'd had education in psychology which had enabled them to see inside my mind and emotions and tell me (as I had no knowledge of who I was and what I was thinking and feeling) what I was feeling and, due to my having these vile emotions, what I was; one telling me I was mentally ill, and the other, that I imagined I was hiding how jealous of her I was but that I wasn't hiding my green-eyed-monster self from her at all.

Now, once again, in Dr. Schenectady, I had another person from whom I'd wanted to have some respect tell me, basically, that while I was clueless about my insides, he could see my insides quite clearly, and he was going to perform a beneficial service for me by telling me exactly who I was - a piece of mixed-up junk. By this time, I'd pretty much had all I could take of another human's intimidating me into feeling that while I might be thinking I was presenting an acceptable appearance to the world, they, with their superior knowledge and experience, could see right through my facade into who I really was, and as I needed to know who I really was, they, out of altruistic concern for me, were going to tell me.

A need to know me took over my life. I felt that if I could know everything there was to know about me, that knowledge would put a stop to presumptuous humans being able to lord it over me with their "You think you can hide yourself from me, but you can't" games.

There were a lot of other things I felt I just had to know in addition to knowing myself. Psychiatrists, psychoanalysts, and psychologists cured depression, didn't they? So, why were they not doing with me what they did with those depressed women they cured? Was there some reason they were withholding real help from me? Were they withholding from me the kind of help that would help because I needed to be taught a lesson about acquiescence to their authority or something?

What was all that stuff about for which Dr. Schenectady seemed to be scorning me for my lack of awareness - my inadequate response in marital relations, my emotions being inappropriate compared to what would have been appropriate? I had to have answers, and I had to have them from a source that would not present them to me in a way that left me feeling sneered at. I knew of one source of information that had never underestimated my intelligence, insulted my character, assumed my female mind needed material dumbed down, or done any of the other things I'd often gotten from human information givers. That source was the authors of books. Only in books had I found the wisdom of the alphas in the packs in which I wanted a place.

During my four month layover between New York and Florida, I checked out every book in libraries and bookstores I could find in the towns close to where I was staying that seemed to have anything to do with psychotherapy. I read synopses of Freud's theories, how he would have arranged the room for treatment of his clients, what he would ask his clients to do, and what he himself might have said to stimulate a client into sending her thoughts in the most productive direction.

My readings led me to understand that Freud had spent years psychoanalyzing himself. Considering this, I couldn't see any reason why other humans couldn't psychoanalyze themselves. What was there standing between Freud's finding out how to psychoanalyze himself and my finding out how to psychoanalyze myself?

I found many books by MDs, psychologists, and psychoanalysts giving their decisions about how the sexual responsiveness of women who were psychologically mature and healthy differed from the responsiveness of women who were neurotic, repressed, and stuck in childhood. At last I was getting my first clue as to what in the hell Doctor Schenectady had been implying when he had said of my intimate relations with my husband, "You really didn't enjoy it very much, did you?"

Mulling over all the material I'd read, I came to a couple of conclusions: one, no therapy was going to have much effect on depression that did not carry the recipient of the therapy back to a childhood trauma which had launched the condition. I hadn't yet come across any authority writing about depression who had addressed any of the other possible causes like genetics, brain damage, childhood social isolation, childhood maternal neglect, here-and-now environment, and so forth. If I had come across anything in my reading that said that recovery of repressed feelings and memories actually hardly made any change at all in an analysand's habitual mood, level of energy, or functionality in love and work, I must've not wanted my brain to process the words.

All I got out of what I read was, "Whatever your hang-up is, go back to your childhood and find that memory and those feelings that are clogging up your fuel line so you can't put your pedal to the metal, and your anguish will be over". I bought that idea with a belief not unlike the belief of born-again Christians who state they are saved and that they will spend eternity in heaven with their savior when they die.

The second conclusion to which I came was that I needed to orgasm differently. Reading all this material that stated that emotionally healthy women had no-hands orgasms had left me feeling as if I were a shameful failure as a female. (Postscript: three or four decades later, I was reflecting on how many women I had known who either had never had an orgasm, or had only rarely, and realized I'd never had any reason at all to agonize over my sexual performance's not seeming to be up to male doctors' descriptions of what it should be.)

The books I read about psychoanalysis made it all seem so great; a life's project of the highest order. If I could just accomplish this task of returning to my childhood and resurrecting my repressed energy, my repressed joy, my repressed sexuality, surely then I could outshine my older sister, Leah, who'd left me in the dust at every turn of the road on our way to becoming wives and mothers whose houses and children would show the world that we were better wives and mothers than our peers.

FROM BASKET WEAVING TO SHOTS IN THE DARK

Psychoanalitically Oriented Psychotherapy or Psychoanalysis?

From my first exposure to psychoanalysis-inspired memoirs, right up to the writing of this piece fifty or so years later, no work I ever did, or ever heard about anyone else doing, has grabbed my attention with more appeal and staying power than the work done by analysands and their therapists trying to reach back into childhood memories and find there the relationships and their attached emotions which have left the analysands functional cripples (or, at least, limpers).

That is why, in 1967, when my husband Bobby applied for and got a transfer from New York to Miami, and I found in Miami a psychiatrist with the best of credentials who said he would employ with me psychoanalytically oriented psychotherapy, I was filled with optimism and hope for my future. I knew very well that, technically, my therapy would not be psychoanalysis. However, I also knew that the term *psychoanalytically oriented* surely meant that recovery of repressed childhood memories would be the outcome for which my doctor would be aiming.

It's hard to know where to start in my relationship with Dr. Searcy. Giving a male psychiatrist, who seemed in the early days of my association with him to have a pretty keen interest in Freudian psychoanalysis, a fictitious name that substitutes for the Circe of Greek mythology (instead of a Germanic name) may seem strange, but given the ways in which I changed while in therapy with Dr. Searcy, Circe's changing Odysseus' men to hogs comes immediately to mind.

I had read about people's lives going to pot while they were in the process of recovering childhood repressed material in *The Fifty-Minute Hour; a Collection of True Psychoanalytic Tales*, by Robert Lindner. However, Dr. Lindner's way of recounting his clients' tragedies took all the tragedy out and made the patients' painful experiences seem as if they were merely bumps in a road that never failed to end up at paradise. When Dr. Searcy told me at our first meeting that he would be conducting "psychoanalytically oriented psychotherapy" with me, I couldn't have been more satisfied. I didn't know I was on my way to hell. I thought I was beginning a thrilling adventure that would change me so much for the better that I would eventually be on heights far above most of my fellow women.

I should have kept a journal at the time my treatment under Dr. Searcy began. It's almost impossible, with the viewpoint about those 1960s and 1970s therapy events that I now have, to reconstruct the state of mind with which I assigned meanings and interpretations to them while they were in progress. However, I was far too hopelessly consumed with unresolved limbic system struggles to be able to rise above those issues and rationally concentrate on a prefrontal-cortex-dedicated project like keeping a journal. Or, my failing to keep a journal might simply have been more of the "leaden paralysis" effect which I have read about at depression information sites on the Internet.

Although my fifty-minute hours were going to occur only a couple of times per week as opposed to the five times per week clients of psychoanalysts saw their therapists, I felt sure there was no reason why I couldn't go on with the work I'd read about, not just during the hour and forty minutes I'd be with my doctor, but also during all the time I wanted to devote to it for the other hundred and ten or more hours a week I'd be awake.

The concept of free association is a concept most people can grasp quite easily - no visual-spatial genius required there - transference, likewise. Following dream content to its links bridging the here-and-now everyday experience and the unacknowledged desires in the subconscious mind seemed like work I would love to do and at which I felt I would be great. After all, I (if I were the analysand) would certainly be a hundred times more familiar with the experiences and feelings exposed by my dreams and associations than any psychiatrist, as his associations could only lead him to conclusions more relevant to his own life than to mine, I reasoned. It would be my life from which the free association and identity puzzles and their solutions would come, and I felt it would be silly for any doctor to assume he could interpret to me my transference, my dreams, my unresolved longings and fears, and all the other aspects of memory recovery better than I.

Before I even began my psychoanalytically oriented psychotherapy with Dr. Searcy, I'd made up my mind I was going to undergo psychoanalysis even if I had to do it myself, without a psychoanalyst, no matter how long it took, even if that turned out to be years or even decades. I had the same mind in my head, in the same personality I'd had, when I sat on my Kiddie Kar at the top of a long flight of stairs when I was three or so, and just had to do what my mother had sternly warned me not to do; just had to find out what would happen if I edged the front wheel of my Kiddie Kar over the edge of the top tread.

By the time I went, in the summer of 1967, to my Miami psychiatrist for my first session of his psychoanalytically oriented psychotherapy, I had already formulated in my own mind what I was going to do, how I was going to do it, and what the outcome was going to be. My case was going to progress exactly as the cases of psychoanalyst Doctor Robert Lindner in his book, *The Fifty-minute Hour*. At the beginning, as his clients began to unload repressed material, they had gone downhill in functioning and in mood until they fell into a zone of psychological purgatory. Some clients of Lindner's had stayed stuck at their bottoms for years, according to his accounts. Their odysseys became the template for an odyssey I could see myself making - became determined to make.

My reading of Lindner and other psychoanalyst/authors did turn up a few caveats mingled in with the many tales of descent and resurrection there. One situation which should deter therapists from administering psychoanalytically oriented psychotherapy or psychoanalysis to a client was the absence, in a client's childhood, of having had a strong and reliable bond with a parent or parent surrogate, I read.

Not having yet had any therapy which sent me back to see my inner child, I didn't know whether I would be a client without much positive transference to transfer to a psychiatrist/analyst or not. I had no idea whether or not I had had a childhood with such negative experiences with caregivers I would not be able to transfer much besides negative identification to a psychiatrist thus dooming me to sinking my own boat.

What I saw was me becoming the me I had always dreamed of being, and that dream entailed my dumping of everything I had ever been up to that point and becoming a 180-degree different person.

Earlier in the spring, as I had read books by Karen Horney, Anna Freud, Erik Erikson, (among others), and some synopses of the theories of pioneers like Sigmund Freud and Carl Jung, my despair with myself over having failed to get cured of depression, when I'd spent months each with five different therapists, began to be replaced by hope - greater and greater hope - that I could become that person I wanted to be. I could see a butterfly pulling itself up and out of a chrysalis.

Looking at therapies in my past, I transitioned from blaming myself for not having had that rebirth I thought I needed, to seeing the therapies as being ineffective because they hadn't addressed the real cause (I thought) of my perpetually poor performance; that being my unfinished emotional and psychosexual business from childhood. By "psychosexual" I mean, of course, Freud's stages of childhood sexual development: the oral, the anal, the Electral (Oedipal angst for females), and that identification-with-momma period that resolves the Electra conflicts.

Once settled in, in Miami, I had set to work to find this psychiatrist, vowing that this time I would not accept one who would not address with me the really serious stuff holding me back from being the person I so wanted to be, That serious stuff I needed to get out of me (I thought) was surely childhood repressed love, fear, and anger and the events in which these too-emotional-for-a-child repressions had occurred.

In the beginning, Dr. Searcy was a dream come true for a female client who wanted psychoanalysis but who couldn't afford those four- or five-a-week sessions of the real thing. (In 1967, a female client wouldn't have called herself a client though, but rather a "patient".) In the sixties, psychiatrists were gods, or at least knights in white satin, and their female clients were the helpless damsels in distress whom they had chosen (great rescuers of the emotionally-challenged that they were) to save. We women played our roles, too, by unquestioningly picking up our scripts for "patients".

My route into the doctor's brought me (after a forty-five-minute drive through South Miami and Coral Gables) to US 1's intersection with Brickell Avenue - a lushly landscaped drive lined with high-rise condominiums - and to the thoroughfare and causeway entrance to Key Biscayne. That island almost shimmered in the brilliant light of Florida's sun and clear blue skies, the buildings poking up bright white here and there above stands of palms and other tropical trees. No woman has ever been more in love with any city than I was with Miami.

On my first visit to Dr. Searcy's, I was late. As soon as he ushered me into his inner office, I began to apologize but was stopped short by his calm remark that I need not apologize, the time there was mine, that he was paid for the time whether I was there or not and that I could do with the time what I wished. This seemed to ease my anxiety a bit.

I still carried with me the image of my late treatment in New York by the tall, supercilious, older man who sat behind a huge desk with a ceiling-high cathedral window behind him, and who called me by my diminutive (rather than, as is expected in the South, my married name) and presumptuously indulged in wild analyses of me. I entered treatment with Dr. Searcy squared off to defend myself with what I hoped were now better self-knowledge weapons than I had had before I'd done all my reading. One by one, I laid my weapons down in the atmosphere cast by this man's tender voice quality, the youthfulness of his occasionally mirthful comments and his non-straying attention to everything I had to say. At that time, did I recognize the man's tender vocal style of speaking as being acting? I don't know.

In the first appointment, he explained that the treatment he proposed for me would be "psychoanalytically oriented". Those were the magic words as far as I was concerned. I'd read copious amounts of literature about the process of retrieving emotional and psychosexual material from early childhood by freely associating with a doctor's guidance. I was filled with hope that now, at last, I could achieve a breakthrough to my unconscious where something that lay there was crippling my efforts to live a life that would impress: my aunt, the matriarch who had appointed herself guardian over my father, my mother, and every issue from their irresponsible unions; my older sister, Leah, the ever-superior psychic seer of everything in me that I wanted to hide for the sake of escaping from humiliation and shame; and that would finally interest my mother enough to bring the light to her eyes that I saw there when she looked at my older sister.

I wanted the doctor to help me, but I found myself having a hard time following his direction to say whatever came to mind. I was having a hard time even answering his questions, which were not that frequent. I soon realized that I was expecting him to analyze every word I spoke and to then point out to me the real, embarrassing, unhealthy states of mind which lay behind each defensively chosen utterance. Anxiety began to build about this eventuality even while this psychiatrist's calm nonjudgmental way of relating to me lulled other anxieties.

At our second appointment, I was again late. Again, Dr. Searcy assured me that I could do with my time what I wanted. But this time, he followed this assurance with a question, "Why are you giving up part of your time? Perhaps it would be helpful to us to find out why you would choose not to make use of all of the time you are paying for."

This was new. Dr. Searcy was saying to me (or so I deduced from attributing to his words an underlying meaning), "You are the person here who has to do the significant work if effective work is to be done". I did want to be the one, of the two of us, who would be doing the work. I had no desire to be worked *on*. Now, I felt I was being invited into a partnership on a project I wanted to successfully complete more than I'd ever wanted to accomplish anything. I began to talk, and talk, and talk. As those of you who have had any experience with psychoanalytic strategies could guess, resistances arose and blocks halted my unspooling of my thoughts. At each prolonged pause in my speech, Dr. Searcy would remind me how important it was to speak every thought that came to mind, would remind me that every utterance was acceptable there, that I didn't need to self-censor when speaking as one normally does. Nonetheless, in the beginning, I would go silent if what had just come to mind seemed to be politically incorrect or offensive. When the doctor would then prompt me to go on, asking what I had just been thinking, I would say something along the lines of, "I'm afraid you will think ..."

"Me, Dr. Searcy?" my guide would exclaim. "Would I think that, or is that the person I represent to you? Is this transference that you are experiencing or is this the reality, right now, of the situation?"

Gradually, I did come to believe that everything I had to say, regardless of how personal or unacceptable as subject matter with others, was welcome fodder for the grinding of the analysis mill as I tried, with Dr. Searcy's mentoring, to push away the debris of transference to him of past relationships and come to grips with the here-and-now professional relationship between us.

Fears continually arose in me of how Dr. Searcy might view my opinions, my creative ideas, my stereotyping of people - my every word, actually - as I freely associated away. At such times, I was taught to attempt to express the emotion I was feeling. Generally these emotions fell into the categories of fear of his anger, or shame in the face of contempt in what he might be thinking of me or feeling about me.

On one such occasion, he stated that he didn't have those kinds of feelings for his patients; that he had had his own analysis. I really wondered about his assertion that his patients, regardless of what they said in sessions, never aroused negative feelings in him. Something about that avowed complete detachment didn't ring true to me, but at the time, I was far too imprisoned by self-doubt to openly express my dubiousness.

Session by session, I seemed to fall deeper and deeper into a totally self-centered world of subvocal fantasized conversations with Dr. Searcy. "Conversations" isn't exactly the right word to describe my unending imagined revelations to the doctor. "Bringing gifts that pleased the god" is a good psychoanalytic metaphor for what I was accomplishing in my daydreams.

In my *fantasized* audiences with him, the doctor hardly ever had anything to say to me. His role consisted of emanating warm approving feelings of everything that I said; of having the kind of light in his eyes that said he thought I was doing spectacular, superior work at this free association business. I created the illusion for myself of his being completely engaged in the work we were sharing, and I pictured a bond between us, because of our mutual work, that was on a higher level than our marriages to other people.

At the time, I thought the compulsive fantasizing I had fallen into was because of positive transference to Dr. Searcy of the identity of someone I had loved in childhood. I saw myself as having the same relationship to Dr. Searcy that female patients in the books I had read had to their psychoanalysts. I had no idea at the time - or maybe I did have some idea but not a clear enough idea to go anywhere with it - that this fantasizing about talking to the doctor was, yes, a sincere effort on my part to go on working during all the hours between sessions on the same thing Dr. Searcy was having me work on in sessions when I was actually speaking to him; but, I'm pretty sure that what I was also doing was the same thing I had done after my aunt Emmelia had brought Leah and me back home to misery after I'd just spent the first months of my fourth year basking in the love of Aunt E and her friends and the approval of Leah as she played the role of my teacher and nanny at Aunt E's in Lexington.

Back home, with my loss of all of that social nourishment overnight, I had fallen into living in fantasy - the visuals and feelings all about Aunt E and the animated adults with their children who filled Aunt E's world, about the beautiful houses filled with expensive personal possessions, and, most of all, physical affection. Aunt E's words of love for me and the hugs changed, in my daydreams, to imagining what it was going to be like when I would have that boyfriend or husband of the sort that Aunt E, Leah, and all of us females of all ages were always talking about. I could see my boyfriend and me hugging, kissing, and doing some even more exciting things than that. In fantasy, I was trying to create an inclusion of myself into what I imagined the world of my doctor must be, I suppose. I was pretty sure that it was a world like that Aunt E must have shared with her stockbroker husband while he was alive.

While I was rapidly moving all my thoughts to what I planned to speak about in my next session with Dr. Searcy, my husband's thoughts, outside of his work, didn't seem to be on anything except indulging our children's desire to watch TV with him every minute he was home. My husband wasn't interested in ANYTHING - and I do mean ANYTHING - that was on an intellectual level above that of preschoolers. Everything in the world of which I wanted to be a part, to my husband, was worldly, phony, nothing in it as good as his little tiny world bounded by his women folk's primitive, fundamentalist, Taliban-like religion and their avoidance of looking into or experiencing anything new.

By the time I was seeing Dr. Searcy, living with my husband felt like living with his grandmother's spirit in control of my household, making sure everything was going exactly as she decreed. And with my children, my husband wasn't a parent - he was a peer of theirs, covertly leading them to see me as their enemy.

The doctor, I assumed, was keeping me on the path to working through all the negative transference that would interfere with my having a healthy way of relating to him - a superficial, non-emotional way, I guessed. I did not deny myself indulgence in one bit of the positive transference. It was my addiction.

My illusion that I had a kind of symbiotic relationship with the doctor took a few crashes. For one thing, I discovered on my first visit to my church that Dr. Searcy, his wife, and their two children attended there. This had good points and bad points for me. To the good, was the fact that my doctor's being a member of my church raised him immeasurably in my eyes in as far as my assessment of his qualities of intelligence, insight, and discernment.

On the disturbing side, was the presence, right before my eyes, of the woman my doctor really loved - his wife. She fit the description perfectly of a Beach Boys' California Girl; tall (considerably taller than he, actually), willowy, blond, and beautiful.

Unsettling questions deluged my mind. "Does he tell her who his patients are? She doesn't know I even know her husband, does she? She must know he's down there at his office hearing all these women telling him all these most intimate details of their lives, feeling all this love and adoration for him borne of positive transference. How does she feel about that?"

It doesn't matter how much you have read about transference, and it doesn't matter how many discussions you have had with the object of your transference about the fact that your feelings are only transference, your awareness of the reality of that doesn't stop adrenaline from flowing, your heart from beating faster, your stomach from fluttering, or fear from transforming your limber body into a graceless board. After conditioning, Pavlov's dogs salivated when the bell rang whether they saw any food there or not.

It's like that with transference. Intellectually, you know your body's responses to the doctor are occurring as a result of conditioning by past relationships, but as Michael Douglas's son remarked to him after being told by his dad that Dad's onscreen love scenes were only acted, "Yeah Dad, but when you kiss the girl, you really kiss her".

Dr. Searcy reproved me once, at a much later date, when I tried to describe my feelings for some man in my life as being transference. "You only feel transference for the psychiatrist", he impatiently corrected me. That statement sounded like bullshit to me, but by that time in our relationship he was beyond discussing that issue with me as if I were a credible observer. Logic tells me that love or hate or fear or longing doesn't occur for anybody without some component of that feeling coming from transference of emotions felt in past relationships to present ones.

As I look back now, with over fifty years having passed since I began my work with Dr. Searcy, I can remember no point at which he expressed concern about my need to fantasize about him to the exclusion of every real relationship I had in my life. After only a few months of treatment, I was living in a daze. I had signed up, at about the time I began treatment with Dr. Searcy, for an adult education art class. I began the course very motivated to produce art that would impress my teacher and fellow students. I labored over my productions with enthusiasm and with a dedication to excellence.

Gradually, as the weeks went by, my obsession with the doctor - even though we had discussed innumerable times how all the feelings I had for the doctor were simply transference - increased until I was throwing my art assignments together at the last minute in such a sloppy way that I felt shame over the poor quality to which my work had sunk. I grieved over the state I was in, but all the resolves I made to get it together and keep my wits about me faded to fantasizing before I could ever put my get-a-grip resolves into motion.

At first, I continued to take good care of my children, but gradually I lost the ability to keep my mind on my present responsibilities to such an extent that I asked my husband to call his parents and have them come to get the kids and to keep them in North Carolina until I could get past my collapsed state of mind.

I intellectualized myself into acceptance of my out-in-space state of mind by recalling the stories I had read about the breakdowns most patients seemed to go through as they went deeper and deeper into psychoanalysis and came closer and closer to the unblocking of the frightening childhood experience. I was existing on visions of future wellness and happiness when (I expected) I would have recovered the childhood repressed memories, the release of which, I felt sure, was now imminent.

Dr. Searcy increased my number of appointments from twice a week to three. I remember going one Saturday morning – a day on which I've never known psychiatrists to work - when downtown Miami and the doctor's office building were relatively deserted. Sitting with the doctor, alone, with all the people who usually would be bustling around outside gone for the weekend, brought a powerful, enveloping sense of elevated identity with it. But in trying to match that spiritual sensation up with which childhood caregiver Dr. Searcy was calling forth out of my subconscious, it seems it was I, rather than Dr. Searcy, who was representing someone else to me. The soul-satisfying connection to the doctor that I felt spelled Leah more than anyone else, but not *my* relationship with Leah. Rather, what I saw was Leah in relationships I had observed her having with one after another of people that loved her - people I wish could have loved me the way they seemed to love Leah - but to whom I was just part of the woodwork. As I sat with my psychiatrist on that day that held for me such a thirst-quenching feeling, was a part of my being (that part of me that unconsciously imitates Lea) hanging in the room speaking to me, saying, "Emmy, this is what it feels like to be Leah"?

I don't think Dr. Searcy started out representing any one caregiver to me; I think the initial transference in which I found myself was more of evoked time and place than of any individual. I think it was all about summer when I was four and staying with older sis Leah at Aunt Emmelia's big house in Lexington, with smiling, happy adults giving me attention - positive attention - every day, and Leah playing the role of nanny to me. My doctor was just (in transference) one of those men before whom (Aunt E had taught Leah and me) I should do everything I could to be as likeable as it is possible for one human to be in the eyes of another… initially.

When we began work, it was early summer in Miami - a city to which people dream of going - and here I was in sunlight and new beginnings just as I had been, at four, having left cold, drab, highland Virginia behind to go to warm, sunny Lexington in Virginia's verdant Great Valley.

I've sat down at a typewriter or keyboard many times over the decades since I left Miami and Dr. Searcy behind, and I never have been able to come up with any more than a garbled, confused narrative about why Dr. Searcy's opinion of me mattered so monumentally to me that I would go into self-destruct mode when I thought I had lost it after our work relationship had seemed to me to be going so swimmingly at the onset. I do know that the answer to that question - whatever other questions remain unanswered - was Mother.

Many very sane and intelligent people believe that we all have an aura emanating from us that can be unconsciously detected by other living things, including humans.

In the first months of my work with Dr. Searcy, I detected nothing but good things as I sat in his office during my fifty-minute hours - a positive attitude toward me and great satisfaction with my progress. I even felt I detected, on his part, surprise that I was moving along so fast, as if this was not something with which he had had much experience in treating clients.

Then, one day as I was exuberantly describing erotic content that had come back to me from my Electra stage of development, I thought I saw a frown cross his face. He cut me short and changed the subject. His voice seemed to me to carry annoyance and impatience ... Mother's reaction to just about everything I had said or done as a child.

Consistently, over the months I'd been in treatment, if I visualized his office with us there seated on either side of an end table, each facing forward while the Dr. sat quiet and almost motionless waiting for me to do my work, the free association vision that came along with the in-real-time image was a mental picture of my mother seated on a low stool silently reading a book in her lap, waiting.

What was Mom waiting for? Mom was waiting on my youngest sister - seated on a potty to Mom's left, facing forward - to get on with the business at hand. Sis had cerebral palsy, and at three, had still not been able to gain any mastery over the potty thing.

At wit's end as to what she could do, Mom had decided, for this session, to keep Sis sitting until something happened no matter how long it took. I think this was Baby Sis' fifty-minute hour. To me, they seemed to sit there forever. Through it all, Sis sobbed softly but steadily, and Mom maintained an attitude of quiet stoicism. It looked grueling but it worked. Sis finally got the hang of the potty thing.

My childhood longing where my mother had been concerned was to do "work" that would inspire her, delight her, impress her, whatever that work might be. With Leah, all her accomplishments, goals, social connections - her activities across the board - brought those gleams-to-the-eye, smiles, and good attention that I so wanted but seemed to accomplish the reverse in winning with every idea of mine I put into motion.

Where my mother has been concerned, I have never been able to let her hostility toward me and her low opinion of me go. Why have I not been able to let that go? ... because prior to some event she had loved me and found me just as valuable as she found Leah? ... I don't know.

With Dr. Searcy, I started with transference to him of the identity of a loving caregiver and saw that change, because I did things in my life of which he disapproved, to hostility and low opinion. Mother's endless complaint of me was, "You just won't do what I tell you to". In real time, no transference involved, that was exactly what Dr. Searcy's complaint against me came to be. I've never been able to let go of the indignation I've felt over that, nor the hurt and feeling of loss, nor the despair. Finally, after seven years of believing that my continuing in my therapy with Dr. Searcy would eventually pay off in my recovering some memory that would free me from myself, there was nothing left of my dream but a sensation of some life being lost at which I'd never get another chance.

In my last appointment with Dr. Searcy in 1974, seven years into what I had been continuing to believe was psychoanalytically oriented psychotherapy, I happened to mention that phrase in conjunction with my sessions. "You are not in psychoanalytically oriented psychotherapy", I heard this psychiatrist inform me. "You are in supportive therapy."

Astonishment and a sense of being maliciously betrayed gripped me. "No wonder I've been going nowhere for years", I thought. "I wonder at what time in this past seven years he dropped me into this without saying a word to me about the decision?"

Dr. Searcy didn't stop there. "You are delusional", he went on. "You are in a delusion that you are in psychoanalysis", he stated very authoritatively. I didn't make any attempt at all to refute what he was staying. We were totally out of touch.

I thought back to 1970 when I had let my ex move to North Carolina with my children, and I had elected to stay in Miami instead of moving to be near them because I'd thought I was working on resolving a transference to this doctor. I don't remember making a fuss of any kind to Dr. Searcy over this ending of the greatest hope I'd ever entertained over any work I'd undertaken in my life. To the best of my recollection, I quietly cancelled any further appointments, went home, and turned my mind to starting life over in some other place.

PSYCHOTHERAPY OR PSYCHOANALYSIS?

Event at a Cistern, Re-Visited

In an earlier composition, "In the Beginning", I related an incident from my preschool years where I would have fallen into a cistern and drowned if it had not been for my father's instantaneous reaction to hearing my cry for help from a distance so far from where he and my mother and sister were working, I am surprised he even heard me. I believe that the fact that he heard my cry, dropped his tools, and ran as fast as he could to reach me while my mother stood without moving as he did so, made quite an impression on me with respect to my perception of what value each placed upon me.

Perhaps my mother and older sister were just as concerned as my father and the only reason he reached me so much more quickly than they was simply because he could run faster, but my feelings go with the "he loved me much more" theory. Seeing your parent put everything he has in him into saving your life can definitely make a child feel loved. This event in my childhood as well as others involving my father all did seem to have those dual components of love and fear that cause repression in young children. Still, I think it was the opinions about Daddy expressed by his older sister (my Aunt E), Mother, and Leah, and the behavior of these three women toward him, that had a more powerful psychological effect on my carryover of transference from him to later relationships in my life than what he himself said and did.

Of course, ask me about any of my life's failures in love and work, and I'm sure I will find a reason to blame Leah. But, if I envision myself growing up without Leah ever-present, there to show me with sneers and words that my relationship with our father was depraved, would I have been attracted to males based on transference rooted in my preschool relationship with my father?

Men I met after my time with the psychoanalytically oriented psychiatrist (to whom I was supposed to transfer the identity of my father but couldn't) showed me that on my deepest animal-instinct level, I definitely was attracted to men who had physique and some other attributes very like my father - so attracted that the need I felt reminds me of a starving animal falling on a handout of food. In these men, there was a level of game-playing and a drive toward hurtfulness to women that made the strength of my physical attraction to them terrifying. I think that the major reason I never transferred to my Dr. Searcy the identity of my Electral-stage father was that throughout my childhood I was physically and emotionally terrified of my father. For a depressed woman, perhaps a relationship with a man of whom she's partially terrified - whether the reason is because she thinks he might physically hurt her, or for other factors such as his being a womanizer or married - may be the only stimulant powerful enough to get the energy going in her that will give her relief from her motivation-bereft condition.

Pondering the question: Why could I not transfer the identity of my father to my psychiatrist? (Thus giving us the material the doctor kept looking for that wasn't there) ... I see my lack of fear of the doctor, coupled with there being no chance whatsoever of there ever being an orgasmic reward for lusting after the doctor, as being the big hurdle which necessitated my finding a transference stand-in love-object other than the psychiatrist. I never have been able to understand why the doctor could not comprehend that my very intelligent cerebral self could see there was never going to be satisfaction of animal instincts with the doctor, therefore aim-inhibition automatically set in. Freud had a lot to say about aim-inhibition, as I recall, so why didn't my psychiatrist grasp this? I have no idea.

Once, when a therapist asked me what hurt after I had complained of how unbearably depression hurt, I didn't know how to answer her. The question provoked in me a need to know that sent me on a lengthy contemplation of what did hurt so awfully when I was in my most miserable moments. Of all the feelings I've ever felt that were so powerfully excruciating I was driven to attempt suicide, shame was that feeling. In all the things I've ever seen, heard, or read, I've never come across anything that revealed what chemical it is that the brain releases that causes one to feel ashamed. But, for me, that's the brain chemical that can wipe my whole body clean of any good feeling I have.

I identify my older sister as the most significant person of my childhood in as far as that feeling of shame is concerned. Using shaming, Leah had control of my whole world from before I was out of diapers, and I think I must have had Stockholm syndrome right out of the starting gate. Leah's reaction to anything that would have been emanating out of my body from before I would even have been of an age to have muscular control over oral, anal, or urethral effluents, would have been shaming me and expressing disgust, I'm pretty sure.

Much psychoanalytic lore focuses on the Oedipal period of a child's development. I have a feeling that I have already described this period in a preschooler's life in several preceding pieces, but just in case I haven t ... the three-to-six period is the stage referenced when the word Oedipal is used. Oedipal concerns, in my mind, little boys who unconsciously want to get dad out of the way as their mom's erotic partner; who want to be more attractive in this arena then their dads are to their moms. As you know, undoubtedly, Oedipus was the principal in a Greek play, who, through a bizarre chain of events, killed his own father and married his mother.

While the term Oedipal is often applied to little girls' three-to-six stage of development, the more correct reference would be Electra. It is the Greek legend of Electra that supplies the nomenclature applicable to females in the Oedipal-equivalent complex when, Freud postulated, a woman exhibits a repressed, incestuous desire of a daughter for her father.

While I'm unsure about why I have felt such a desperate need for a boyfriend or husband who could arouse in me erotic chemistry throughout my life, I believe that significant problems I was not able to work through to resolve the Electra complex at the appropriate age lay in my inability to win warmth and acceptance from my mother and older sister, not in any inappropriate behaviors of my father. My sister's reaction to my trying to be wherever my father was if I was able to get there, was often sneering at my relationship with him. I felt, too, that she saw something degenerate in his being physically affectionate toward me and in my accepting that affection. I thought Mother felt the same.

If it had not been for the sneers and disgust I saw so frequently on my sister's face when the topic of my father's warmth toward me came up, I don't think I would've had nearly the anxiety over my relationship with my father that I did, and I don't think unresolved Electra would have continued to send me ending relationships and looking for new ones for the rest of my life.

Returning to the connection between my Electra stage of development and my episode of being rescued by my father at the cistern at our barn:

Some days after relating the facts of the incident to my psychiatrist, I began to think and do some unusual things. I stayed up until the wee hours of the morning trying to play some songs on the piano that were in an old songbook from which I had seen my father try to play. My older sister was amazingly gifted at the keyboard of a piano or organ, whether playing by ear or from sheet music, but neither Daddy nor I could ever play competently so much as one of the simplest songs we could find. That gave Daddy and me something in common that Leah couldn't share; a lot of ineptitude in a lot of things we attempted.

After several days of my all-night piano playing, I remember being awakened in the early morning hours by a linguistic alarm going off in my head.

"Oh my God," I was dreaming, "it's going to come out of my mouth." Whereupon, erotic fantasies began to flood my brain like water spilling over a dam. This unstoppable flow seemed to be endless. It went on for a day or two, maybe more. I surmised that the weeks and months of free association mode of thinking coupled with my considering who, in the present, might be representing persons in my childhood, had brought back a formerly repressed memory. There was erotic stimulation so intense I'd never experienced anything like it in my life. Even more strangely, it all had the feel of being a spiritual experience.

As waves of fantasy kept coming from my brain on and on, I was inspired to try to get my husband in on this great burst of unexpected lust. Strangely, things just didn't work out in our real-life effort that gave me anything like the passion that I was experiencing in the fantasies coming from my brain. I had thought that bringing up repressed Electra feelings from their depths would enable me to have the no-hands orgasms that psychoanalysts claimed were a sign of good mental health in a woman. Finding that my eruption of unconscious into the conscious hadn't achieved that for me was terribly disappointing because I had suckered myself into believing devoutly that that was true.

In any new experience I've ever had, it has just come automatically for me to analyze it and give it the Dr. Spock (as in Dr. Spock of Star Trek) logical explanation for, "What happened here? Why did it happen?" Having been reading, for months, literature that dealt with psychiatry, psychology, and, most especially, psychoanalysis, my conclusion about the whole thing was that my psychoanalytically oriented psychiatrist's therapy had released repressed Electra stage material from my unconscious. It was all about Daddy and my here-and-now representative of Daddy was my husband. In other words, I'd married a boy just like the boy who'd married dear old Mom.

It was not that memory of this incident (Daddy's saving me from the cistern) had ever been lost to me. Visually, I remembered every detail of it. What I had repressed had been the whole swirl of overpowering conflicting emotions I had felt toward my father in this event; fear and loathing over the vicious paddling he had given me following the rescue, while being filled with gratitude and love for him for saving me from being pulled down into a bottomless cavern where water that would drown me lay out of sight in its depths. I always had conflicting feelings toward my father because of the behavior extremes to which his brain damage pushed him, but my feelings on this day had been more than I could consciously bear, I guess.

The whole point of my undergoing psychoanalytically oriented therapy was supposed to be that I would recover repressed memories, the theory being that these memories, seething in my unconscious, were the cause of my depression. I bought that theory absolutely at the time. Since then I have come to see repression in a completely different light from the way literature presented it to me at the time that I was buying all of the explanations.

Now I think to myself, God bless the evolution that

brought the process of repression to humans, hiding hatred from us that we can't afford to show, and hiding it so well, even from us, that we don't give ourselves away by displaying even so much as a twitch of rage toward someone who is hurting us who is more powerful than we.

When hatred absolutely must be hidden for our own welfare, repression comes to our rescue. I've found repression to work that way completely behind the scenes and automatically even as an adult. What a divine intervention for the protection of little children. Repression may have saved many a child's life. I'm pretty sure it saved me, as a child, from a frequency and intensity in my father's bursts of ill-controlled anger that my less repressed sisters weren't lucky enough to avoid.

As an adult, I think my brain's instinct to automatically repress anger, with no conscious awareness on my part that repression of emotion is taking place within me, may have saved me several times from striking out physically at people who were subjecting me to psychological torture. By some miracle going on behind the scenes in my mind, all the while that my mother-in-law was alive and teaching my children things to say to me and ways to behave toward me that would hurt and humiliate me to the most devastating degree she could devise, I maintained an attitude of calm and respect toward her. In her presence, I never consciously felt anything but perplexity and horrible pain.

She taught my children to believe that being verbally inhumanly cruel to me and divorcing themselves from all feelings of compassion and familial warmth for me (as well as from recognition of me as their mother) constituted the performance on their part of good, God-approved acts, because I was a "fallen woman" and I wasn't "fit to speak to them." I would spend hours driving to be with my children, and my mother-in-law would be waiting with them at the door so that she could say these things to me in their presence thereby modeling for them how to talk to me completely free of any feeling of respect; not only free of respect for me, in that I was their mother, but free of even the simple respect each of us owe to any fellow human being.

It wasn't until she was dead that my anger against my mother-in-law for destroying my relationship with my children, and for destroying my children's observance of civilized values, rose from my subconscious, and I felt the power of my rage. It was truly ungodly. I screamed and cursed and sobbed it out in my house alone hour after hour with no one to hear me but my pets. (At, least, I hope no one heard me but my pets, but I'm not really sure of that.) I could see then that if I had felt such rage at any time while my mother-in-law was alive, I don't know how I could have contained it.

But, enough on that sad theme … I believe my focus was going to be on negative transference or someone connected to it in some way. Let me see if I can stop freely associating away from my subject matter and find my way back to the connections I had planned to write about…

As long as I remained, in my therapy, seeing my psychiatrist through eyes influenced by transference related to my father, things went quite well. However, negative transference was on its way. God help the little girl who, as an adult, puts herself in the care of a psychiatrist who practices psychoanalytically oriented psychotherapy and who can't use signs of negative transference in a way that helps his client. There is nothing in the world that can throw a depressed person into more obsessively negative thinking, addiction, and self-destruction than negative transference.

And, incidentally, going back to that thought, ... "just like the boy who married dear old Mom" ... that is supposed to be the kind of transference that is the glue which holds a woman to her husband: in my case, my unconscious little-child self had wanted to identify - following the relinquishing of competition with Mom or Dad - with Leah, not with Mom; and, Leah had had a relationship with our Dad of mutual fear, hatred, scorn, and global rejection. Resolving my Electra issues by finding out I'd gotten that man "just like the man that had married dear old Mom", couldn't have been any more murderous to a relationship between a woman and her "till-death-us-do-part" mate, than it was to mine.

ROOTS, RELIGION AND DEPRESSION

EVENT AT A CISTERN, REVISITED

The New Alpha

In one of my first encounters with the woman my ex-husband married a year or so after our divorce in the early 1970s, she gave me a good taste of how she would be appropriating me in her grand plan for her future. I had had experience in my own family with being used as a scapegoat by dominance-asserting females, but the adult female alphas in my family at least had moral compasses rooted more in British style pretension than Nazi style terrorism. I had never known a human being like this one my ex had married, and I had no defenses anywhere within me to protect myself and my children from the destruction she would deliver to me, my children, and the dream I had of a positive bond forever with my descendants.

This initial experience - one of an endless number like it to come - began with my taking a flight from Miami, where I lived, to Charlotte, North Carolina, where my ex and his new wife, Shelley, lived with my children, whom I'll call Millie and Mack. Personally, I know nothing of Shelley's background. Everything I relate here about it was told to me by my children. They said she came from some western part of the state and that her family grew burley tobacco. She had a degree in psychology from some state university, the name of which I don't think they mentioned, and in telling me this, I believe I saw expressions on their faces that said that this was a matter that impressed them.

I chose for this woman the fictitious name Shelley through the process of free association. Those associations start with Shelley's maiden name - Germanic in genealogic origin - which leads me to Hitler and his tricking of a whole nation of people into believing his depictions of the Jews in their midst as being bestial, depraved, degenerate, and filled with secretive plots to wipe out Aryan culture and economy.

From Hitler, the association path in my mind goes to Nazis and Anne Frank's family hiding for two years or so in the attic over a factory in the Netherlands. Next, the visuals that accompany that image move to the couple who shared that attic refuge with the Franks, and you come to the name Shelley. I never think of Shelley without thinking of Hitler's fooling of an entire population of supposedly civilized people into buying his tale that they were being plotted against in a vast conspiracy of Jews worldwide to take over and demote Aryans to the status of slaves, when that whole scenario was a projection by Hitler of what he himself was doing. People of Germany surely had heard of the personality defense of projection, and how that works to protect one from seeing him or herself as a "bad" human being - a predator. As Germany was not a country thought of as populated by uneducated or uncivilized people, how could it be that millions of human beings, not only in Germany, but throughout countries of Europe, Asia, and North and South America, could see Hitler, a projector to a pathological degree - dangerously insane - as a man they so loved and idolized that they trusted him to lead them to an Eden on earth? They worshipped him and turned their lives and wills over to him. Under Hitler and his buddies, the German people left humanity behind and became a pack of dogs on the hunt, all after the prey that Hitler had targeted for them.

The tale that I have just outlined is, point by point, a parallel of what has taken place in my ex's family - my children's influencers - once Shelley came into their lives. The modus operandi of deceiving self-deceivers who are after the recruitment of enablers seems to always begin with their demonizing of a person or a group of people who lack means of protecting themselves from having their image besmirched by lies and slander.

If it were not for humans who are dazzled by false accusations - maybe what enablers are dazzled by is not the falsehoods but rather the audacity of the projecting deceiver in feeling free to utter outrageous accusations in the very face of their victims - the demonizer would get nowhere with their project of turning people against the victim of their accusations. Apparently, my ex was one of those limitless hordes of my species who are dazzled into idolizing malicious falsehood creators and will step right up to support one.

When I agreed to my husband's taking custody of my

children, I had no idea that his character would become whatever the biggest bully in his environs wanted it to be. That is because I hadn't a clue as to the operational value system of so many of us humans. Do we all have two sets of values? One we talk about a lot but seldom act on (a value system of the conscious mind, constructed for our self-image's sake), but then a second, which we don't think or talk about because it's in the unconscious where we hide it from ourselves? That second one, possibly a primitive predatory pack value system, seems to be the one we are more likely to act on automatically than the civilized value system we claim to believe in when an alpha exhibiting certain predatory pack behaviors comes into our lives and shows us the way to become our worst selves.

Please excuse the detour. Now back to my story.

I may have asked my children why Shelley had not chosen to take a job as a psychologist after she graduated rather than the lower-pay-grade one she had settled for and held for a brief time prior to marrying my ex. They gave me no reason other than that she hadn't wanted to. After becoming acquainted with how she operated in her relationship with my children and others my children told me about, I had to wonder if her failing to go to work in the field of psychology didn't have some reason behind it other than that she didn't want to.

The legal terms of my custody arrangement with my ex for my children were: "The husband shall have custody of the children, out of the State of Florida pursuant to mutual agreement of the parties, with reasonable visitation of the Wife. The Wife shall have custody, if so desired, during one-half of the summer period and one-half of the Christmas and Easter periods," Fortunately for me, someone responsible for wording the document included that phrase, "pursuant to mutual agreement of the parties". Were it not for that inclusion, the account my ex began giving out in the presence of third parties (if what my son-in-law related to me is true) - that "The Court" awarded custody of my children to him because I was an unfit mother - would be the only information my descendants would ever hear.

It probably will be the only thing any of my descendants hear anyway, since (it has finally become totally clear to me) neither my children, my grandchildren, nor any of the spouses brought into my children's paternal family, *WANT* to believe anything about me rooted in reality. Where I (or someone whose brain operates in the way mine does) don't want to believe false characterizations of other humans created for no more reason than that the falsehood-creators and their toadies can have some justification to give for behaving inhumanely to the target of their cruelty, apparently, many humans (at least my progeny do) seem to love believing in slander even when they know full well that the malicious slanderer is an habitual liar.

When I finally realized how enamored my children, my grandchildren, and so many others are of those individuals who blatantly mouth accusations against innocent people and exhibit insulting, abusive behaviors as low in character as law will allow, I could not get my mind around the fact that any civilized human would actually find these behaviors to be irresistibly magnetic for them. How infinitely depressing it is to realize my children, grandchildren, and all those they hold closest *WANT* to believe that my children suffered all kinds of physical and sexual abuse at my hands. Every time I have any contact with any of them, someone in the pack has thought up something new to accuse me of, and, along with the accusation, comes some ridiculous statement of "proof" that what they have made up is absolutely so. All this has come about - has grown like a tree out of a mustard seed - from one individual to whom my ex decided to turn over his thinking and feeling self; Shelley.

Getting back to my tale of my visit to my ex-husband's home to pick up my children: as soon as I had made my greetings to the adults and turned my attention to my children, Shelley, for no reason that I could see, became my authoritarian, glowering interrogator; demanding of me that I tell her exactly where I would be taking my children, what I was planning to do with them. I couldn't believe my ears. Shelley was apparently acting out a script in her mind in which I was one of those parents that often make the news, a parent without custody who kidnaps their children from the parent-with-custody when an allowed visit gives them that opportunity. This was so bizarre an idea, given all my prior history with my children, I couldn't understand why my ex was just standing by, listening to this woman talk to me as if I were there, not to visit my children (just a pretense), but with the real intention to kidnap them ... just standing by with an idiotic grin on his face and saying not a word in defense of reality.

As the very fact that my children were living with my ex and not with me was due to my own judgment that I couldn't provide for them the kind of home and environment every child deserves, the idea that I was there harboring a plot to kidnap them, and being talked to by this woman as if this vision of me that she had in her mind was necessitating her being verbally abusive to me in front of my ex and my children, was a situation in which I suddenly found myself for which I was completely unprepared.

Being caught off guard by her unwarranted display of suspicion and supervisory presumption toward me, I, unfortunately, allowed myself to fall to her level and made some angry statements about how I was entitled to do with my children whatever I wanted and that I didn't have to answer to her for that, whatever that was. Legally, I may have been correct in what I said, but I was a captive prey to her. My ex's having physical possession of my children meant that she, now, had physical possession of my children, and as long as I wanted to try to hold on to a relationship with them, her having the ability to subject me to insult and injury was going to be, for her, like shooting fish in a barrel.

I had had hardly any exposure to adults who did not make it a habit to communicate with others courteously and respectfully. In the families among which I grew up, adults' communicating with each other graciously and respectfully was unwritten law. My coming to my ex-husband's home to pick up my children at the pre-arranged time was something which had taken place completely uneventfully on my former trips there. Before Shelley's entry into the picture, my ex-husband and I had worked out everything almost unfailingly harmoniously.

My insides were aflame as I got my children out the door as quickly as I could and into my car. We arrived at my motel, threw on bathing suits, and headed for the pool. Once there with Millie and Mack, I put the gut-churning face-off I'd just been through with Shelley out of my mind and entered into the pleasure of swimming. Both my children were competent swimmers and had been from the time our Miami next-door neighbor had installed a pool several years earlier. At the time Millie and Mack learned to swim, my marriage to their father was still working satisfactorily, so he was a part of their lives for hours every day and knew full well that they were going next door almost daily to swim with the neighbors' four children of the same age range. What I'm trying to say by bringing this up is that my ex surely knew that both of his children were completely capable of judging for themselves what was within their ability, in so far as swimming feats were concerned, and what they had best not attempt. In a pool as small as the motel pool in which we were swimming, I had no fears whatsoever about their safety. I was in the pool with them and all three of us were focused on each other and nothing else.

Mack told me that he wanted to show me that he could swim the whole length of the pool underwater. I was as excited about watching him perform this swimming exploit as he was about performing it. Millie and I stood watching at the shallow end of the pool as Mack set off, underwater, for the far end. Just as he arrived successfully at the place he had set out to reach and rose to the surface to catch his breath, sputtering and panting as all swimmers always do who've been swimming any distance under water, in my peripheral vision I caught sight of two very familiar figures rushing toward the pool area from the direction of the street. They must have seen Mack rising to the surface at their end of the pool before my mind fully registered who they were. By the time it became clear to me that this was Shelley with my ex tagging behind, they were in a full run – not toward Mack, but toward me – with Shelley screaming at me over and over, "He's drowning, he's drowning! Your son is drowning and you're standing there doing nothing. What kind of a mother are you? You're going to stand there and let your son die!"

Fortunately there were only a few motel guests at the pool besides Millie, Mack, and me at that time. Nonetheless, the effect Shelley's scene had on my confidence that fellow human beings would recognize me as a good and caring mother, rather than as the monster Shelley was accusing me of being, was horrific. Even the best parent in the world would be shaken to the core, I think, to have some woman come running up with a large man alongside for support and start screaming at the top of her lungs what Shelley was screaming at me. Humiliated, confused, and helpless doesn't begin to describe what I was feeling as Shelley, with my smiling ex-husband standing utterly silently and supportively by her side, screamed at me loudly enough to have been heard by the guests, not only at the pool, but those who were in their rooms as well.

Why my ex-husband did not let Shelley know that Mack was an entirely competent swimmer and was not sputtering and gasping because he was drowning, but because that's when swimmer's do when they come up for air, I can only surmise. For all the hysterical crying out Shelley was producing in order to alert my fellow hotel guests as to the kind of woman I was to stand casually by as my son drowned before my eyes, I don't recall either her or my ex moving toward Mack as if they intended to give him any help. Shelley seemed to want everyone's eyes focused on how thoroughly she was stripping me of my status.

The exuberance of all three of us - Millie, Mack, and

me - brought forth in our hearts by being together again, was so trashed by Shelley's histrionics that even after we had thankfully seen the last of her broad backside vanishing out the poolside gate, we couldn't recover. The children were overcome with gloom, I was overcome with gloom, and all amount of our mutterings to each other about how ridiculous and silly Shelley's performance had been couldn't make that dark cloud go away. If anyone had told me on this day that in time my sweet children would become people who would pride themselves on their capacity for behaving toward me exactly as Shelley was behaving toward me on this occasion, I would have dismissed the warning utterly.

On the long drive back to Miami following this visit with my kids, my thoughts kept returning to the scripts that Shelley had seemed to be following that day. What had been Shelley's source material for her dramatic positing of me as an evil, unscrupulous mother? I had no idea. Shelley's enlisting Bobby to help her call motels all over Charlotte until they found the one where I was registered? Why? Their racing to my motel with what seemed to me to be the urgency of EMS responding to a 911 call? What had the woman's imagination been cooking up in her brain? I had a great fear that Bobby had married a woman who was in far worse mental shape than I, and who now would have control over my children's lives.

With the passage of years, my anxiety and regret over my failure to protect my image from what Shelley did to it on that day in Charlotte has only grown. Shelley's running, with Bobby in tow, up to the swimming pool where Mack, Millie, and I were so enjoying our time together? The act she had put on screaming about my doing nothing while

Mack was drowning right in front of me? Did Shelley really think that? Or, was this a planned sort of exhibition she intended to give to humiliate me ... to make me look weak and ineffectual in my children's eyes? I had no idea. Could she be paranoid schizophrenic? ... delusional? ... or just plain mean? I had felt sure, all along, that Bobby was going to marry a woman who would be a better mother than I. Now I was thinking, "Dear God! What have I done?" From what Millie and Mack were telling me, their new life under Shelley was nothing short of miserable; they were being ignored while Shelley and Bobby sat for hours drinking and talking.

What Mack and Millie were telling me in subsequent visits about their home life added to my angst. Obsessing over what to do led me nowhere. The thinking of professionals at the time I decided to hand over my guardianship of Millie and Mack to Bobby was that weekdays with mom and weekends with dad was no good for children; what children needed was to live in the same home with the same parent all the time. I had thought I was doing a good thing to make myself scarce in my children's lives.

Then, in 1976, came a great break for the kids (I thought). Shelley and Bobby decided Bobby should quit his news editor job and go into tobacco farming with his family back in the eastern part of the state. Shelley and Bobby had a baby by now, and, according to my daughter, Shelley wasn't finding housekeeping and childcare for her own child to be nearly as engrossing as playing the role of rescuer of my children from their evil monster natural mother.

Millie complained that Shelley wasn't taking care of her little brother. She spoke about Shelley's making no attempt to potty train the boy, and worse yet, Shelley's not changing the child's diapers; that she had to change them herself if they were to be changed. Millie expressed the opinion that Shelley was too involved in the multi-family tobacco enterprise to give her child the care he should be getting. I myself could see that he was getting his breakfasts, not with Shelley and Bobby, but at his great aunt's, who was constantly stuffing him with sweets.

Not long after that, Mack gave me the news that his little brother had been in an accident - that the child had had his head run over by a piece of farm equipment. I could hardly believe what my son was telling me. His little brother, who was only two or three at the time, had been allowed by either Shelley, Bobby, or both to ride on a tractor manufactured for dedicated use in agriculture. I had never seen a farm tractor that had even any seat for anyone other than the operator, much less safety restraints. I'd never seen any tractor built for farming purposes retrofitted in any way that would have made it safe for a child of two or three to be on while in motion. I couldn't imagine a parent having so little foresight that they would fail to consider the possibility that their two-or three-year-old child would fall off a vehicle never designed to prevent riders from falling off and being run over by the very vehicle they had been riding on.

This accident, which Shelley's and Bobby's child miraculously survived, did not leave my children's little brother unscathed. That this kind of accident happened, in light of the words Shelley had screamed at me, "What kind of a mother are you? Your son is dying and you're standing there doing nothing!" seemed to me like a strange ecclesiastical judgment event. It left me stunned.

The scientist Stephen Hawking has hinted at the possibility that laws of physics make predestination a viable belief. It occurs to me, if predestination is at work in the world, Shelley's behavior toward me and the words she had screamed at me in Charlotte comprised an instance of her projecting onto me her persona before she had even had the child with which her projection was involved. Einstein and physicists since have posited attributes of time that are mindboggling to me. Could it be that there really IS punishment for a trespass, but that a sin and punishment for that sin have no particular order?

Revelations

In Lyman Chalkley's *Chronicles of the Scotch-Irish Settlement in Virginia* (a three-volume collection of transcriptions of actual court records relevant to a great area of the east-central United States and encompassing a period from 1745-1800) I believe I found the reason why, in states where I lived other than North Carolina, I never knew anyone whose life had been destroyed by slander. In one citation after another, I see names of those who had been charged with slander (a criminal offense in Virginia) with a note following that that person so charged had fled to North Carolina to evade justice.

"Well, well", I thought to myself. "No wonder any laws on the books here in North Carolina protect the rights of the slanderers to make up any preposterous accusations they can dream up and fear no punishment of any kind for doing so no matter what the losses their victims suffer." I even found the maiden name of my children's stepmother among Chalkley's citations bearing on slander. "Must have been one of her direct forebears", I thought to myself.

One would think that in this modern age, in a supposedly civilized nation such as the United States, slanderers would be shunned and ostracized. However, this is eastern North Carolina, and I have found in living in this environment for a couple of decades that here, slanderers are put on pedestals and the populace rushes to help and support them against their hapless victims. The more vicious and outrageous slanderers' accusations against a targeted individual, the more people will rush forward to loudly proclaim that they know for a fact that the accusations are true and even more horrible things besides. Such is the nature of almost anyone indigenous to this area, and even not, who has allowed himself or herself to fall under its spell. Such, I'm afraid, has been the fate of my children.

Watching my children change, in character, from the open, honest, emotionally spontaneous human beings they once were into what their stepmother and others in their environment here have wanted them to be, has been a torture for me beyond anything I can describe in words. It has left me broken in spirit, disappointed, and horrified. I have only myself to blame for their change. Had I had the faith in myself that I should have had - the faith that I was a better mother for my children than any other woman would be, intractable depression notwithstanding - perhaps my children would never have been open to being influenced by the inhumanly callous and unscrupulous people they came to admire so much.

Several factors decided my disastrous decision to allow

my husband (and therefore Shelley and the women of my husband's family) to have custody of my children. Contrary to what my ex-husband's wife and mother told my children (and also related to me and apparently just about everyone else in their world) I did not "Come down here and dump the children" on them (their grandmother, her husband, her sister, and the children's great-grandmother) "because I didn't want them". I didn't bring my children to them at all. My ex-husband and his wife did that. What I had done was allow my husband to take custody of my children after he informed me that he wouldn't be able to continue living if he couldn't have custody of his children.

Prior to this interchange between us, on another occasion, he had told me that he couldn't continue with a custody arrangement he and I had whereby I kept the children during the week and he on weekends. No, he avowed. It was so painful for him to be without the children during the week while I had them that he would have to terminate taking them on weekends. If he couldn't have the children with him one hundred percent of the time, he said, he just couldn't be with them at all; because, his separation from them at the end of each weekend was too painful for him to bear. Better for him, he averred to me, having none of their company at all than just two days a week. Those two days just opened his emotional wounds afresh every week, he said.

Next, my ex-husband informed me that he had applied for a transfer from Miami, where we then were, back to his home state of North Carolina and had been granted it. He wouldn't have asked for this transfer if I hadn't promised him that he could have custody of the children, he all but sobbed to me. Shame on me that I was so gullible as to be taken in by this maneuvering. Shame on me for failing to recognize in my ex-husband the capacity for such intelligent and crafty scheming. Shame on me for failing to recognize that my "good ole boy" ex-husband had possession of profoundly destructive psychological weapons and the ruthlessness to use them. My arrogant lack of appreciation for the potency of the venom of fellow human beings I wrongly assumed to be harmless, proved to be my undoing.

That I did not recognize my ex-husband's manipulation of me as lowdown and dirty as manipulation of a person through their emotional weaknesses can get, was just too bad for me. With my too-well developed conscience and too-well developed empathy telling me I was doing a good thing for all concerned, I allowed my ex-husband to take my children into his custody. At the time, their going was the end of my life, but at least I had some comfort in thinking that I had made a sacrifice that would make many other human beings happy - my children, my husband, his family.

I, with my usual self-underestimation, believed that my children loved their father far more than they loved me and therefore shouldn't be separated from him. My parents had plenty of grandchildren, so I knew my giving my ex-husband custody of mine wouldn't tear irreparable holes in their hearts. They didn't care much for children anyway. In contrast, my ex-husband's family members seemed to worship children as if they were gods. The impression I got when they visited us was that there was no joy in life for them that even came close to being with their grandchildren - my children. I thought that my taking my children away from them through insisting upon custody would destroy them. If I didn't allow my husband to have custody, my conscience told me, not only would my poor husband be emotionally bereft, but his mother, father, aunt, and grandmother would be too.

Imagine then my feeling when my ex-husband's mother angrily accused me, with my children looking on, of "dumping my children" on them because I didn't want them. Imagine how I felt, when I heard years later from my son-in-law that my ex-husband was stating, not that he and I had come to consensus on our own without interference from third parties about which of us would have custody, but that the court awarded him custody of my children. If ever there has been a prime example of the old adage, "No good deed goes unpunished", my giving of the custody of my children to my ex-husband has been that.

But, it hasn't been socially convenient for my ex-husband, his wife, or his family members to speak the truth about anything I've ever done. That would be counter to the laws of survival of the fittest for those living in human packs. Identifying me as the parent who weaseled out of having to do what decency demanded of me for little children by "dumping them" on family elders, rather than attributing that act to the real perpetrators - their father and stepmother - served the purpose of strengthening family ties. Nothing brings about tighter bonds within a human pack than creating the myth that the pack's young ones are under threat from an evil outsider.

A major reason for my giving up de facto custody of my children was that my husband hadn't been the one who wanted to get out of the marriage. All the guilt and shame that my ex-husband, his family members, my family members, and my psychiatrist laid on me for trying to bring an end to my marriage, was a load of guilt and shame I couldn't begin to offset with feelings of self-worth or deservedness; I didn't have any feeling of self-worth or deservedness.

My ex-husband, his family members, my family members, and my psychiatrist all made it clear to me that I had an inviolable moral commitment to stay in my marriage, feel wifely feelings for my spouse, and think nothing of the world going by without me. They gave me to understand that my not being contented in my marriage and fulfilled by having a husband, children, and a house to care for was because I was a "s___" (my ex-husband's verdict), and too hopelessly mentally ill to be reachable (my psychiatrist's opinion).

It never ceases to boggle my mind when I hear adults, who otherwise seem to have possession of a reasonable amount of intelligence, expressing the opinion that you can love somebody if you want to; if you will just accept your moral obligation to do that instead of choosing to be a bad person instead. When I hear such nonsensical edicts being delivered by the self-appointed morals-bearers among us, I have to wonder to myself if they have ever allowed themselves to feel one spontaneous urge that the earth and its mammalian evolution have bequeathed to them; or, if they have squelched every natural desire or animal instinct that has ever arisen in their heart and guts with cold cerebral self-assurance that they are feeling what their religion and their pack-leaders have told them it's right to feel.

Next, on the list of considerations that went into my decision making of whether I or my ex-husband should have custody of my children, was the fear that my children's being raised by a severely depressed woman such as I would throw them into the same state in which I found myself and in which my mother had existed through all the years that I had known her. I took stock of the fact that I had been in misery through most of the time I'd spent on earth, and multiple psychiatric treatments and medications hadn't done anything to change that.

Any parent who has experienced long-term depression and who has any feeling of compassion whatsoever for her children would sacrifice anything to spare them such a life. The psychoanalytic literature I had read at that point led me to believe that depression might be acquired by children through a process of instinctive acquisition of a parent's state of mind by her offspring. My husband didn't suffer from depression. I did. Therefore, to me, he became, in my mind, the correct parent to have custody. I discounted all the positives my constant presence in their lives could have brought my children. When my ex-husband moved back to North Carolina with my children, I stayed in Miami.

I believed that it was essential that I stay in Miami because I believed myself to be in a type of psychiatric treatment I had to stick with until I had "worked through the transference". That's a description of the treatment I had been given by the doctor at its onset. So, I, of course, did not want to end the relationship I thought I had with my psychiatrist. I didn't have a working partnership with my doctor, but I was too lacking in faith in my own judgment and intelligence to see it at that time. He wasn't working on anything *WITH* me. He wanted to work *ON* me without any interference or input from me on what the work was to accomplish or how it ought to be carried out.

His view of our relationship was that I had no more to contribute in my own behalf to our work than a sick cat contributes by yowling and hissing at the veterinarian who is trying to help her. His notion of psychotherapy for me was that I should bring my perfectly submissive mind to him; and, without any resistance to his will whatsoever, allow him to manipulate my emotions in the way a physical therapist would manipulate a patient's limbs. The most dedicated of patients can't accomplish any working through of transference when she is trusting in her psychiatrist to help her over the negative humps and he can't recognize the understandable in negative transference when the client all but explains it to him.

There is nothing to be gained by a client when her psychiatrist believes that her negative reaction to his therapeutic strategies represents willfulness, ignorance, and mental illness on her part. Denial and addiction - unrecognized by the eminent psychiatrist, I might mention - kept me going back to him for years while his attitude toward me brought me ever lower in mental health. His and my relationship was a classic case of destroyer and destroyed holding on to contact with each other for all the sickest of reasons. I bore the responsibility for protecting my self-image from this psychiatrist's damaging arrogant attitude toward me, and I failed in that responsibility. I failed to extract myself because I had no knowledge, at the time I continued to seek this doctor's help, that he simply lacked the wherewithal to offer me anything professionally.

Enough said on that score. To allow myself to think much about what happened to the personalities of my children and the last throes of my relationships with them plunges me into such mental agony I become incapable of performing the simplest of tasks. The task before me today is to rewrite my will, and dwelling on a grief that will never be quenched as long as I am alive will accomplish nothing and will prevent me from taking care of this disagreeable but necessary piece of business.

For the greater part of the last decade, I have felt that to bequeath anything to my children would be to reward them for abusing me. I sensed that a great part of the attitude they had been tutored to hold toward me was based on their grandmother's myth that I had committed unforgivable sins against them, against their father, and all his family. My children's grandmother didn't come up with this myth until after Bobby and Shelley had moved from Charlotte back to the community where she and other of Bobby's relatives lived.

Prior to this opportunity Shelley had engineered to spend every day with my children's grandmother and other adult female relatives, the grandmother's and my relationship with each other had always been mutually respectful and observant of what I have always known as Christian decency.

Now, out of nowhere, my children's grandmother began meeting me at my children's door, when I came to visit with them, with sermons. At first, these sermons to me of how I was a fallen woman who needed to get down on her knees and beg God to forgive her, may have been delivered to me in my children's hearing, but at least, the woman made no effort to involve them in preaching my lowness to me. That changed.

Soon, when I arrived at their door, their grandmother

had positioned one of my children on each side of her, and when she prompted them, each had something to say to me to the effect that they didn't want me to visit them; that I was just forcing myself on them. Shelley had made a puppet of my ex years before. Now, I could only wonder as to what had transpired in my children's grandmother's mind that she was suddenly talking and behaving toward me in a way I never would have thought possible given what I'd always heard coming from her mouth about the arrogance of humans who thought they could influence God's will. I had to wonder if Shelley could be feeding her the script she was having my children recite to me. I was seeing a personality in my ex's mother that I had never seen before.

So, what is this awful, unspeakable, depravity I have committed which makes me unfit to even so much as speak to my children; which has brought me to this state of being the most detestable of all creatures - a fallen woman? What is this awful sin against my children I have committed which obligates them to banish me from their lives for my sinfulness?

Well - get prepared for the horror of it - I actually stated once, in the presence of my children, that I didn't see anything so terribly wrong with unmarried people sleeping with each other or living together before marriage. I didn't just throw that information out unbidden. My children were in their early teen years and had very recently been having drilled into them by my ex-husband's wife and family members that having sex with someone you weren't married to was so reprehensible that from thenceforth everyone who knew you or had ever known you would think of you as trash. My children were given to understand by Shelley, their grandmother, and possibly my hypocritical ex as well, that the whole world would be focused on nothing but them and their shamefulness if they were a person who had sex with someone to whom you weren't married. My son asked me if I slept with my boyfriend. I just answered his question honestly ... yes. They wanted me to know how wrong I was in doing this and proceeded to deliver to me the sermons their father's wife and family members had delivered to them. I wondered how it was that they did not remember that their father had had a girlfriend who moved with them when their father made the transfer from Miami to North Carolina. I guess my children remember only the family history as told to them by Shelley.

What I was thinking while my children were telling me how unspeakable it is for people who aren't married to each other to sleep together - how all the world would have their minds on my sexual conduct and would think me dirt if they even suspected I was having unmarried sex ... what I was thinking was how this was exactly what had been drilled into me as a preteen and teenage girl, and how disappointed I was to find that my children were being fed all this moralistic crap about shame and sex that had so tortured me through my teenage years.

I had lived in fear, from before I entered puberty until a minister spoke the words, "I now pronounce you man and wife", that some boy might try to make me do necking or petting things, so he could then scorn me for being easy and could tell everybody he knew, so they would laugh at me with him. I lived in fear that boys would claim they had done things to me related to this "sleeping" thing that was supposed to be so horrible for a girl to do with a boy.

On one occasion, a date told me that so-and-so "says he threw you". I had no idea what my date was talking about, but I sensed it was related to this "sleeping" activity with which, I'd been given to understand, all boys wanted to soil and shame females. My mind went to work overtime and every contact I had had with this former classmate of mine who had claimed that he had "thrown me" played through my mind, not just that evening, but for days.

Throughout my teens, I had no knowledge of what made girls get pregnant, but I knew that if you were an unmarried girl who let yourself get impregnated, you had "ruined your life". For the remainder of your days, you would have nothing before you but the lowest opinion of everyone in your environment. You wouldn't need to wear a scarlet letter - everyone would know exactly what your shame had been. The community would scorn you, and your family members would live in shame because of your failure to keep yourself rigidly resistant to all attempts by boys and men to get "familiar" with you. I guess my aunt took it upon herself to feed me all this because my mother wouldn't even discuss urination, defecation, or menstruation with her daughters, much less anything having to do with vaginas, penises, or sex. As my aunt was a nurse, I suppose she felt it fell to her to terrorize me about boys and what they wanted to do to girls, since my mother didn't seem to be shouldering that responsibility appropriately.

In none of the horror stories I was told about what happens to girls who let boys do things to them they shouldn't allow, was I ever told that pregnancy occurs when a male ejaculates semen into a girl's vagina or close enough to the opening of her vagina so that those little spermatozoa that are really ambitious might be able to swim up into the opening and from thence up to the uterus. I had my first period in June after I had turned thirteen. I didn't have another for eight months. I had no one I could talk to about it. A gym teacher had told us girls that if a girl's periods stopped, that was the sign she was pregnant. Who was I going to go to and say, "I didn't have another period after June so I must have let some boy (I don't know who) do something I wasn't supposed to let him do (I don't know what) and I'm going to mortally humiliate myself and my whole family by getting bigger and bigger and having a baby I shouldn't be having?" How can I describe to you the perpetual terror that hung over me through the rest of the summer and far into the fall?

The last thing I wanted for a daughter of mine was for her to go through in her teen years what I had gone through in mine due to my lack of knowledge and lack of women to whom I could go for information that would have reassured me and eased my fears. Before my ex-husband and I had gone our separate ways, while my children were quite young, I had explained to them where babies come from so that they would never live in the fear and confusion that I had.

So, as my teenage children related to me all this fear-and-shame-instilling crap they were being fed by a woman who seemed to me to have an obsessive interest in not only my children's sexuality but everyone else's as well, my heart sank. The last thing I had wanted, in as far as my children's sexuality was concerned, was for them to be brainwashed into the beliefs about women and sex that have brought women thousands of years of physical and mental torture on account of a natural bodily function that ought to be regarded by society as a natural bodily function - not as the ultimate yardstick for measuring whether a woman is good and clean or evil and dirty. I wanted my daughter to have access to sexual information from a woman who didn't have sex, shame, religion, and femininity all tied together in a great stifling knot. It sounded to me, from what my children were telling me, that the only woman in my daughter's life who had an attitude about sex that wasn't polluted with misogyny and fundamentalist religion was I. When my daughter was fifteen or sixteen, I sent her a book by Nancy Friday entitled, *My Mother, Myself*, which dealt with the way daughters acquire or don't acquire from their mothers healthy attitudes toward sex.

Is that it, you ask? Is that a confession of your unpardonable acts of sexual depravity?

Not entirely. My original sin was that I ceased being satisfied with being married to my children's father. After nine years of marriage, I realized that my husband and I were completely unsuited to each other; that our match was as one between two different species of animals. I initiated the breakup of our marriage. At the time, I thought that if our marriage ended, he and I could find mates more in keeping with our natures. That was correct thinking on my part; we shouldn't have ever married in the first place, and it was a breakup that needed to happen. However, I lacked the self-assurance and self-confidence to go about dissolving the marriage in a careful, well-thought-out way. Had I known then what I know now, the process would have taken place very differently. I failed completely in my responsibility to myself to protect and hold on to what I had a right to hold on to. It's my nature to want to give away "the shirt off my back", and I did that to a degree that makes me sick to think of it today.

In my husband's family's fundamentalist scheme of things, however, I suppose the women perceive of themselves as being of the ilk of prophets and priests of the Old Testament; righteously identifying for all those women who need to be brought forth to face public indictment for being "fallen", so the crowd can dish out to them their just deserts for being so evil - dish out to them their verbal and emotional stonings. Would that my children would see this witch-hunting viciousness for what it is instead of worshiping at these women's altars and helping them achieve their destructive ends.

It took quite a few years for me to grasp that any kind, thoughtful, or loving thing I tried to do for my children - any effort I made to hold on to the relationship I had once had with them - would be instantly recharacterized in their disordered minds as the effort of a cast-out demon to bribe and trick them into letting her back in because that was the delusional interpretation Shelley preached (and my ex supported) for every loving word or act of mine toward my children that reached her eyes or ears. That my ex-husband, his wife, my children, their spouses, and probably all my grandchildren are living in an alternate reality where I represent the devil to them, is something that I now realize I cannot change.

Of all my life situations that have left me too demoralized to feel much of anything other than hopelessness and helplessness, I don't think any has hit me harder behind the knees than recognizing that the brainwashing that my children underwent at the hands of their stepmother, their father's mother, and probably even their pretend-to-be-what-she-wants father, changed them permanently, and that they would never again treat me with the love and respect they once had.

I used to imagine that, for sure, someday, they would feel remorse for at least something out of all the things they'd done and said to me that had hurt me so badly and humiliated me in front of so many people, and would approach me to say how sorry they were. Instead, every opportunity that arose where that could have happened turned into a new opportunity for them to show themselves and everyone in the encounter that they had no intention of extending respect or commonly performed courtesies to me.

The motivation humans exude when their intention is to demonstrate fealty to alphas seems to me to be at its greatest when the alphas they want to impress are the deceiving self-deceiver unscrupulous type. When their self-selected alpha is simply a person operating mainly in do-unto-others Second-Commandment mode, not demonizing any individual or group, number and enthusiasm among supporters seem to me to fall away.

For far, far too long I believed that I could argue my children out of the brainwashing they had been given about me in their youth. I lived in the belief that they, being educated and intelligent people, surely would be open to dialogue and logic if I just explained everything adequately. I labored under the misguided belief that all human beings have a natural desire, as I do, to hold beliefs that will withstand true-or-false tests. I went on and on trying to communicate with my children and denying to myself that my children thought well of themselves for having closed their minds to me. Finally, I had to accept that the alternate reality in which my children live is a world they want and need much more than they want any relationship with me; that when people want to believe in a myth that makes them feel elevated, there is no argument on earth, by any human on earth, that will persuade them of the error or inhumanity of that belief.

REVELATIONS

Elsie

After decades of living with depression and following every lead that I could come by to get to that not-depressed person I thought I was capable of being, I am left with only one bit of wisdom in which I have confidence. That bit of wisdom is that support from someone who really likes you, just as you are, depression and whatever other flaws you have notwithstanding, can make such a difference in a depressed person's life it may have the effect of a miracle sent by the Almighty. At least, that is what I had the good luck to come by in my own life.

Beginning with my first-grade teacher and continuing throughout my life, when good fortune put a woman of more advanced years than I into my life who behaved toward me in a warm and approving way, giving me the impression that the level of work I could do made me interesting to her - enticed her into wanting to help me be all that I could be in my work - the effect has been like putting Miracle Grow Bloom Booster on flowers. I don't mean to suggest that support from a loving mother surrogate could free me from depression, neurological deficiencies, and defects of character, but I do remember, with each mentor who came into my life and chose to involve herself in helping me to achieve what I wanted to achieve, my whole quality of life would move up a notch.

When I entered first grade, it was the beginning of November and my classmates (all strangers to me because we had just moved from Virginia's plateau down to Roanoke Valley) had already had two months of instruction, whereas the only schooling I'd had was a few sessions conducted by my older sis on alphabet, phonics, and a bit of reading about Dick, Jane, and Baby Sally. Daddy, not Mother, took me to school on my first day and introduced me to the teacher, who expressed great doubt in my ability to catch up to the other children.

Showing considerable pride in me, my father informed her that I could read. The teacher produced a book and I was able to do exactly what my father had promised her I could; I read - not perfectly, but enough. How wonderful it is when your parent is proud of you and you can perform the activity he said you could in a way that doesn't let him down. How wonderful it would have been for me if I ever could have done that for my mother. From that day, this teacher, who managed three grades with no assistance, involved herself personally with me in a way that no female in my family was interested in doing.

When I was in fifth grade, I was given some more opportunities to win some good attention from women. A mother in our neighborhood decided to sponsor a 4-H club for community children. In that era, 4-H for girls involved selecting projects from a list of goals in home economics: preserving food, cooking balanced meals, sewing clothes for oneself, and the like. The sponsor of our club was the mother of a son, not a daughter, and I believe she took a special interest in me because I was more than eager to excel in home-making skills that she was eager to share with a receptive protégé. This woman's sponsoring of my 4-H group and the one-to-one warmth and interest she showed me gave me confidence and access to social opportunities that I would not have had through my middle school years without her.

Moving ahead a few decades brings me to 1976 and the point in my life where, one might say, I was down for the count. I had spent the first months of the year in a state mental institution as a result of having made several attempts over the preceding couple of years to get rid of myself. I'd been in good spirits all the time that I had been in the hospital, but once out, I had nowhere to go except back to my same old life. Then, by some desperately-needed unexpected stroke of good fortune, a man I had met while in the hospital called me and asked me for a date.

Our date went very well. I couldn't have asked for a more interesting conversationalist, and soon our conversation turned to the subject of his involvement in Alcoholics Anonymous and its meetings, around which his life outside the hospital had become centered. We had talked a lot while patients at the hospital, and he knew that I had exhausted every possibility I could think of that might offer me a way to live a life I could bear. He suggested that I go with him to an AA open meeting. I was dubious. I knew I abused alcohol, but I felt pretty sure I was not addicted to it.

All it took for me to see AA as a possible salvation for me was one meeting. I began going with my friend to other meetings besides the once-a-week closed one. "You cannot go to closed meetings", I was told by big tall men there, "unless you're an alcoholic". I made a decision that, for me, AA was absolutely the last house on the street (as I heard recovering alcoholics describe it) and, as I could see my life was surely at stake, I could not be splitting hairs with myself or anyone else over whether or not I had been enough of a drinker to call myself an alcoholic. All that is required for membership in AA is that one have a desire to stop drinking, according to the writings of th founders. I knew I could have a desire to stop drinking, so I did stop drinking and started going to every meeting in town. I went all in.

I had to choose a sponsor, I was told, and I needed to put a lot of thought into that as the criteria I used in making the choice would probably determine whether the sponsorship worked well for the both of us or not. By some miracle that surely represented work going on in the universe at which I can only marvel, there was a woman attending most of the meetings that I attended (Elsie), who stood out as a good choice to me on account of her many years of sobriety, of being married, and of working in the same employment. I couldn't rack up much length of time at any of those benchmarks for success in love and work, and Elsie apparently could, so I had no doubt that she was qualified to lead me. I asked her to be my sponsor and she accepted.

Right away, Elsie did what I needed someone to do for me; she reached out to me and she never stopped reaching out to me right up to the last days she spent here on earth. For reasons I don't completely understand, I don't reach out for help when I'm down. I seem to need someone to take hold of me and pull me in toward them. Perhaps I don't reach out to people for help because I'm so afraid their response will be like the response would be from members of my family (and many others) who must believe that preaching at the person in pain and apprising them of all the things they are doing stupidly or wrongly is "help". A lot of mental health professionals think that is "help".

Elsie's "help" wasn't like that at all. At the first meeting I attended after asking Elsie to be my sponsor, the topic introduced by the evening's discussion leader was love. Rather than members raising their hands to speak - which could have the downside of some members speaking too much and some none at all - in this meeting, everyone around the tables spoke in turn if they wished to speak or passed if they didn't. After the meeting, as everyone was saying their goodbyes to each other, I came up to where Elsie was standing. She turned to me, looked into my eyes with full emotional engagement, then embraced me warmly and said, "I love you Emmy".

What an impression that made on me. I left the meeting feeling somewhat in shock, even then, but the effect this act of Elsie's had on me didn't end with that evening but remained with me and actually deepened in the days that followed as Elsie spoke with me for hours each day by phone and following meetings. Our conversations were largely devoted to the working of AA's twelve steps, but we got some gossip and family history in there too. We talked about spiritual experiences such as that Bill Wilson described that launched his sobriety and recovery. I must be extremely open to suggestion because I awoke one morning, during this period of time in which I was talking for hours every day with Elsie, to a sensation that I could see all the atoms jiggling in everything around me and that that motion was generated by a great universal energy of love.

Elsie had imperfections of character and personality just like every other human who ever lived. I didn't see one of them. When I needed her companionship or support, she was there for me, seeming to value my companionship and my support just as much as I valued hers. There were professors from William and Mary and an Episcopal minister in our AA groups. They sought Elsie's counsel on issues having to do with their sobriety, yet here she was, treating me as if her time spent with me was just as important to her as the time she spent talking to them. I'd never been treated so lovingly and respectfully before.

I soon found out that Elsie worked in the administration building at the hospital where I'd stayed for months and she might have known a good bit about me before I ever turned up in her AA meeting. She never said exactly what she did at the hospital, but I gather she worked in financial administration. To me, she seemed to have more insight into what patients needed in order to live independently outside the hospital than did any of the mental health professionals I'd met while I was there. "What people need most is support", she said. That sounded right to me then and still does today.

With Elsie in my life, giving me hugs, smiles, and the

kind of attention in the presence of others that added to their positive view of me, I began to see projects in my future other than the search for some man for whom I could feel the way I wanted to feel. Twelve step programs stress the need for turning one's life over to a higher power. For most, this means God. I move in and out of feeling there could be a higher power managing the universe, but my thinking rests pretty steadily in that there could be a higher power but not one who cares anything about living things' suffering.

Elsie expressed skepticism about the loving God idea too, and this was very important to me because senior relatives of my mother's saw individual family members troubles as an opportunity to swoop in with a script of preaching and teaching in which they saw themselves as being saviors of a poor soul lost in sin. Giving comfort to a hurting fellow being wasn't in their repertoire. A family member in deep distress was treated like an untouchable ripe for the picking by my salvation-gifting missionary aunt and uncle.

Elsie never looked at me as if I were a project to be worked on as had my Aunt E, my missionary relatives, and my Miami psychiatrist. All these "helpers" had related to me as something broken to which they could apply their fixer expertise, not as a fellow human being with whom they wanted to get personally involved. If Elsie had related to me as if my depression or other of my characteristics made me unacceptable to her as I was - imperfections she was not going to give up working on to correct until she got me undepressed and extroverted - I couldn't have stood a relationship with her.

Elsie and her husband held the opinion that all of us

who attended AA meetings were broken people, but that our brokenness didn't make us any less fun to be with, or any less spiritually and intellectually enriching as companions, than those who didn't see themselves as being broken. In fact, while those of us in AA were being looked down upon by our relatives and others who knew we had affiliated ourselves with the program, we felt that in AA we had come by a source of support, social nourishment, and personal growth that made us much wealthier than those who barely hid their scorn for us.

What I found in Elsie and many of my fellow AA attendees in Williamsburg, Virginia, throughout my years living, working, and attending College there is, unfortunately, rarely found in AA meetings in other places. After I moved to North Carolina to continue my education in Triangle universities, I could not find another group of the philosophy I had found in Elsie's home group. Elsie (with the support of her husband) had managed to wrest control of that group from the dictatorship by the loudest-voiced men who, in many AA groups, prevent the discussion in meetings of any issues promoting a fulfilling life after alcohol is left behind. These domineering men insist that every meeting be devoted to alcohol and nothing but alcohol. Such a group philosophy would have made having a sponsor and attending meetings useless to me.

Fortunately for me, even after my move, Elsie continued to call me every week for long talks. And during holidays, I could drive to Williamsburg to be with her in person and get those wonderful hugs and smiles from her that helped me so much in my efforts to face life. With Elsie's love in my life, I managed to accept supervision and the patronization of colleagues at work and at school, and to continue to visit my children in the face of the hurtful and hateful statements and behaviors they were being taught to meet me with when I reached their house (if they even decided to be home when I got to their house).

With Elsie's support I made it through a BA, an MS, settling into a profession, buying a house, staying with my career long enough to earn Social Security and a pension, and surviving many unworkable relationships without falling apart or contemplating self-destruction. As I told my sister a few years ago, if it hadn't been for AA and Elsie, I'd now be living on the streets and pushing all my belongings around in a grocery cart, if I was still alive.

ELSIE

Acknowledgement

In the writings I've included in this book, I've painted a very dim picture of what kind of mental health help a woman suffering childhood-onset or long-term depression can expect to find who goes searching for such help here in eastern North Carolina. Sad to say, I haven't painted the picture nearly dimly enough, given what I'm currently hearing from fellow sufferers and finding in local news items about the lack of services available to mental health clients here.

Healthcare people in this region seem to be in love with the theory that depressed women are dangerous dual-personality types of low character, untrustworthiness, dishonesty, and deceit who neglect, abuse, or molest children (if they ever get around any). If a depressed woman is a mother, simply showing that she has had a diagnosis of depression - or even citing some evidence she might

ACKNOWLEDGEMENT

suffer from depression - is taken as proof that she must also be an unfit mother. Mental health professionals here seem to also think that children of depressed mothers (even adult children) need to be told that they surely were abused by her when they were children, and those children need to be brought up to speed on what an unsavory, dangerous person their mother is.

Fortunately for me, in the early 2000s I found a mental health professional in this area, Dr. Michael Nunn, who had retained his capacity for sane thinking, and who declined to fall in line with the popular practice of presenting insult and psychological abuse as treatment for depression in women.

One of the first very helpful things he did for me that had never been done before, even though I'd been seen by many mental health professionals, was to recognize that I have rather severe attention deficit disorder. In university, I'd studied that condition, so I should have recognized my own symptoms of it, yet I hadn't until Dr. Nunn told me I was ADD. With that diagnosis, he prescribed a new and different medication for me to try, a stimulant.

The only medication I'd tried up to that time that had helped me at all was an MAOI (monoamine oxidase inhibitor) which had been denied to me when my general practitioner who had prescribed it was replaced by one who wouldn't. Following that, any doctor I saw prescribed the same old antidepressants I'd been prescribed before that only seemed to increase my lethargy and drowsiness, leaving me feeling worse instead of better. The stimulant Dr. Nunn prescribed produced a bit of motivation in me that hadn't been there before. Any little bit helps when you can't get yourself up and moving even to do ADLs (activities of daily living).

In addition to approving a medication more appropriate to my symptoms than I'd previously been given, Dr. Nunn next began to express an interest in my case that seemed to be personalized and I found him to be more open to input from me about my treatment than I had ever experienced before. Dr. Nunn ran a large operation at his clinic in the early and mid-2000s and had several therapists in his employment.

In most of my sessions at his clinic I had been seen by one of his associates. For awhile I attended group therapy led by a psychologist. She seemed to want to teach us. I knew that being taught has no effect on depression and I wrote the psychologist a long letter on that subject.

Next came a male therapist to whom I mentioned my lifelong desire to write and publish a book. He asked me why I didn't set my sights on something I could actually do. That certainly was depressing.

Somewhere in the string of therapists, I got a young woman who believed that telling me I was pretty was support. If I had never seen a mirror it might have been. The next time I saw Dr. Nunn I said to him (with disgust on my face, I'm sure), "If I'm going to have 'supportive' therapy, can we please at least raise the intelligence level of it a little?"

Dr. Nunn set up my next session with him. As he began to respond to this and that matter that I brought up, I became aware that he had listened to what I had said about raising the intelligence level of my talk therapy and was giving me what I had always longed for from doctors and psychologists and never before gotten - at least I felt I hadn't - validating statements.

ACKNOWLEDGEMENT

Instead of disparaging my ambition to write a book, he gave me solid encouragement to give it a try. In discussion of how my evangelistic family members perpetually preached at me but otherwise didn't seem to want to communicate with me, he commented to the effect that there was something wrong with my family there, not with me.

It was absolutely amazing to me to be receiving validation from a doctor and being talked with as if I were someone for whom he held respect. This was so uplifting to me after all the experiences I'd had of being talked to with condescension, and of being rejected in my attempts to get a therapist to work with me as they would with a colleague, I came away from that session with a confidence in myself I couldn't ever remember having before. In fact, I saw myself as having a brain in which I could safely put my trust; that I did not need, any longer, to be going to therapists to find out if I had at last reached a state of being okay.

www.ingramcontent.com/pod-product-compliance
Ingram Content Group UK Ltd.
Pitfield, Milton Keynes, MK11 3LW, UK
UKHW021301180426
11947UKWH00015B/955